Developing Software
for the User Interface

 **Software Engineering Institute**

The SEI Series in Software Engineering

Developing Software for the User Interface

Len Bass
Software Engineering Institute

Joëlle Coutaz
University of Grenoble (IMAG-LGI)

ADDISON-WESLEY PUBLISHING COMPANY

Reading, Massachusetts ■ Menlo Park, California ■ New York
Don Mills, Ontario ■ Wokingham, England ■ Amsterdam ■ Bonn
Sydney ■ Singapore ■ Tokyo ■ Madrid ■ San Juan ■ Milan ■ Paris

Software Engineering Institute

The SEI Series in Software Engineering

VT100, VT52, and Decstation are trademarks of Digital Equipment Corporation. Sun3, NeWS, and SunView are trademarks of Sun Microsystems, Inc. Apple, Lisa, Macintosh, QuickDraw, ResEdit, HyperCard, HyperTalk, and PICT are trademarks of Apple Computer, Inc. X Window System, X Intrinsics, and Xlib are trademarks of Massachusetts Institute of Technology. PostScript is a trademark of Adobe Systems, Inc. NextStep and Interface Builder are trademarks of NeXT, Inc. OpenLook is a trademark of AT & T. OSF, Motif, and UIL are trademarks of Open Software Foundation, Inc. GDI (Graphics Device Interface), Microsoft Windows, and Microsoft Word are trademarks of Microsoft Corporation. IBM, Presentation Manager, System's Application Architecture, Common Communication Support, Common User Access, Common Programming Interface, and Interactive Transaction System are trademarks of International Business Machines, Inc. UIMX is a trademark of Visual Edge, Inc. Serpent is a trademark of Carnegie Mellon University.

Select portions of this book were adapted from Joëlle Coutaz, "Interfaces homme-ordinateur. Conception et réalisation" (Dunod, Paris 1990).

Library of Congress Cataloging-in-Publication Data

Bass, Len.
    Developing software for the user interface / by Len Bass and
  Joelle Coutaz.
      p.   cm. -- (SEI series in software engineering)
    Includes bibliographical references and index.
    ISBN 0-201-51046-4
    1. User interfaces (Computer science)   2. Software engineering.
I. Coutaz, Joëlle. II. Title. III. Series.
QA76.9.U83B37   1991
005.l--dc20   90-48300
                                                    CIP

Reprinted with corrections July, 1992

2 3 4 5 6 7 8 9 10–MA–95949392

PREFACE

The field of user interfaces is expanding rapidly. This expansion is driven by three factors: expectations of users, costs of development of the user interface, and emergence of new input/output technologies.

Having seen sophisticated iconic interfaces, such as that of the Macintosh, users now expect such interfaces to be readily available. The cost of providing these interfaces is high, however. The cost of the user interface in an interactive system can account for as much as 70 percent of the total life-cycle costs. The more sophisticated the interface, the higher the percentage of the life-cycle cost for which it accounts.

The range of technologies available for user interfaces is growing rapidly. In the last twenty years, the most common user interface has gone from cards to electric typewriters, to glass teletypes, to today's bit-mapped graphics. Other more exotic interface technologies have been developed; it will be only a short time before they become inexpensive enough to be readily available.

When new technologies are introduced, existing systems must be revised to take advantage of them. The cost of providing new features drives up user interface costs, and the effort involved in discovering how to use the new technologies effectively is immense.

Our intention in writing this book was to accomplish two purposes. First, we wish to explain the concepts behind the development of user interfaces from both the operator's perspective and the developer's perspective. We hope to enable the individuals involved in the development of user interface software to understand their role in the broader context of the software engineering life cycle.

Second, we wish to provide a categorization of the levels of abstraction of various tools and systems. One problem with the field of user interfaces is that words and concepts are used by different people in different ways. The categorization we employ is drawn from various sources and, in general, reflects mainstream usage. Our hope is that by providing a coherent discussion of these levels of abstraction and showing how they relate to one another, to the general problem of building user interfaces, and to various psychological concepts, we can reduce the semantic confusion associated with user interface discussions. A second benefit of categorization is that if software engineers build systems based on appropriate models of abstraction, the cost of constructing and modifying the user interface component will be reduced and thus more systems will be constructed with high-quality user interfaces.

Our focus in this book is on the life cycle of the user interface. This focus manifests itself primarily in an emphasis on software concepts, models, and architectures used in the development of user interfaces. That is the area in which we work and in which we have expertise. By focusing on concepts, we hope to ensure that the material in the book transcends any particular system. We use multiple systems as examples to clarify the various concepts discussed. The user interface software, however, is intimately connected with the front end of the life cycle—the design of the user interface. Since the user interface is often designed by a software engineer rather than a user interface specialist, we give a brief overview of design principles to guide the software engineer who is designing a user interface. We also include discussions of terminology and references to more extensive material on user interface design.

This book is unique in showing the influence that software and software architectures have on the resulting user interface and in identifying for the software engineer some of the implications of the technical choices that result in a complete working system.

This book is geared to software engineers who are developing user interfaces and to students of user interface software concepts. We assume that readers are familiar with basic software engineering concepts, but not necessarily those used in user interfaces. Readers are assumed to have used at least one of the modern bit-mapped graphics workstations with a window system and to be either professional software engineers or students in their senior year of college or first year of graduate school. The book provides an introduction to general concepts; it is not a programming manual for any particular system.

Acknowledgments

The people who have assisted in the preparation of this book are too many to enumerate. Worthy of special thanks are Marianne Deacon, Dennis Doubleday,

Spencer Peterson, Roberta Schwerer, Skip Shelley, Charles Weinstock, and the students of the DESS-GI at the Université Joseph Fourier of Grenoble, who implemented the first version of the mobile robot user interface: Annie Chabert, Nathalie Martin, Laurence Nigay, and Thierry Peuzin. The assistance provided by Karola Fuchs, Sheila Rosenthal, and the staff of the SEI library was outstanding. Also deserving of special mention is Josette Coutaz, who provided much of the sustenance that made this book possible. Finally, we thank David King, James Larson, John Sibert, and Dan Olson for their helpful comments on an early draft of this book.

The impetus for this book was provided by a tutorial organized by Peter Poole in his joint capacities as chairman of the Computer Science Department of the University of Melbourne and head of the International Federation of Information Processing's Technical Committee on Languages and Systems. The tutorial was given by IFIP Working Group 2.7 of which we are members. This book is affectionately dedicated to the other members of that Working Group.

Pittsburgh, Pennsylvania   L. B.
Grenoble, France   J. C.

CONTENTS

1

The Elements of User Interface Development

The process of designing and constructing user interfaces is critical to building systems that satisfy customers' needs, both current and future. This process includes the original design of the interface, implementation of the system, and modifications of the operational system. These modifications are endemic in interactive systems. Since the user interface can account for approximately 50 percent of total life cycle costs for interactive systems [Myers 1989a, Sutton and Sprague 1978], the software engineer has a vested interest in creating a user interface that both satisfies the customer and is constructed using the best available tools and techniques.

The user interface mediates between two main participants: the operator of the interactive system (a human being) and the computer hardware and software that implement the interactive system. Each participant imposes requirements on the final product. The operator is the judge of the usability and appropriateness of the interface; the computer hardware and software are the tools with which the interface is constructed. Consequently, an interface that is useful and appropriate to the operator must be constructed with the hardware and software tools available. Because of the complexity of both components, the construction of the user interface involves making many decisions about how to employ the tools available to best satisfy the operator. Developing the user interface is further complicated by the fact that the customer may not have a complete idea of the requirements for the system being constructed and may have preconceptions about the interface that are expensive and difficult to implement. The tools available to support user interface development vary widely in complexity and power; new tools are being developed very rapidly.

In this chapter, we discuss the life cycle of an interactive system, emphasizing those elements that relate to the user interface. The user interface elements are divided into those affecting the requirements and specification phases (the human side of the interface) and those influencing the implementation phase (the computer side of the interface). Finally, we introduce the example of a mobile robot, which we will use throughout the book.

The elements introduced here are expanded in the rest of the book. Chapter 2 discusses the user interface design process (the requirements and specification portion of the life cycle), Chapters 3, 4, and 5 deal with software structure (the implementation portion of the life cycle), and Chapter 6 covers user interface tools (the whole life cycle).

1.1   The Software Engineering Life Cycle

The user interface development cycle is a process involving a number of individuals. In this chapter we first look at the software engineering life cycle, then discuss the individuals involved in user interface development, and finally specify how user interface development fits within the software engineering life cycle.

Researchers in software engineering recommend six phases for the design and development of computer systems. These phases are requirements definition, specification, implementation, testing, installation, and maintenance [ANSI 1983].

1. *Requirements definition* is the formulation of a formal or semi-formal statement of the problem to be solved. This statement specifies the properties and services that the system must satisfy for a specific environment under a set of particular constraints. Requirements are defined with the customer—however, the customer may not necessarily be the operator of the final system.

2. *Specification* consists of high-level functional design and internal design. During high-level design, the computer functions that the operators will see are delineated. During internal design, the organization of the software program is delineated to meet the high-level design specification. In software engineering, this phase covers the definition of data structures, algorithms, modules, programming languages, and so forth.

3. *Implementation* is the expression of the internal specification in terms of a set of programming languages and tools.

4. *Testing* involves debugging both modules by themselves and sets of modules.

5. *Installation* is placing the software system into production.

6. *Maintenance* essentially involves making changes and dealing with their side effects.

Although these activities are defined as phases, in reality most development follows an iterative process of refinement—the specification phase may lead to the discovery of additional requirements; constraints discovered during implementation may affect the construction of the user interface; once the system is deployed, modifications of the user interface constitute further refinements; and so forth. (See Boehm 1988 for an incremental development model.) Thus, the process of refinement continues throughout the life cycle.

1.2   Roles

In general, humans play five roles in the development of a user interface. In some environments, the same person may perform all the roles; in others, the roles may be split among several individuals. The roles follow:

1. The *operator* runs the final interactive system. Thus, it is the operator who must be able to understand and use the user interface furnished by the people who perform the other four roles. We prefer the term *operator* to the term *user,* because there are many users within the domain of user interface. There is the operator, the programmer user of the various computer services, and the individual who uses the information generated by the interactive system. Even the term *end user* is not always correct, since the end user of the information generated by an interactive system is difficult to determine. It could be the operator, the manager who receives the information, or a customer who purchases a product based on the information received by the manager.

2. The *system designer* sets up the overall architecture of an interactive system, specifying which tasks are to be accomplished within which portion of the system. These decisions determine the tasks that are to be required of the operator.

3. The *user interface designer* employs the task specification of the system designer to define the interface with which the operator interacts. This individual needs to understand the task to be solved, the special needs of the operator, and the costs and benefits of particular user interfaces—both in terms of the operator and in terms of the implementation and maintenance costs.

4. The *functional-core software designer* creates the software structure needed to implement the tasks performed by the portions of the system other than

the user interface. In general, we will be concerned with this role only to the extent that it affects the user interface.

5. The *user interface software designer* structures the software that will implement the user interface defined by the user interface designer. Chapters 3, 4, 5, and 6 discuss material relevant to this role.

The people performing these roles interact in a process that results in the development of a sequence of user interfaces for a particular interactive system. This sequence terminates only when the interactive system is no longer being modified. Modification of an interactive system ceases when some portion of the interactive system can no longer feasibly be updated to incorporate additional or alternative functionality.

1.3   User Interface Life Cycle

The user interface life cycle generally follows that of software engineering. Two important observations about this design process will influence the presentation of the material in this book:

1. Designing and developing the user interface is an iterative process of refinement that persists as long as there is sufficient motivation to modify an interactive system. Thus, any implementation should be based on a software architecture that supports modification of the user interface.

2. On each side of the interface are abstract representations of the components. On the human side, these abstractions are studied, albeit imperfectly, by psychologists. On the computer side, these abstractions are described by a hierarchy of abstract machines that provide various levels of service and that cost differing amounts to implement and maintain. Any user interface must be based on an awareness of both components.

In each stage of the user interface life cycle, the people in the roles defined earlier may be responsible for further changes:

☐ The operator may ask for changes at any stage. The operator may want additional information available, a change in the appearance of the information presented, or additional functionality.

☐ The system designer may modify the functionality of the total system.

☐ The user interface designer may make changes because of error rates or dissatisfaction of the operator.

☐ The functional-core software designer may modify the structure of the tasks of the non–user interface portion of the system.

▫   The user interface software designer may make changes because of constraints introduced by the available tools.

The next sections discuss specific considerations relating to requirements
definition, specification, and implementation of the user interface in the software
engineering life cycle.

1.3.1   REQUIREMENTS DEFINITION

For user interface design, the requirements phase encompasses problem definition, operator modeling, and task analysis. Task analysis involves high-level
design of the user interface. To design a user interface for an interactive system,
the system designer must first understand the desired functionality of the system
and the capabilities of the operator. The system designer then constructs abstract
models of the operator and of the tasks to be performed—the base application
functionality.

The model of the operator contains assumptions about the operator's understanding of the application domain, human characteristics, and computer knowledge. The model of the interactive system contains a rudimentary version of the
functionality to be implemented. These models may be made explicit by the
system designer or, more likely, may be manipulated implicitly and be made explicit only at a later stage of the process.

It is important that software engineers involved in user interface construction understand the concepts and terminology used by user interface psychologists. The more knowledge the software engineer has of such concepts, the better
able he or she will be to design the interface. Even when they are working on a
team that develops requirements and specifications, software engineers must
interact with the user interface designer. In this case, it is important for the
software engineer to understand the terminology and outlook of the user interface
designer so that the two can communicate.

Chapter 2 discusses how this high-level design relates to the requirements
portion of the software engineering life cycle, and it suggests how the designer
could proceed with the user interface portion.

1.3.2   SPECIFICATIONS

In the specifications phase, the user interface designer specifies the interface with
which the operator will interact. The interaction objects to be used, such as
windows, commands, or menus, are determined. Usability and learnability tests
of these objects should be performed during this phase. Chapter 2 provides suggestions on how the user interface designer should proceed. Also during this
phase, the functional-core software designer defines the functions in greater detail.

Thus, during specification, the models of both the operator and the system functionality are refined. The user interface designer is responsible for refining the model of the operator, and the functional-core software designer is responsible for refining the model of system functionality. This refinement should be influenced by interactions with the customer and by consideration of the types and availability of tools to be used. At some stage in the process, the user interface designer expresses a user interface that captures the current notions of both the operator's model and the model of application functionality. The user interface can be expressed through a variety of means, including a prototype or a storyboard. The expression of the user interface is evaluated by the operator for suitability.

Throughout the specifications phase and all other phases of the life cycle, refinement continues. At any stage of the process, gains can be achieved by looking ahead. Such planning permits cost/benefit analysis of various desirable user interfaces or system functionalities in terms of their complexity and cost of implementation. Figure 1.1 shows how either tasks or interaction objects can be added or modified at any point.

1.3.3   IMPLEMENTATION

The software structure necessary to generate a user interface is better understood and easier to analyze than the operator's behavior. The user interface presents an abstract machine with which the human interacts. This abstract machine is realized through interaction of the software with the particular hardware on which the interactive system is executing. One way of structuring the software is as a hierarchy of other abstract machines, each providing certain services to the layers above it and requiring certain services from the layers below it.

We use the term *interactive system* to emphasize that we are discussing systems with which a human interacts. We are not discussing computer-to-computer communication. It should be clear, however, that an interactive system is a total functioning system. It includes any components necessary to make the system functional and is more than just the user interface portion of the system.

The layers we discuss are layers of abstraction and can be implemented in a variety of manners. One is to treat the abstract layers as actual layers and implement them as we describe them. Other implementation architectures are described in Chapters 4 and 5.

The division of the software into abstract machines yields a mechanism for protecting one layer from modifications in the layers below. The fundamental software engineering principles of *modularity* and *information hiding* are the basis of the notion of abstract machines.

In this book, a taxonomy of user interface software is used that divides an interactive system into the following levels:

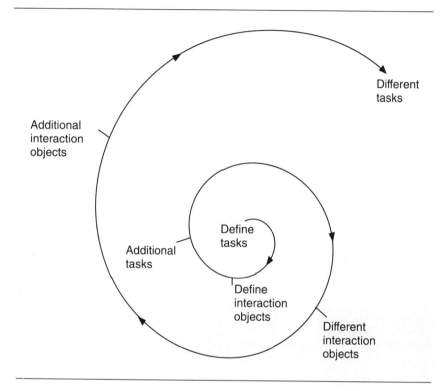

FIGURE 1.1
Process of iterative refinement of user interface. The user interface is defined in terms of tasks to be performed and interaction objects used to perform those tasks. The designer of the user interface continually switches between the definition and modification of the tasks and the definition and modification of the interaction objects used to perform those tasks.

1. A *device driver* controls the physical device. For example, the device driver sends pixel-level instructions to display the cursor in the desired position.

2. A *resource manager* controls the actual resources involved in the interactions. It both manages the physical device's resources and provides the abstractions used for interaction. For the most common interface technology, bit-mapped graphics terminals, the resource manager is a *window system.* Window systems are discussed in detail in Chapter 3.

3. An *interaction object* is an entity that the operator can perceive and manipulate with physical interaction devices such as a mouse or a keyboard. An interaction object includes both a presentation (output) and an interaction (input). A menu is an example of an interaction object. Interaction objects are discussed in Chapter 4.

4. The *dialogue controller* is the portion of the user interface software that controls the media used and the sequencing of user interactions. It determines the logic of the interactions, such as when an interaction object is accessible to the user. It also controls the style of the interactions— for example, whether menus or command lines are used. Dialogue control is discussed in Chapter 5.

5. The *functional core* implements domain knowledge, such as aircraft characteristics in an air traffic control system. The functional core should, ideally,

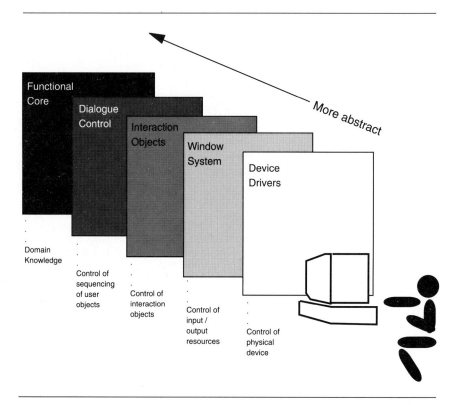

FIGURE 1.2
Operator interacting with computer. The software that generates the user interface can be divided into layers of abstraction. The device driver handles specific input/output requests, the window system manages the resources of the device, the interaction object layer manages the objects with which the operator interacts, the dialogue controller manages more abstract user interface concepts, and the functional core manages domain knowledge for the interactive system.

remain totally ignorant of the way its data structures and functions are exposed to the user via interaction objects. The functional core should be ignorant of both the media used for the input and output and the specific form in which the information is transmitted. For example, it should not know whether a window system or audio is used for output, what language is used to present text, or whether input comes from menus or from command lines. On the other hand, the functional core should not be ignorant of the fact that there is an operator with which it communicates. Although the knowledge that the functional core has of the operator should be manifested in a media-independent fashion, it is necessary for the functional core to have some knowledge of the existence of a user. Such knowledge is necessary, for example, for the detection of errors related to the application domain and the indication of legal targets of particular operations.

Each layer presents an abstract machine that provides certain services. The user of these services is called the *client*. The layer providing the services is called the *server*. The client, then, can be any layer above the server. For example, the client of the window layer could be the functional core, dialogue controller, or toolkit.

The operator of an interactive system communicates with the functional core through the user interface layers of device driver, window system, toolkit, and dialogue controller. The layers control increasingly abstract concepts. Figure 1.2 shows an operator interacting with the various layers.

Each of the intermediate layers—that is, those other than the device drivers and the functional core—has two functions. It must control its portion of the total user interface, and it must provide a mapping between the layers above it and the layers below it. Thus, the interfaces between the layers are important in any implementation.

1.4   Mobile Robot Example

The interaction between an operator and a mobile robot will be used to illustrate the concepts presented throughout this book. This example is based on the mobile robot [Crowley 1987] shown as a bit map photograph in Figure 1.3. The robot is designed to navigate through a collection of obstacles within a closed environment, such as a building. The robot is intended to perform surveillance of an environment that is hazardous for people, such as a chemical plant after an accident. Within the environment of the robot are walls, equipment, and people. The people are either intruders or accident victims. The robot must navigate through the environment using its own sensors and information available from an operator.

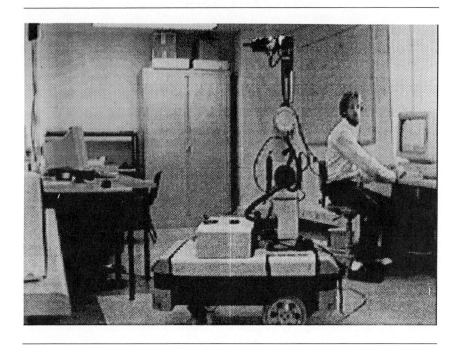

FIGURE 1.3
A bit map photograph of the mobile robot in a laboratory environment with its
operator. (Courtesy of Professor James L. Crowley, LIFIA, INPG, Grenoble, France.)

The operator interacts with the robot through a user interface implemented
on a workstation, which communicates with the robot by means of a radio serial
line. The operator provides the robot with an initial description of the structure of
the environment. This description includes nonmovable objects such as walls and
movable objects such as furniture. The operator may subsequently modify the
description of the environment by adding and deleting walls, for example. The
robot is also given a description of named places in the environment, as well as
routes between these places. Routes describe the passages between places and
suggest locomotion parameters for moving. For example, a route between assembly line 1 and assembly line 2 might direct the robot to move parallel to assembly
line 1 at a rapid speed for a certain distance, to slow down, to turn right, and to
proceed slowly for another specified distance.

The operator specifies a mission for the robot in terms of a set of surveillance and navigation tasks. A typical mission might consist of a command to
patrol a set of places during an interval of time. The robot translates the mission
into a plan composed of a sequence of locomotion and surveillance actions. At

the designated time, the robot executes the mission plan, while dynamically updating the description of its environment and re-deriving its plan. The operator observes the progress of the mission on the workstation and can intervene at any time to modify the specification of the mission or its execution.

1.5   Functional Core of the Mobile Robot Software

From the high-level description of the interactive system, the portion of the software that implements the functional core can be determined. In particular, the functional core implements all the functions discussed except for those involving media dependencies. The functional core is also responsible for these user interface services that require domain knowledge.

Note that we described the robot functionality almost entirely in terms specific to the application domain. That is, *environment, mission, route,* and so on are domain terms that the designers must understand to implement the interactive system. One of the problems for the user interface designer, discussed in Chapter 2, is how to make those application concepts clear to the operator. Solving this problem involves making assumptions about the domain sophistication of the operator.

The definition of the functional core of an interactive system, by necessity, begins with the definition of the interface between the functional core and the dialogue layer. In the robot example, the interface between the functional core and the dialogue layer should consist of a statement of the functional core's understanding of the environment and a statement of the calculated routes and basic operator commands, such as modify environmental information, modify routes, and perform movement, either along a single path of the route or along the total route.

Figure 1.4 is a high-level decomposition of the functional core of the robot software. Notice that the user interface exists solely as a single item off to the left of the design. The isolation of the user interface reflects three considerations. First, we will expand the user interface structure in succeeding chapters and so choose not to show the expansion here. Second, this structure clearly separates the user interface from the functional core, which simplifies modification of the user interface. One of the goals of the taxonomy described in this book is to allow the isolation and easy modifiability of the user interface software. Third, the figure represents the domain expert's view of the interactive system—that is, that the user interface is not as important as domain functions. This view is common among people who are not user interface specialists.

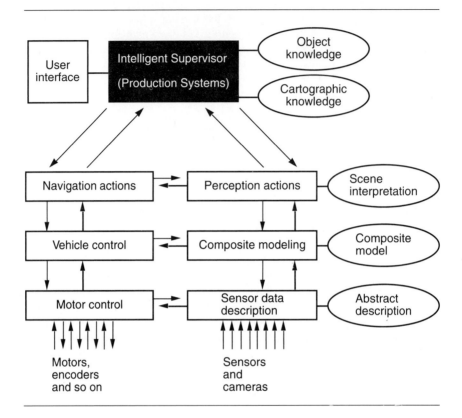

FIGURE 1.4
High-level decomposition of the functonal core of the mobile robot. The user interface software is contained in a single bubble, reflecting the domain specialist's view of the user interface.

1.6 Summary

In this chapter, we discussed the software engineering life cycle and how user interface development fits into it. We emphasized the importance of the human operator. Another important concept introduced was the abstract layers of an interactive system, with device drivers on one end and funtional core on the other.

Finally, we introduced an example of an interactive system that controls the action of a mobile robot. This example will be used throughout the book to illustrate important points.

2

In Search of a
Design Method

In this chapter we discuss the process of designing a user interface. Design starts with the system designer's defining the requirements and is made concrete by the user interface designer during the specifications phase. We present a series of steps that, though not simple, lead to a design intended to improve the overall usability and learnability of the user interface for the desired interactive system.

The goal of this chapter is to bring together material from diverse sources about user interface design. Although it is certainly not comprehensive nor complete, we expect the chapter to provide software engineers with a starting framework and pointers to sources with more information.

2.1 An Overview of the Design Stages

There is no exact method for designing interactive systems, but a number of researchers and practitioners in the areas of cognitive psychology and human factors have made an attempt to define a general framework for user interface design (for example, see Shneiderman 1987; Gould 1988; and Scapin 1986). Common steps in this process are:

1. Define the problem the customer wants solved.

2. Model the operator.

3. Perform task analysis.

4. Define the computer objects and functions that correspond to the task domain.

5. Design the appearance and behavior of the user interface.

6. Evaluate the design.

Figure 2.1 shows how these steps refine and relate to the software engineering stages. Problem definition, operator modeling, and task analysis are part of requirements definition. Computer objects and functions definition and user interface design are related to the specifications. The last step, evaluation, may be performed at any time in the design process.

From both the software engineering perspective and the user interface design perspective, the sequence of steps for user interface design is idealized. Designers do not move smoothly from step to step. At each stage, information is discovered that was unknown or overlooked at prior steps; consequently, design decisions made in prior steps must be adjusted. The process should also be forward looking. In particular, questions dealing with constraints should be considered early in the process. Hardware characteristics, the level of services provided by the software tools, the schedule, and the budget will all affect the final design and should be considered as early in the process as possible. Thus, the

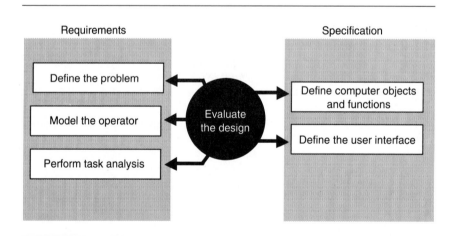

FIGURE 2.1
Refinement of the software engineering stages into the user interface design steps. The requirements phase includes defining the problem the customer wants solved, creating a model of the operator, and performing a task analysis. The specification phase includes defining the computer objects and functions that correspond to the task domain and designing the user interface. Evaluation should be carried out throughout these steps.

design task is a process of iteratively refining the current step as well as the previous ones, and knowledge of future steps influences actions at the current step.

This process does not stop with the design of the user interface but continues with the implementation and consequent modification of the user interface. Iterative refinement does not end as the process moves from the system designer to the user interface designer to the user interface software designer. During and after the initial implementation, information will be discovered that affects the design. To facilitate this iterative process, the system designer should gather as much information as is feasible at each step and should document any assumptions that lead from one step to the next so that they will be available for review and analysis at subsequent stages.

It is important to consider the user interface design explicitly in the requirements and specification stages so that implementation issues related to it can be considered. Looking forward to implementation during the design phase allows the designer to make user interface cost/benefit decisions at an early stage.

For the user interface software designer, the iterative refinement process dictates that software design be as flexible as possible. The user interface that the software initially implements is not usually the final user interface. The task breakdown underlying the user interface is difficult to modify substantially, but the expression of the task breakdown in the user interface will change frequently. Consequently, flexibility is vital in software design. Techniques for ensuring this flexibility are discussed in succeeding chapters. We now proceed with describing the steps for designing the user interface.

2.2   Define the Problem

The definition of the purpose of an interactive system can be expressed either formally or informally. This phase of the system design is beyond the scope of this book and in the sphere of requirements extraction [see Davis 1990]. From the point of view of subsequent steps, however, it is important that domain concepts be identified as explicitly as possible.

2.3   Model the Operator

The purpose of the second step is to determine the characteristics of the operators. Clearly, one cannot expect to build a system that is easy and enjoyable to use without having identified the salient properties of the operators. Psychologists are insistent on this point: interactive system design should be "user centered" [Norman and Draper 1986]; the designer should "know his user" [Hansen 1971]; and "early and continual focus on the user" [Shneiderman 1987] should be achieved. "Talking to users is not a luxury, it's a necessity" [Gould 1988].

The rationale behind "knowing the user" is that the designer must be able to decide what level of support the operator requires, both semantically and syntactically. We now discuss the concepts of semantic and syntactic knowledge, give some techniques for identifying an operator's characteristics, and provide some general classifications of operators.

2.3.1   SEMANTIC AND SYNTACTIC KNOWLEDGE

There are numerous theories of how knowledge is acquired, organized, retrieved, and exploited [Simon 1984, Tulving 1984]. This section describes a general simplified theory of knowledge: the semantic/syntactic model of user cognitive behavior [Shneiderman 1987].

Syntactic knowledge represents the linguistic conventions that the operator must know to communicate with the interactive system, either to specify requests to the interactive system (input expressions) or to interpret responses from the interactive system (output expressions). Thus, syntactic knowledge is specific to each computer system.

Semantic knowledge is an organized hierarchy of factual and procedural concepts or symbols. Factual concepts can be viewed as objects (or data), whereas procedural concepts can be viewed as a set of operations on objects (or procedures on data). Within an interactive system, *domain-dependent* semantic knowledge is inherent to the task domain and *system-dependent* semantic knowledge is the knowledge of the functioning of the interactive system. For example, understanding the meaning of "undo" is semantic, not related to the task domain. This is the category of system dependent semantic knowledge.

The concepts of syntactic and semantic knowledge correspond to the layers of user interface software defined in Chapter 1. The user interface layers provide syntactic processing, whereas the functional core is in charge of semantic processing. Figure 2.2 shows how semantic knowledge is translated into syntactic specification for presentation to the operator.

Syntactic and semantic knowledge are part of what Norman calls the conceptual model of the user. This model shows the user's mental representation of the interactive system and the task domain. In this representation, concepts of interest at a given time for a particular task are called *psychological variables* [Norman and Draper 1986].

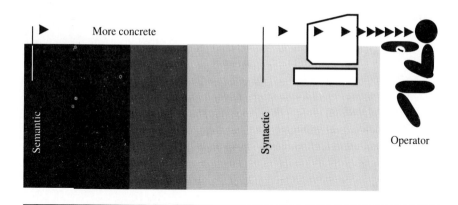

FIGURE 2.2
Semantic knowledge is generated by the functional core and converted by the user interface layers into syntactic form for presentation to the operator.

2.3.2 TECHNIQUES FOR IDENTIFYING THE OPERATOR'S CHARACTERISTICS

The degree to which one can characterize the operator depends on the whether potential users of the designed system can be identified. If the interactive system is to replace existing manual methods or systems, then it is possible to achieve direct contact with potential operators. Gould [1988] gives an excellent overview of simple techniques for gathering data about operators. These include interviews, questionnaires, observations of the user at work, videotaping, and thinking-aloud sessions. *Thinking aloud* is a technique whereby the operators explain their actions as they perform them. In all cases, the goal is to gain insight into the thinking and experience of the potential operators.

When the task is a new one, identifying potential operators is not always possible. In the case of the mobile robot, for example, the task domain is new. Thus, observation of the real-world use of a mobile robot is not possible. In such a situation, the operators can only be modeled based on general classifications, such as those proposed by Shneiderman [1987].

2.3.3 GENERAL CLASSIFICATION OF OPERATORS

Shneiderman [1987] organizes the community of operators into novice users, knowledgeable intermittent users, and frequent users. This classification is based on the operators' semantic and syntactic knowledge of both the task and computer software.

☐ Novice users have no syntactic knowledge, possibly little semantic knowledge about the computer domain, and/or shallow knowledge of the task domain.

☐ Knowledgeable intermittent users have good semantic knowledge of both the task domain and computer issues, but may have trouble remembering the details of syntactic knowledge.

☐ Frequent users are familiar with both syntactic and semantic aspects of the system.

Users may be novices in their semantic knowledge, but experts in their syntactic knowledge, or vice versa. For example, an operator may be ignorant in a domain but skillful at using a particular interactive system. Conversely, an operator may be knowledgeable in a field but ignorant in the use of a particular interactive system. Clearly, operators' mental models evolve with time from these two extremes.

In the case of the mobile robot, it was assumed that the operator was an expert in the domain of mobile robots but not a software engineer. Thus, the operator would require some training in using the system but little training in the goals and underlying assumptions of the system. One implication for the design was that easy syntactic constructs (for example, menus rather than command lines) were desirable, and that help should be provided on the appropriate use of these syntactic constructs. Another implication was that little explanation was necessary of the meaning of key terms from the domain.

In summary, there is no a priori rule for designing a system to be used by the average operator. Collecting informal data is an art requiring sensitivity and expertise. Some form of modeling of the operator is a necessary step in the design of an interactive system, however; the system designer always has a conceptual model of the operator. The issue is whether this model is created through the system designer's intuition or through some more systematic method. It is a rare system designer who has an accurate intuitive model of the operator of the system under design.

2.4   Perform Task Analysis

Once the system designer has identified the problem to be solved and has some knowledge of the operator, the next step is to define the specific tasks to be performed by the interactive system. As always, analyzing tasks may require refining the problem to be solved or learning about some new characteristics of the operator. The goal of task analysis is to identify what needs to be done and to structure the task domain in accordance with environmental properties—namely, the operator's mental model and the hardware characteristics. The result of this process is a set of specific tasks and concepts that the operator will perform and manipulate with the aid of the computer system.

Task analysis sets the foundation for the utility and the usability of the system. It may be seen as a two-step process: task decomposition and analysis of the decomposition.

2.4.1 TASK DECOMPOSITION

Operators tend to break large tasks into smaller subtasks until they reach unitary tasks. This observation has led to a number of models such as GOMS (goals, operators, methods, and selection rules) [Card, Moran, and Newell 1983] and representational frameworks such as CLG (Command Language Grammar) [Moran 1981]. CLG provides the designer with a way to model an interactive system as opposed to GOMS that models task decomposition. These models and frameworks describe what the operator should do, not what the operator actually does. Although they are idealized representations of real phenomena, they provide the system designer with a starting point.

One way to perform a task decomposition is to:

1. Consider the domain-dependent concepts and enumerate the operations to manipulate them.

2. Build up a hierarchy of tasks and subtasks.

Operations correspond to unit tasks. Domain dependent concepts together with their operations define the task objects of the domain as perceived by the operator. For example, the domain dependent concepts for the mobile robot system include environment, mission, place, routes, and walls. Operations for these objects include create, destroy, and modify. The concepts, plus their operations, are the task objects—that is, the objects on which a task is performed plus the valid tasks for that object. On the software side, task objects correspond to the abstract data structures of the functional core. On the operator side, they determine the services that the interactive system is able to provide.

Decisions made at this stage of the design process set the functional foundations for the whole interactive system. If the operator does not understand the tasks, then performance errors will occur. If the tasks are too low level, the operator will have to do too much work to achieve the desired result. If the tasks are too high level, the operator will not have the degree of control necessary to perform some tasks.

In designing the mobile robot system, we faced two alternatives: we could ask the operator to specify each step of the mission in a way that was comprehensible by the physical robot, or we could define for missions a higher level operation description that would automatically build the low-level script. Consideration of the operator's needs led us to define the high-level operation description.

Developing the task hierarchy is more difficult than selecting the basic operations on task objects, for the hierarchy contains assumptions about how the operator will solve the problems posed by the task domain. Consequently, we must rely on informal analysis of the data gathered during the building of a model of the operator. One way to exploit the experimental data is to identify the major task groups that sit at the top of the hierarchy and place the task object operations at the bottom of the hierarchy. The intermediate levels are then filled in by working down from the top levels and up from the bottom levels, attempting to match the results from the two directions. That is, scenarios are generated that describe the type of problems the operator will wish to solve and these scenarios are then examined in an effort to infer an appropriate task hierarchy.

As shown in Figure 2.3, the task domain of the mobile robot is composed of three main tasks: environment specification, mission specification, and mission execution. The specification of an environment requires modifying an existing environment or creating a new environment from scratch or from an existing one. Modifying or creating an environment involves editing environment items (for example, walls, routes, places).

Task decomposition is difficult and time consuming. For example, it took almost one labor year to define the task domain of the mobile robot. One method of determining the basic tasks is to define meaningful scenarios, which are then analyzed for the more basic tasks. The analysis should begin with simple scenarios and then proceed to progressively more complicated ones. Beginning with complicated scenarios focuses attention on special cases before the basic tasks have been discerned. During the mobile robot design process, each of the four designers specified the apparent steps to accomplish a scenario. By comparing the results, we were able to define a task model that we thought would be appropriate for the hypothetical user. Clearly, the quality of the model could have been improved by asking real users to participate in the exercise.

An important notion that should not be neglected at this stage of the design process is dealing with errors. The Latin expression *errare humanum est* acknowledges the fact that errors are unavoidable. Several theoretical analyses explain the causes and occurrences of errors [Norman 1983, Reason 1982]. Lewis and Norman [1986] divide errors into two major categories: slips and mistakes. *Slips* are non-intended actions, whereas *mistakes* result from inappropriate intentions. Slips are related mainly to syntactic-lexical knowledge (although not exclusively), whereas mistakes result from semantic knowledge deficiencies. In both cases the goal of the system designer is to:

- Minimize error occurrences.
- Facilitate early error detection.
- Support error repair.

Since errors involve all levels of the operator's knowledge, "designing for errors" should be taken seriously at every step of the design process, including task analysis. It is essential that task decomposition and the delineation of task domain concepts, which serve as the basis for the semantic conceptual level of the interactive system, be consistent with the operator's model and the purpose of the

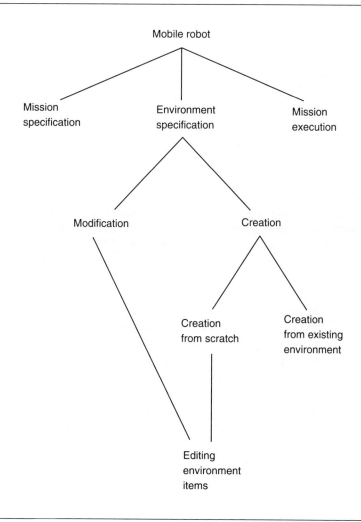

FIGURE 2.3
A sketch of the task decomposition for the mobile robot. The highest level tasks are: mission specification, environment specification and mission execution. Environment specification has the subtasks of modification and creation.

system. This helps to prevent errors. It is also essential that the individual tasks be analyzed for possible error conditions that might occur during the execution of a task. In particular, decisions must be made about:

☐ Task ordering—how much freedom does the operator need to switch between tasks?

☐ Task anticipation—how much information should be provided about the next tasks allowed, once a particular task has been specified?

☐ Explanations—how much domain-dependent information must be provided when errors occur?

☐ Assistance—how much domain-dependent information must be suggested for error repair?

For example, for the mobile robot system, the following decisions were made.

☐ Task ordering. Having observed that editing tasks are primarily user-driven, we decided that task ordering should be essentially free. As a result, the operator of the mobile robot is able to switch between any of the three major categories of tasks: environment specification, mission specification, and mission execution. The task domain, however, imposes some constraints on the operator. Mission specification tasks cannot be undertaken if there is no environment. Similarly, one cannot plan execution tasks if no mission exists. As discussed in Section 5.2.2., these constraints can be modeled in terms of preconditions.

☐ Task anticipation. Mission specification is a semantically complicated task. At each stage in a partial specification of a mission, further legal specifications are identified by the mission specification task. These are presented to the operator as a menu, but the presentation is not the responsibility of the task. The important point is that during the execution of the task, legal subtasks are explicitly anticipated.

☐ Explanations. These are provided on a domain-dependent basis. For example, when the operator builds a wall that intersects a route, the system is able to detect this error and return a message about the nature of the problem.

☐ Assistance in error repair. Domain objects involved in the problem are identified for the operator (for example, the route and wall that intersect).

2.4.2 TASK DECOMPOSITION ANALYSIS

Once a task sketch or graph has been constructed, it can be analyzed and possibly revised to simplify operator usage. In this section we discuss some specific items to look for during this analysis and some of the implications of the task graph structure. A task decomposition should be examined for:

- Alternative decompositions of a single task.
- Common tasks at different points in the graph.
- Non-determinancy within the task graph.
- Categorization.

Alternative Decomposition and Common Tasks.   Alternatives and commonalities in the task graph are related. Alternatives occur when a task has several possible decompositions. For example, for the mobile robot system, we have identified two methods of accomplishing the task "modify location of a place": "get/set info" for fine tuning the location and "move" when precision of location is not required. As shown in Figure 2.4, "get/set info" presents the location of a place as two editable (X,Y) fields. The "move" command allows the operator to move the location of a place by manipulating the mouse.

Having alternative methods for performing a given subtask can be either good or bad. It is helpful if the methods correspond to different cognitive needs and are available at every occurrence of the subtask. Both of the methods in the example "modify location of a place" are available for every occurrence of the subtask. Having alternatives is detrimental if both methods are not consistently available [Scapin 1986, p. 14].

Context-dependent alternatives lead to semantic inconsistencies, increasing learning time and the likelihood of error. For example, the subtask "modify

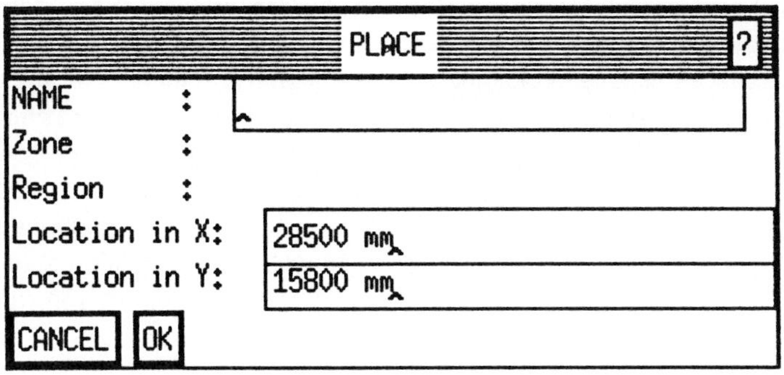

FIGURE 2.4
The form obtained with the "get/set info" command allows the operator to fine-tune the location of a place by editing the location in the X and Y fields.

location of a place" may be performed in the task contexts mission specification and environment specification. If the subtask had different decompositions in the two main tasks (for example, if "get/set info" were not available for mission specification), the alternative methods for modifying the location of a place would be context-dependent and semantically inconsistent.

Commonalities should be indicated in the task graph by a single node rather than by having the same task twice within the graph. When nodes that express the same task are combined, all possible decompositions of that task will automatically be available whenever that task is to be performed and context dependencies will be avoided.

Nondeterminancy and parallelism.   Nondeterminancy occurs when a single task has multiple subtasks that can occur in any order. It is important not to arbitrarily impose ordering upon tasks at this level. An imposed ordering may not be the one most conducive to the operator's solving the task easily. In the context of the mobile robot, the operator is allowed to partially build a wall in the robot environment, switch to editing a place, and then finish defining the wall. Nondeterminancy gives the user flexibility in choosing which task to perform when.

Parallelism occurs when multiple agents are involved in the task or when the user acts simultaneously on different task entities through multiple input devices. Examples of inherently parallel domains are (1) systems in which a collection of users collaborate on the solution of a single problem and (2) the execution of a mission in which the robot and the user are simultaneous actors.

User interface software must support the types of nondeterminacy and parallelism inherent in the task decomposition. This problem falls in the area of dialogue control discussed in further detail in Chapter 5. The operations defined as the primitives during the task analysis are the atomic elements and, once issued, will execute with no further operator intervention. It is possible, however, to define other operations (also atomic) whose function is to monitor or interrupt the original atomic operations. Thus, a level of operator control beyond the original task decomposition is possible, but this level should be used only for monitoring or error detection. If these interruptive operations have extensive semantic implications, they should be included in the original task decomposition.

Task Categorization.   The task graph may also be useful for categorizing tasks and for flagging those requiring special attention. Special attention may be required for various reasons. Frequency of the tasks is one reason [Shneiderman 1987]. Complexity of the task is another.

The complexity of tasks can be used as a category for organizing the functional space of the system into layers. According to the *training wheels technique* advocated by Carroll and Carrithers [1984], simple functions should be made available in a straightforward way, whereas advanced functions should be made less accessible. With this arrangement, newcomers may perform easy tasks without being confused and frustrated by failures, and they can progressively explore the system up to the most complex features. In other words, they learn by doing. In the mobile robot, the mission execution task, which involves the collaboration of two actors (the robot and the operator), is marked as a case requiring special attention because of the complexity of parallel operations.

So far, we have analyzed the operator's needs and have structured the task domain in a way that is amenable to an interactive system. We now need to consider the specification phase of the software engineering life cycle. Requirements definition can be considered the semantic phase of the user interface life cycle, whereas specification is the syntactic phase. In the next sections we discuss different types of syntactic constructs that can be used within user interfaces.

2.5 Define Computer Objects and Functions

Up to this point the system designer has determined the task objects and basic operations that will be made available to the operator in some fashion. The next phase in the design is to make those objects explicit—that is, to determine which computer objects will exist within the user interface (although without specifying the details of these objects) and which within the functional core, the functionality that will be accomplished by these objects, and the specific methods of communication that will exist between the user interface objects and the objects in the functional core.

The basic design principle to be followed in this phase is that of *direct correspondence* [Hutchins, Hollan, and Norman 1986]. That is, the task objects and structure should relate directly to the way in which the operator specifies the operations to be performed. A direct correspondence reduces the mental effort that the operator has to exert when translating intention into the concepts offered by the system. The more substantial this mental effort, the greater the *semantic distance* is said to be. Semantic distance also reflects the operator's mental effort when interpreting the system state in terms of a mental representation. In somewhat simpler language, the operator has to determine the correct input to gain a desired result and has to interpret the system output in terms of the result expected.

Defining computer objects involves:

☐ Making a correspondence between task objects and computer objects and dividing the computer objects into semantic and syntactic,

☐ Providing general computer services to enhance task accomplishment, and

☐ Deciding who drives the interactions—the operator or the interactive system.

2.5.1   MAKING TASK OBJECTS CORRESPOND TO COMPUTER OBJECTS

The purpose of the first step is twofold: identifying the computer objects that correspond to the task objects and defining the system commands in accordance with the task graph. Computer objects may be classified as either semantic or syntactic. We now discuss this distinction in some detail.

Semantic Computer Objects.   Semantic computer objects (or semantic objects) model task domain objects. Direct correspondence suggests that each task object have a semantic object counterpart. Designs that are based on the task objects of the domain are clearer, easier to modify, and easier to explain than are designs that, in some sense, confuse task concepts.

Since semantic objects are domain dependent, they are processed by the functional core of the interactive system. In the mobile robot example, the functional core implements the semantic objects "places" and "walls" to represent the task objects places and walls. Note that although the semantic objects have been defined, the mechanisms used to present them to the operator have not.

In Section 2.4.1 we mentioned the importance of error modeling. At this stage in the process, the mechanisms for error reporting become more refined. Error conditions are some of the semantic concepts that must be mapped into task domains. Task domains exist in the operator's mental model; computer objects exist in software and mapping is from the operator's mental model to computer software. We have found it convenient to model an error as a data structure whose type denotes a level of seriousness and whose components reference the concepts involved in the error. As shown in Figure 2.5, the seriousness code can be transformed into some type of display in the next step of the design (user interface definition). Thus, the error type can be transformed into a visual hint for warning the operator, and the components detailed in the error data structure can provide

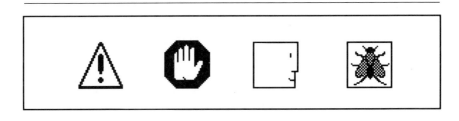

FIGURE 2.5
Examples of visual hints to express the level of seriousness of errors.

There isn't enough room on the disk to duplicate or copy the selected items (additional 145,408 bytes needed).

OK

FIGURE 2.6
An example of an explicit error message. The system gives the cause of the error and provides the user with additional information useful in recovering from the error. (Reprinted by permission Apple Computer, Inc.)

information about the exact cause of the semantic error. As Norman [1986] observes, the greater the precision of the semantic feedback, the easier it is for the operator to evaluate and recover from errors. Figure 2.6 illustrates a semantic error message that precisely identifies the cause of an error. Figure 2.7 provides an example of how error messages may be classified in the user interface according to their seriousness. This is another example of the type of feedback that helps the operator. Note that at this stage the type of error has been determined and the information to be presented to the operator has been determined, but the exact presentation of that information has not.

Syntactic Computer Objects and Syntactic Tasks.   Although interactive systems are designed for specific task domains, there are tasks and concepts inherent

---

CRITICAL ERRORS:

In statement **x := a** (highlighted line 24),
the variable **x** has not been declared.

TOLERABLE ERRORS:

Variable **y** is declared (highlighted line 2) but is not referenced.

FIGURE 2.7
An example of error messages classified according to their gravity for a programming environment.

in computer technology that are independent of the task domain. For example, output rendition is performed through windows, but windows may overlap and behave like peepholes that limit visibility. As a consequence, the operator must perform operations on windows, such as scrolling and resizing, to overcome the limitations of the technology. Recall that syntactic knowledge represents linguistic conventions.

□ *Syntactic tasks* are actions that result from the use of computer technology and are independent of a particular application domain.

□ *Syntactic computer objects* (or syntactic objects) are objects used to represent psychological variables that do not exist in the task domain but are useful in accomplishing a task with the computer.

An example of a useful syntactic object is support for multiple and simultaneous views of the same semantic computer object. Each view matches a particular need at some stage of a given task. For example, in editing text, it should be possible to view a document as a table of contents and, simultaneously, read a particular chapter or subsection. The table of contents and the subsection are two views of the document semantic computer object. As another example, Figure 2.8 shows an environment from the mobile robot that is presented simultaneously in two different windows but at different levels of detail. In one window routes are suppressed, whereas the other shows all of the components of the environment.

In all cases, visual consistency should be maintained between the multiple views; when relevant, any change in one view should be reported to the others. For example, in the mobile robot system, movement of a wall in one view should be reflected in the other views, provided they show walls. Multiple views are not always easy to implement. This issue is discussed in Chapter 5.

Multiple presentations of a single semantic object should not be confused with the existence of multiple semantic objects for a single task object. The point we are making in this section is that there should be a direct correspondence between semantic objects and task objects, and any refinement of those semantic objects for the purposes of simplifying operator interaction should be accomplished by introducing syntactic objects.

The Boundary Problem between Semantic and Syntactic Objects.   The distinction between semantic and syntactic objects has a useful implication for software design. Semantic concepts, which model the task domain, are implemented in the functional core. Syntactic objects, which do not involve the functional core directly and do not have direct counterparts in the functional core, should be implemented in the user interface portion of the interactive system. However, life is rarely so simple. In practice, the distinction between syntactic and semantic concepts is not always clear. It is possible, and frequently done, to aggregate task concepts into a single concept available to the operator. For example, a useful support for the evaluation of errors is an overall indicator of the system state.

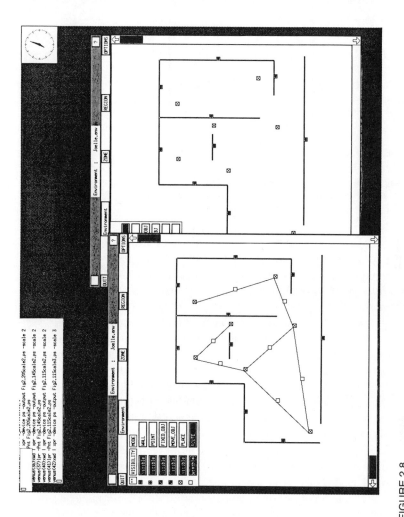

FIGURE 2.8
Multiple simultaneous views of the same semantic concept for the mobile robot system. The view of the environment on the left displays more information than does the view on the right.

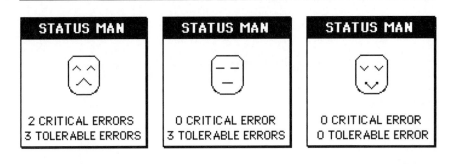

FIGURE 2.9
The status man is a syntactic concept that serves as an overall indicator of the system state. It is either happy, neutral, or sad, depending on the error conditions of the interactive system.

Figure 2.9 gives an example of such an indicator: the *status man.* Although it is clear that a status indicator is a useful feature, it represents an aggregate of task error states and not a task error state by itself. Coutaz [1987a] calls such aggregates *semantic repair objects,* although semantic enhancement objects is a more descriptive term.

   Another example of semantic enhancement is the concept of zone in the mobile robot. The task decomposition contains no concept of zone, but by analyzing the mobile robot task decomposition, a system designer observed that the specification of identical values might be repeated for a number of places. For example, the operator might tell the robot that at places p1, p2, and p3, it should follow any humans, warn the operator in case of fire, and move as fast as possible. According to the Keystroke model [Card, Moran, and Newell 1983], describing expected robot behavior in terms of the zone concept and specifying which places belong to which zone should be more convenient for the operator than entering such information several times. The zone concept has subsequently been the subject of much heated discussion among the system designers.

   So far we have identified the computer objects useful in modeling task objects and discussed, in general, the distinction between semantic objects (ultimately in the functional core) and syntactic objects (ultimately in the user interface software). We now need to identify the commands that the operator should use to manipulate the computer objects.

Command Levels.   The most direct method of defining the commands available to the operator is to associate commands with atomic tasks in the task decomposition. This approach is straightforward and simple. However, it relies on a "proper" task decomposition. As Shneiderman observes, "choosing the appropriate set of atomic actions is a difficult task"[1987, p. 56]. In particular, the definition of what commands should encompass is a difficult problem: "If the atomic actions are too small, the users will become frustrated by the large number of actions necessary to accomplish the higher level task. If the atomic actions are too large and elaborate, the users will need many such actions with special options, or they will not be able to get exactly what they want to do" [Shneiderman 1987, p. 56].

We saw one example of this problem in the specification of the mobile robot's physical actions. The task decomposition for the mobile robot provides another example: the creation of an environment is one task, and the editing of an environment is another. Should the operator perform these as two separate commands, or should there be one command to both create and edit the environment? Identifying each task as a command will reduce the semantic distance, but it may increase the keystroke difficulty of performing the task. The solution we advocate is to identify each operation as a separate semantic level service, then identify keystroke problems and reduce them with syntactic objects.

2.5.2   PROVIDING GENERAL SERVICES

We have described some concepts involved in relating task objects to computer objects. Extra computer objects may be defined to extend and correct for the operator's capabilities. These objects typically have semantic as well as syntactic components. The extra facilities may be of general use—for example, macro commands, undo-redo, cut-and-paste, provision for on-line help, and default values—or they may be services specific to the application domain. In this section we focus on services in general use. In Chapters 4 and 5 we will see how user interface toolkits and dialogue controllers provide (or do not provide) mechanisms to support general services. Some general services, however, require semantic support and, hence, must be included in the functional core. Defining the computer concepts explicitly makes it possible to determine and support the requirement that the functional core supports these services.

Macro Commands.   A *macro command* is a command that is defined as the combination of several existing commands. It minimizes the number of physical actions needed to specify input expressions (see the Keystroke model [Card, Moran, and Newell 1983]) and has been identified by human factors research as a factor that simplifies the use of user interfaces (as long as it is not overdone).

A macro command is an abstraction mechanism for interaction languages. As such, it matches human cognitive processes that encapsulate related pieces of knowledge into bigger chunks. In the creation of an environment for the mobile robot, the primitive tasks are "create environment" and "edit environment." Yet, most frequently, the operator will wish to edit an environment after creating it. Thus, the definition of a macro command to perform both the creation and the editing makes sense.

The use of macro commands can be supported either by the task domain or by syntactic means. An example of a syntactic macro command is "mouse button down, mouse button up" within the interaction object "select." Error checking for macro commands is best done when semantic knowledge can be invoked. An example of a semantic macro command is creating and editing in a single command. Consequently, the definition and expansion of macro commands are often included in the task domain.

Undo-Redo.   Undo-redo allows easy and straightforward recovery from errors and slips. It saves the operator the trouble of trying to figure out a plan of action to bring the interaction back to a safe or previous state. As a side effect, undo-redo facilities encourage exploration of the interactive system and, thus, discovery of new facilities.

Although undo-redo effectively supports task accomplishment, its implementation is not trivial. Recovering from or undoing the effect of a previous command is often difficult. In general, undoing involves all the levels of abstraction of the interactive system, from the device layer through the functional core. Undoing cannot be solved as a simple sequential "un-processing" through the software layers. A current technique for undoing is based on the commitment mechanism developed for transactional systems. A commitment is a statement to the system that it is allowed to perform irreversible actions. In a database system, the updating of the physical database usually cannot be undone. In a mail system, the sending of a message cannot be undone. In a process control system, a change in the physical state of the system being controlled cannot be undone.

A consequence of using commitment as a mechanism for undo-redo is that the portion of the system that controls the action to be done must be the one that performs the undo. Thus, this portion of the system must, in some form, have the commit operation for its objects.

Commitment may be performed at both the semantic and the syntactic level, and consequently recovery can be performed at both levels.

□   Syntactic commitment results from the syntactic object's producing a particular feedback, which leads the operator to believe that the command has been processed. Actually the effect of the command is determined locally in the user interface without involving semantic objects. Typically, in graphics editors, a "draw line" request results in the appearance of a line on the screen but does not change the internal structure of the picture under construction. The commitment occurs at some later point in the dialogue, when the syntactic object managing the picture informs the semantic object that a change has been made. In the meantime, the operator can undo modifications.

□   Semantic commitment could provide a basis for undoing at specified points. These points can be specified explicitly by the operator (the save command) or determined automatically by the system (shadowing—a technique for maintaining both modified objects and the original objects until an explicit commitment is performed). This type of commitment does not have the flexibility of a full-fledged undo mechanism. However, it allows for safe and simple recovery from disastrous situations. In addition to performing saves during the session, the system may automatically duplicate files when they are opened. Thus, the operator can undo to an initial state.

In the mobile robot example, it is not always possible to undo the actions of the robot. (Sometimes it would not even make sense to ask.) In the editing phases, however, undo-redo features are desirable. So far, undo with syntactic object commitment has not been implemented in the mobile robot, but it is possible to restore any file content to its initial state at the beginning of the session.

Cut-Copy-Paste.   Cut-copy-paste is the electronic version of manual patchwork. Information can be deleted from one place in the operator's vision and inserted in another. Reusing outputs as inputs avoids redoing of sequences of actions and supports a limited form of undoing. Consequently, it reduces the number of slips and frustration. However, implementation is not straightforward.

The problem with implementation arises when the source and the destination do not handle identical data types. In such cases, type recasting must occur: when feasible, data in the source format must be transformed to fit the destination format. General type recasting is a topic for research and is still an open question. Consequently, the current practice is to develop ad hoc techniques. Sometimes the adopted solution has undesirable side effects for the operator. For example, consider a round-trip transfer of information between MacDraw® and MacPaint.® MacDraw manipulates graphical objects such as circles and polygons, whereas MacPaint handles pixels only. That is, MacDraw maintains the semantic information that a particular arrangement of pixels is a circle whereas MacPaint semantics deal only with pixels. As a result, a circle drawn in MacDraw and then pasted in MacPaint loses its original graphics type. It becomes a bitmap. When pasted back into the object-based tool, it does not recover its original type. Thus, a circle produced with MacDraw, cut and pasted into MacPaint, then transferred from MacPaint back into MacDraw is not editable any more as a circle, although it still appears to the user as a circle. The cut-and-paste operations have lost semantic information about transferred data.

In summary, from the operator's point of view, the "quality" of cut-and-paste depends on the semantic information maintained within the transfer. This issue will be discussed further in Section 5.2.3.

On-line Help.   On-line help is useful as a reminder or as an elementary teaching definition tool when the operator has forgotten or does not know the role of a particular computer object. Help information can be factual or procedural. *Factual help* describes the role of the objects and functions of the system; *procedural help* indicates how to accomplish a particular task or provides a list of objects currently available for action by the operator.

A simple way to implement factual help is to assign a description message to each computer object and operation. This message is displayed at the operator's request. In order to help the operator build associations, messages may include pointers to related notions. Even this simple form of on-line help requires the production of a large variety of different and meaningful messages. Experiments show that careful attention must be paid to the content [Borenstein 1985], otherwise on-line help may be worse than hard-copy manuals [Relles 1979]. Factual help does not require contextual knowledge of the interactions and thus can be fully implemented in the user interface part of the interactive system.

On-line help typically introduces a configuration management problem into the interactive system. The information about an item exists in two separate places: the executing system and the help message. Any change to the externals of the item in the executing system must be echoed to the on-line help system. Maintaining consistency of the two in a system undergoing modifications requires special attention.

Procedural help supports problem solving. It provides answers to questions such as "how do I do this?" and "why?" That is, given the current state, the system is able to tell the operator how to reach a specified goal or to explain why a particular goal is not reachable. This type of support requires a clear understanding of the tasks the operator wishes to accomplish. Procedural help relies heavily on dynamic knowledge of the task domain and semantic concepts. Consequently, procedural help for problem solving becomes part of the functional core as well as of the user interface.

Default Values.   Default values assist the operator by reducing the number of items the operator needs to remember; they also reduce the number of physical actions necessary to specify a value. Thus, providing default values is a kind of error-prevention mechanism.

There are two kinds of default values: static and dynamic. *Static default values* do not evolve with the session. They are either defined within the system or acquired at initiation time from a profile file. On the other hand, *dynamic default values* evolve during the session. They are computed by the system from previous user inputs. Figure 2.10 gives an example of the default value proposed by a system for the file name of a document being saved in the course of an editing session.

In general, default values should be a combination of "most likely" and "least dangerous" responses. They should be most likely to reduce operator effort and least dangerous to reduce operator error. For example, a default value for a deletion query should be "no."

2.5.3   DECIDING WHO DRIVES THE INTERACTION

The final step in defining the computer objects is deciding whether the operator or the interactive system is in charge of the interactions. We have stressed the ne-

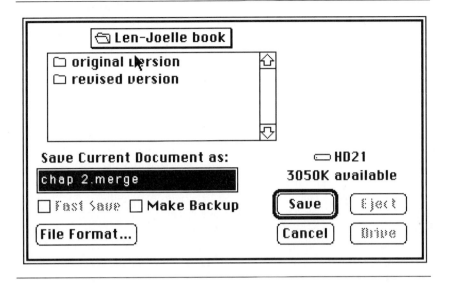

FIGURE 2.10
An example of a dynamic default value. The default file name for saving a document is the name of the document being edited. In order to attract attention, the name is highlighted in reverse video.

cessity of having a model of the operator when fundamental decisions must be made. One of the most fundamental questions in matching the computer world to the task domain is deciding whether the operator or the system drives the interaction. The choice is based on the purpose of the interactive system but is determined mostly by the model of the operator.

In *system-driven interactions* the operator must respond to a particular question from the system. In *user-driven interactions* the operator is free to choose among a number of currently valid options. The distinction between system-driven and user-driven systems is in the breadth of semantically valid inputs across time. In the system-driven case the breadth is one, whereas in the user-driven case the breadth is greater than one.

In general, the operator should have the initiative in a dialogue. This recommendation stems from the view of the computer as a tool: the computer is a submissive server, whereas the operator is the principal actor. In some cases, however, interaction should be driven by the system. For example, in the case of an electronic tutorial, where the operator's domain knowledge is limited and the goal is to learn more about the domain, the operator may feel more confident if the successive steps of the task are suggested by the computer.

A more general way to approach the question of who drives the interaction is to consider the interaction between the human and the computer as a collaboration. In a collaboration, partners act according to their competence. In the case of human-computer interaction, the computer should behave so as to extend the operator's skills. It should let the operator act freely and take control arbitrarily. The difficulty for the user interface designer lies in identifying the transition points where control shifts from the operator to the computer and back.

In the particular case of the mobile robot, the transition points were determined on the basis of the three main categories of tasks: mission specification, environment specification, and mission execution. The first two tasks are editing tasks, and editing is primarily a user-driven type of interaction. On the other hand, mission execution is essentially done by the robot, although the operator must have precedence over the robot. The need for the operator to be able to switch freely between task categories led us to introduce a "transfer" command, which allows the operator to switch between the categories of activities without stopping the current activities. Overall, the whole system is under the control of the operator.

Whether the computer is a tool or a collaborator, the operator should have maximum opportunity to achieve the desired task. Since human problem solving is basically opportunistic, the command space of the interactive system must not be arbitrarily constrained by an inflexible model of interaction. Too often computer scientists turn to techniques such as the use of sequential finite state machines, which artificially limit the options of the operator. For example, it is common practice to force operators to correct semantic errors right away. Clearly, this simplifies the programming task but imposes heavy restrictions on the operator.

In the mobile robot system, semantic errors such as route and wall intersections are detected but accepted, as long as the operator does not build a mission for the faulty environment. As advocated in Section 2.4.1, errors were modeled early in the design process. They are not afterthoughts and are dynamically maintained by the system according to the actions of the operator.

To summarize:

☐ The computer concepts definition phase results in the delineation of a number of computer objects and operations, which should be very close to or possibly extend the task objects. If not, the operator will have learning difficulties and a high error rate.

☐ This phase may result in changes to the task domain, if new semantic computer objects are discovered.

☐ This phase has a strong impact on the internal organization of the functional core. The execution control of the functional core should be driven by the model of the operator.

The elements of the task domain and the matching computer concepts fully define the interface of the functional core with the user interface software. We need now to determine the appearance and behavior of the user interface.

2.6   Design the User Interface

The purpose of this last stage of the design is to define a user interface that conveys a model of the task domain in a way that is both attractive and compatible with the operator's expectations. It should be kept in mind that there are no iron-clad rules. The rules we give can be interpreted in different ways and, in certain cases, are themselves contradictory. The design approach to follow is to use these rules as guidelines and then evaluate the resulting interface. Evaluation provides the best predictor of the success of an interface.

The design of the user interface has two basic components: (1) identifying the interaction objects to show the semantic and syntactic objects and (2) making the system state explicit.

2.6.1   CHOOSING INTERACTION OBJECTS

An interaction object is a computer object that represents a single syntactic or semantic object. At this stage of the design process, the requirements for choosing the appropriate interaction objects are derived from the Theory of Action [Norman and Draper 1986]:

- Psychological variables (those concepts of interest for the task and, by extension, semantic/syntactic objects of the interactive system) should have counterparts in physical variables.
- Physical variables should be associated with physical control devices.

Just as semantic and syntactic objects model task objects, so interaction objects present semantic and syntactic objects to the operator. Interaction objects are in turn associated with physical input and output devices (mouse, keyboard, and screen). We observe that the direct correspondence principle applies all the way through the user interface design steps, from the abstract task domain down to the actual hardware.

One difficulty for the user interface designer is choosing the appropriate interaction objects. The selection should be driven primarily by the goals of (1) consistency, (2) support for action sequence specification, and (3) reduction of the distance between the form of an expression and its meaning.

Defining an Overall Consistency.   The consistency we are interested in at this stage is in the look and feel of the user interface. The look of a user interface is its appearance, and the feel is its behavior. Consistency helps the operator find the correct form for specifying a desired command (the operator can often infer the correct form from remembered forms) [Scapin 1986, p. 14]. Consistency, however, is not an obvious characteristic. What is consistent to one person is not necessarily consistent to all [Grudin 1989]. Evaluating the resulting interface is the best way to determine whether it is consistent. General techniques for enhancing the consistency of the interface's look and feel include defining of an interaction metaphor and using a user interface toolkit.

A *metapho*r is a "figure of speech in which a term is transferred from the object it ordinarily designates to an object it may designate only by implicit comparison or analogy" [*The American Heritage Dictionary of the English Language*]. Metaphors are useful for describing a new model in terms of a known model. For example, one can explain the organization of an atom from the model of our solar system. The new model is then updated over time by manipulating the new concepts. This observation has led cognitive psychologists to explore metaphors in the domain of computer human interaction [Carroll and Mack 1985].

There are currently two major metaphors for interaction: the model world metaphor and the conversation metaphor [Hutchins, Hollan, and Norman 1986]. The model world metaphor electronically mimics objects in the real world. A popular example is the desktop metaphor, in which icons represent folders and documents and the mouse is the electronic extension of the hand. The conversation metaphor is based on a linguistic description of the actions to be performed on system objects. Examples of the conversation metaphor include textual command languages such as the Unix Shell. In the conversation metaphor, the user talks about an implicit world (the user describes what is to be done), whereas in the world metaphor the user directly manipulates objects (the user does not tell how to do it, but instead does it). "Direct engagement" of the user seems to shorten the distance between mental and computerized representations.

The real world metaphor may be interpreted as "using the representations normally used" rather than "using real representations." In Figure 2.11, walls, routes, and places are represented as people might *draw* them in the real world — as lines and rectangles. They are not represented by photographs of walls, routes, and places. These walls, routes, and places can be created and moved around by manipulating the mouse.

When a metaphor is used to guide interactions, there are always situations in which the metaphor does not apply. For example, there is no general "undo" operation on a real desktop. In such cases, the use of a metaphor may become confusing rather than clarifying. Judgment must be used in deciding which metaphor to use and how far to carry that metaphor into the interface.

Some user interface toolkits are designed to convey a built-in "look and feel" consistency. They include a set of predefined general purpose interaction objects, such as buttons, scroll bars, and forms, which are useful for many interactive systems. In such toolkits, certain operations are always performed in a particular fashion. For example, selection is always performed with the left mouse button of a multibutton mouse. The operator has only to decide that a selection is

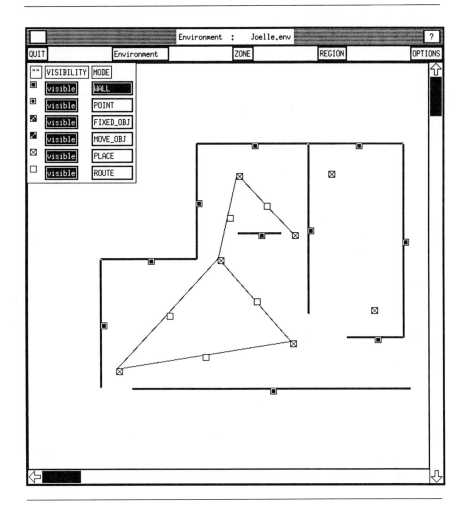

FIGURE 2.11
Places, walls, and routes mimic the real world and are modifiable by direct manipulation.

required and remember the mechanism for performing the selection from prior
selections.

Difficulties arise, however, when a desired user interface extends beyond
the bounds of the available toolkit. Either the user interface must be redesigned to
conform to an existing toolkit or the toolkit must be extended to encompass the

desired functionality or appearance. Extending toolkits is an expensive procedure, so the cost of using a less-than-ideal interface must be weighed against the cost of extending the toolkit. This problem illustrates the importance of looking ahead to future steps during the design process.

Facilitating the Specification of Action Sequences.   Human beings are better at recognizing than at recalling [Scapin 1986, p. 17]. The implication for designers is to devise user interfaces that, when possible, propose alternatives. By proposing alternatives, systems can extend the memory span of the operator [Miller 1975].

Using menus and forms provided by user interface toolkits is a good way of extending the operator's memory. Many of them provide easy ways of specifying useful reminders about the current values of options. Also, fields in forms can propose default values resulting from semantic computation or, more simply, from a previous user's input. When a value is expressed in a particular unit of measure (such as minutes and seconds, or kilometers and meters), this unit should be made explicit.

In the mobile robot, a zone is characterized by a large number of attributes. Studies have shown that operators have difficulty remembering more than seven options [Miller 1975]. The form illustrated in Figure 2.12 both names the attributes and categorizes them, so that the operator need not retrieve items but only recognize them. In the form illustrated in Figure 2.13, fields for specifying distance constraints to the robot for a particular route include the unit of measure.

Reducing Semantic Distance.   The semantic distance between the form of an expression and its meaning is a function of syntactic, lexical, and layout considerations. The facilities for customization also affect semantic distance.

☐   *Syntactic considerations.* When designing syntax, the user interface designer should determine the order of command arguments (delete file or file delete). When commands share arguments, these arguments should appear in the same order in every command [Barnard 1981]. The order does not always match the sequencing of natural languages, and there is a choice between postfix and prefix notation. For graphical environments a postfix notation is more appropriate, whereas prefix notation is adequate for text-based interaction. Forms provide a flexible way of specifying command arguments, since no order is imposed on the user.

☐   *Lexical considerations.* When determining the vocabulary to be used in a system, the designer should choose names that are meaningful and consistent. *Meaningful* implies precise. An imprecise term may lead to conflicting references and may not be remembered [Baddeley 1966]. For example, "destroy" is clearer than "remove" and thus better matches the operator's intention (assuming that destruction rather than simple removal is desired). *Consistent* means that a concept involved in different tasks should have the same identifier. Unix provides a wealth of counterexamples to this rule, and every user of Unix has suffered because of the different means of identifying the same concept [Norman 1981].

☐ *Layout considerations.* Consistency in the spatial layout of output should be preserved. This principle of locality helps the operator anticipate the location of system outputs. In particular, menu items should always appear in the same order. The order depends primarily on a logical sequencing de-

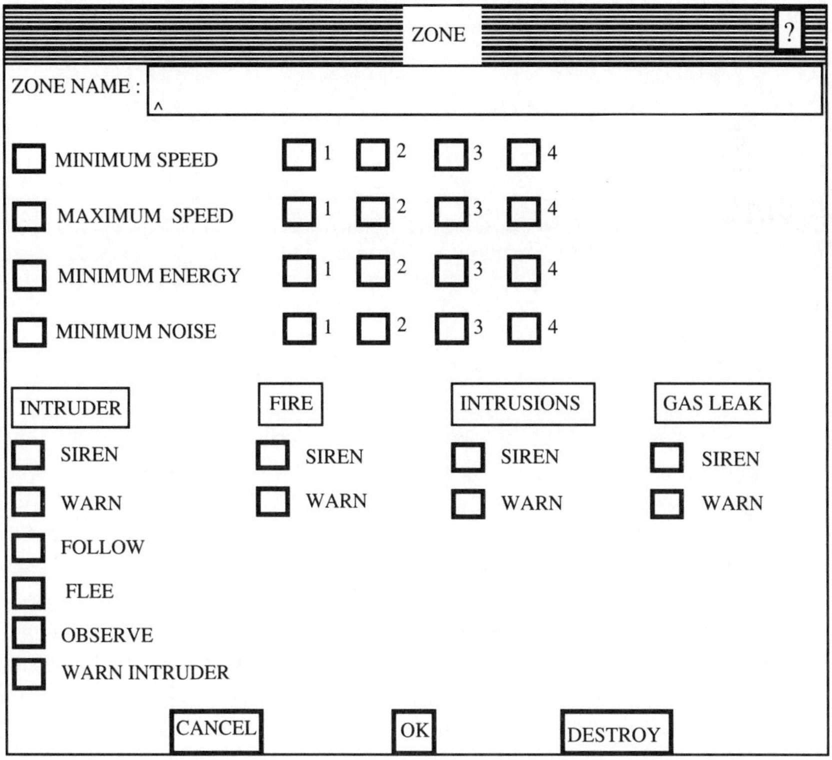

FIGURE 2.12
The form for specifying the attributes of a zone for the mobile robot gives the names for fields so that the operator does not have to remember them.

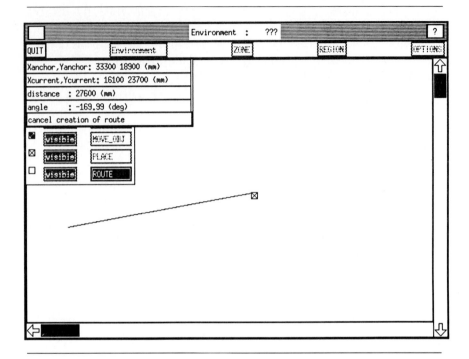

FIGURE 2.13
The interaction object for setting route attributes informs the operator that the unit of distance is mm.

fined by the task. If the task does not show any logical order, a frequency criterion should be applied. If a frequency criterion is not applicable, alphabetical order should be used [Shneiderman 1987]. Similarly, locality rules have been defined for forms: at the top of the form the user should find the fields that must be filled in, whereas optional items can be gathered at the bottom [Scapin 1986, p. 34]. Note that this guideline, by minimizing cursor movements, improves performance in terms of physical actions. It may, however, impede the overall performance of the operator if the layout that minimizes physical actions is in conflict with the logical ordering. In this case, logical ordering should be used.

☐ *Customization.* Customization makes it possible for an operator to have control over some aspects of the user interface. The advantage of adaptable user interfaces is generally a significant increase in the operator's satisfaction. The drawback is a possible loss in consistency and of portability of the interface across users. Interestingly, Hopper [1986, p. 15] observes that in vernacular architecture, "one might want to prevent the moving of walls,...

but encourage the rearrangement of furnitures." Similarly, in user interface design, one may want to prevent changing the syntax of commands, but allow for the modification of the lexical and spatial design.

Lexical and spatial levels of personalization allow operators to define abbreviations and to express themselves in more normal terms.

□ Abbreviations support the execution stage of the interaction. They minimize the number of physical actions necessary to specify input expressions. Consequently, abbreviations reflect the Keystroke model's endorsement of conciseness. Customization allows the operator to define new abbreviations and redefine existing ones. Note that predefined abbreviations should be made explicit, so that the operator knows they exist. One approach, used by Apple in the Macintosh system, is to show menu items along with their shortcut.

□ Natural language and cultural symbols should be used both in the cues given to the operator (for example, labels on menus, fields in forms, icons) and in the expression of error and help messages. At this level language is strictly for presentation and should be maintained outside of the functional core. In Chapter 4 we will see how resource files can help designers improve and adapt the lexical and pragmatic details of the interaction without changing the functional core.

2.6.2 MAKING THE SYSTEM STATE EXPLICIT

The selection of interaction objects does not, by itself, give the operator insight into the state of the interactive system. One technique for supporting task planning, error detection, and error recovery is to have the user interface give explicit indicators of the system's state [Hutchins, Hollan, and Norman 1986]. Explicit expression of the state is achieved through informative and immediate feedback.

Generally speaking, feedback is a reaction to some stimulus. In the context of human-computer interaction, feedback is an output expression produced by the system after it has processed some operator input. The operator then interprets the feedback, evaluates the situation, and acts [Norman 1986]. Immediate and informative feedback can take a large number of forms, including showing the appropriate physical variables, indicating when actions are forbidden, displaying the current mode, informing the operator when response time may be long, and mapping movements of pointing devices on the screen. Error indicators are another feedback mechanism.

The immediacy of error feedback, however, becomes an issue in the granularity of input processing. As a general rule, errors should be reported to the operator as soon as possible in order to facilitate error repair. On the other hand, in some circumstances, error messages should not be given when a particular input is incomplete. For example, in the mobile robot interface, one requirement is that routes be connected. That is, a particular route should have a beginning and an end and no gaps in the middle. The operator may find it convenient, however, to construct the initial portion of a route, then the last portion, and finally the middle portion. An error message indicating that the route was incompletely specified would be distracting and confusing.

Showing Appropriate Physical Variables.   Mental concepts useful at a given time for a given task should have physical counterparts in the user interface. For example, when the user is editing an environment for the mobile robot, the user interface always has a palette that presents the domain-dependent concepts of place, wall, and so on, as shown in Figure 2.14.

Indicating When Actions Are Forbidden.   For domain-dependent and logical reasons, some concepts may not always be accessible to the operator. A concept is implemented as a function or a data structure in the functional core and mapped

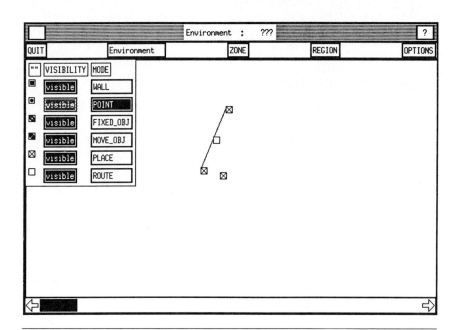

FIGURE 2.14
The palette for the mobile robot makes domain concepts explicit at any time. Wall, point, and other psychological variables are always displayed and available.

into some interaction objects in the user interface. When a particular action on the interaction objects is semantically invalid, the appearance of the interaction object should indicate the invalidity of the action. One common way to express the invalidity of a concept is to dim the interaction object and suppress reactions to the mouse. This is the *do nothing approach* [Lewis and Norman 1986]: nothing happens when the operator attempts to act on the interaction object. If nothing happens, there is no possibility of error. When no environment has been specified yet in the mobile robot model, the icons "mission specification" and "mission execution" are dimmed, as shown in Figure 2.15

An alternative way of expressing invalidity is to remove the currently inaccessible interaction object. In some cases, such as in menus, removing the inaccessible item will change the location of the remaining items, contradicting the principle of spatial layout consistency (Section 2.6.1.).

In any case, expressing the invalidity of semantic actions is a result of the semantic object's using task anticipation, as discussed in Section 2.4.1. The expression of semantic validity has strong implications for software architecture. This issue will be discussed in Chapter 5.

Displaying the Current Mode.   An interaction is moded if the same input achieves two different results depending on system state. For example, some editors treat text input as a command if they are in command mode, but as text if they are in input mode. In general, modes cannot be avoided, but explicit feedback should always convey the current mode. Typically, in direct manipulation user inter-

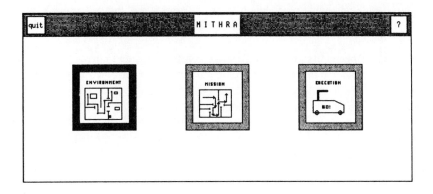

FIGURE 2.15
The icons "mission specification" and "mission execution" are dimmed, since no environment has been specified yet. Choosing either of these icons would result in an apparent lack of action (no reaction to the mouse).

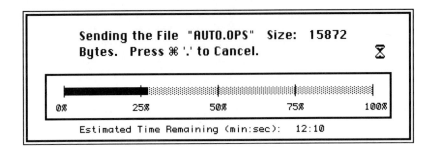

FIGURE 2.16
A progression bar is a helpful interaction object for dynamic feedback. (Courtesy
of Versaterm Software Package. © Abelbeck Software. Reprinted by permission.)

faces, cursor shapes are a common way of expressing the current mode. Input
focus (e.g., the "unselected window" phenomenon), discussed in Chapter 3, is an
example of the type of issue that arises during moded operation.

Informing the Operator of Long Response Times.   Any given interactive system has a general rhythm—that is, the operator builds up an expectation that the
system will respond in a particular amount of time. When cases arise where the
typical response time cannot be satisfied—particularly when the user asks for
heavy computations or time-consuming services (for example, compilation or file
transfer)—the operator should be provided with feedback indicating that the
request is being processed. A special cursor shape (for example, a wristwatch, or
hourglass) is the usual mechanism. More informative dynamic feedback can be
provided with a progression bar (see Figure 2.16).

Mapping Movements of Pointing Devices on the Screen.   Direct manipulation
interfaces make extensive use of pointing devices as electronic extensions of the
hand. Movement of these devices should leave a mark on the screen, to facilitate
the evaluation process. Rubber banding and shape tracking are convenient ways
of providing such feedback. Although they appear as simple mechanisms, they
require substantial programming effort. This issue will be further discussed in
Chapters 3 and 4.

2.7   Evaluate the Design

The discussion above was intended not only to give guidelines for designing a
user interface but also to show the difficulty of always following those guidelines.

The true test of an interface is its behavior in practice, but it is expensive to actually implement and then modify a user interface. Thus it is important that the interface be evaluated at several stages prior to its actual implementation.

The goals of evaluation are both technical and political. The technical goals are to gain insight into the match between the designed interface and the operator's abilities and knowledge of the domain. The political goals are to get management to "sign off" on aspects of the design and have the customer "buy in" to the design.

The earlier in the design process that something can be produced to show to both management and customers, the better for the designer. Management will see signs of progress and will be able to check off milestones. The customer will be able to provide input into refinements in the design and, consequently, will feel more a part of the process and will begin to feel ownership of the design. It is to the designer's advantage that the customer feel ownership of the design, since the customer will then defend the design more strongly against attack. Evaluation also results in an improved design for the ultimate operator.

A number of different techniques can be used in evaluation, depending on the stage of the design [Gould 1988]:

- Printed or video scenarios give an early indication of the concepts to be captured in the user interface.
- Early user manuals provide text and also specific details of operation of a system for review. In the course of writing specific details, the author often discovers better methods of operation.
- Mock-ups demonstrate the appearance of the user interface.
- Simulations demonstrate the dynamic behavior of the user interface.
- Early prototyping gives representatives of the operator something with which they can actually interact.
- Early demonstrations show a limited subset of the functionality to be implemented.
- Thinking aloud provides an idea of the thought processes of an operator while he or she is operating either the constructed system, a prototype, or a prior system.
- Videotapes can be shown to customers and to upper management. Management loves videotapes.
- A formal prototype test provides feedback on how well sample operators can perform specific tasks. It uses techniques from human factors research and statistics.
- Field studies provide evaluation of early versions of the actual system.

We will now consider the formal prototyping process in somewhat more detail. A typical formal evaluation involves a prototype of the user interface and a representative operator. Mock-ups [Boies 1985] and paper-and-pencil (or even computer) simulations may be used as initial test platforms. A collection of task scenarios is set up for testing, and the operator attempts to complete those tasks with an observer (possibly video) looking on. The observer is passive with respect to the task being attempted, but records errors made in the completion of the task. Pauses while the operator attempts to formulate a different strategy are also recorded. After the test is completed, the operator is interviewed to determine his or her subjective feelings about the interface. Errors made by the operator provide an objective indication of the quality of the user interface.

The evaluation is performed with a collection of operators, sometimes with a collection of different interfaces. The results are analyzed for problem spots in the interface, the interface is redesigned, and the process repeated. At some point the process is terminated, and the resulting interface provides the basis for the next step in the design process.

The design process does not end with the design of the user interface, but continues with its implementation. The movement of the process from the interactive system designer to the software designer does not stop the iterative refinement. During and after the initial implementation, information may be discovered that affects other design steps. It is possible, although rare, to instrument the fielded system to record operator performance so that the user interface can continue to be improved. Thus, evaluation is possible even after a system has been placed in production.

We have not performed formal evaluation tests on the first prototype of the mobile robot system. However, an independent team of designers and developers is developing the second prototype, and they have helped in detecting incorrect design decisions. For example, the notion of zone, which was introduced to minimize physical actions, was perceived as awkward by the second design team. What is not clear yet is whether the notion is fundamentally wrong or whether the interaction objects chosen to present the notion are inadequate. What is clear is that the new team uses the copy-paste facilities to duplicate robot behavior across multiple places. The copy-paste facilities do not produce "hot copies" (changes to one copy are propagated to all copies), whereas the zone concept, in effect, does produce hot copies. It is possible that, as the second design team gains experience in making the same modification across multiple places, the notion of zone may gain favor with them.

2.8   Engineering Considerations

The design of the user interface is the primary engineering consideration of this chapter, so we have devoted a large amount of space to design considerations.

Several other areas are also important to the software engineer, however. These are cost and schedule considerations for the user interface design, implications of iterative refinement on the engineering process, and configuration management.

2.8.1   COST AND SCHEDULE CONSIDERATIONS

Not every interactive system needs the best user interface. The cost of developing a high-quality user interface needs to be justified, as does any other expensive feature of an interactive system. Several items need to be kept in mind when one is deciding how much effort to put into the design of the user interface:

1. The cost of any user interface consists of the cost of design, the cost of implementation, the cost of modifications, the cost of operator error rates, and the cost in customer dissatisfaction and lost sales.

2. All the operators of a particular system must be considered in determining the cost of operator errors, customer dissatisfaction, and lost sales.

3. The costs of operator error depend on the application domain. Most would agree that such costs are much higher in controlling a nuclear power plant than in operating a mobile robot.

4. The user interface designer is not the best judge of the amount of time to be spent correcting the user interface design. Designers tend to want to make the user interface perfect, and above a certain level the cost of improvements can be very high.

5. The operator should be considered an error-prone element of the interactive system. Just as the software must be tolerant of hardware errors when the hardware is uncertain, the software must be tolerant of human errors. This tolerance must be designed in from the beginning.

In deciding how much effort to put into the user interface it is important to consider all the costs of the particular interactive system under design. The system designer is responsible for understanding all the costs and all the benefits associated with designing and implementing the user interface in various fashions.

2.8.2   ITERATIVE REFINEMENT

There are a number of engineering considerations that bear upon the design and implementation of user interfaces through iterative refinement.

1. At each stage in the process, as much information as possible should be gathered in order to reduce the number of iterations. It should be realized, however, that the results of each step are subject to change when more

information is acquired, either through further stages in the design process, through experience with an implemented system, or through the acquisition of a new input/output device that makes possible a different type of interaction.

2. The level of simulation necessary to perform an adequate test should be determined. Some behavior must be simulated; otherwise it is impossible to measure error rates. Simulating the total interface, however, would require implementing the entire application interface. The appropriate level of simulation provides enough information to allow testing without requiring the implementation of the entire interactive system.

3. The software engineer must know when to stop the prototyping-testing-revising cycle. In general, although the schedule for the development of an interactive system should allow for the iterative nature of user interface design, schedule requirements ultimately must influence the design and implementation of the user interface.

4. The distance between the design goals and the prototyping and implementation tools must be evaluated. The choice may be between a less-than-ideal interface that is easy to implement with existing tools and a better interface that is difficult to implement.

5. Early in the design process, a decision must be made about whether it is desirable (or possible) to evolve a prototype into the final system. Prototypes are constructed without regard for robustness, error handling, and appropriate software design. The goal in building a prototype is to produce something suitable for testing as quickly and cheaply as possible. This is not the goal of the final system, and yet once a prototype exists, there is often pressure to make it into the system.

The overall implication of iterative refinement for software designers is that the software design must be made as flexible as possible. Techniques for achieving flexibility are discussed in succeeding chapters.

2.8.3   CONFIGURATION MANAGEMENT

In our discussion of on-line help we mentioned the problems associated with configuration management. In general, within software systems, one piece of knowledge should be maintained only in a single place. If a piece of knowledge must be maintained in multiple places, then every time the relationships embodied in that knowledge are modified, all of the places in which the knowledge is maintained must be modified. Sometimes, for performance reasons, knowledge is maintained in several places, but in such cases one location should be designated the master and the others derivatives from the master. Automatic procedures should be established to update all locations when the master is modified.

1. Define the problem.

2. Model the operator. — Develop a model of the operator through interviews, questionnaires, videotapes, thinking aloud.

3. Perform task analyis.

Decompose tasks.

Analyze the task decomposition.
- Detect semantic inconsistencies (context-dependent alternatives).
- Identify parallel tasks (multithread dialogues).
- Mark special tasks (frequency, complexity).

4. Define computer objects and functions.

Make semantic concepts implemented in the functional core correspond to task objects. Type errors for classification and visual hints.

Implement syntactic concepts in the user interface to facilitate task accomplishment. Use multiple views and status indicators.

Define commands based on task decomposition.

Provide general services: macro commands, undo-redo, cut-copy-paste, on-line help, defaults.

Determine who controls the interaction: the user or the system. Stress collaboration.

5. Design the appearance and behavior of the user interface.

Design interaction objects to map semantic and syntactic concepts.

Keep appearance and behavior consistent.
- Choose an appropriate metaphor.
- Use a user interface toolkit.

Facilitate specification of actions through menus and through forms with defaults and units of measure.

Support semantic distance by using prefixed or postfixed syntax, precise and consistent naming, consistent spatial layout, and customization.

Provide informative and immediate feedback.
- Show (or make accessible) interaction objects useful in task context.
- Indicate when actions are forbidden.
- Display the current mode.
- Inform the operator of long response times.
- Map movements of pointing devices on the screen.

6. Evaluate the design. — Use simulations, mock-ups, scenarios, and a representative operator.

FIGURE 2.17
Design method summary. The steps in developing a user interface are enumerated, along with the techniques used in the process.

Several configuration management problems are inherent in user interface software:

- On-line help requires that knowledge of computer objects be maintained both within the objects and within the help messages.
- When commonalities in a task graph are not represented as a single node, the implication is that the knowledge associated with the common task resides in the code that implements both methods of performing the task.
- Semantic enhancement objects, such as the status man in Figure 2.9, often contain knowledge about the relationship of semantic objects that is duplicated within the functional core.

Having multiple locations that maintain the same knowledge sometimes cannot be avoided within a particular software system. In such cases it is important to remember that these locations are a frequent source of errors during maintenance.

2.9 Summary

In this chapter we outlined a design method distilled from the literature. Figure 2.17 gives a summary of the design method. The six basic steps are enumerated, together with the considerations at each step. We attempted to provide enough detail so that the software engineer has some knowledge of the concepts and the terminology of user interface designers. We also provided pointers to more detailed references for the reader interested in probing more deeply into the subject of user interface design.

3

Window
Systems

In Chapter 1 we described the software for an interactive system as a collection of abstract machines, each performing certain functions and hiding the mechanisms associated with those functions. At the level closest to the physical device is the window system. This abstract machine performs three functions:

1. It defines an abstract terminal that provides clients (the users of its services) with device independence.
2. It defines an imaging model to express inputs and outputs for the abstract terminal.
3. It manages the resources associated with input and output devices.

In this chapter we will discuss these three functions, as well as multimedia aspects, the human and engineering considerations, and the future of window systems. The mobile robot example will be presented in terms of window systems.

3.1 Device Independence and Device Sharing

There are many varieties of physical terminals. *Device independence* is achieved by hiding the characteristics of a particular terminal through abstraction. *Device sharing* involves allocating the resources of a physical terminal among multiple clients. An abstract terminal and its clients communicate through *events*. This section discusses these concepts and presents a simple example of the level of services provided by window systems.

3.1.1   DEVICE INDEPENDENCE

Software is said to be *device independent* when it can be executed on various types of devices. Device independence allows for software portability and ease of programming, which is certainly desirable—for example, software should ex-ecute regardless of which model of character terminal is used. Also, program-ming is simplified if the programmer does not have to know the specific sequences that determine behavior on a particular terminal. For example, when "ESC[1;2f" is sent to a Digital Equipment Corporation VT100 terminal, it causes the cursor to be positioned at line 1, column 2 of the display. The Digital Equipment Corpora-tion VT52 uses a different sequence for the same function. This sequence be-comes meaningless when the VT100 is replaced by a bit-mapped display. It is clearly desirable for a programmer to be able to use the same commands in preparing software to run on a VT52, a VT100, and a bit-mapped terminal.

A window system includes a layer that defines an abstract terminal. The abstract terminal provides its clients with a fixed set of virtual operations, which work on the underlying physical hardware. Virtual operations appear to the client as real operations and are translated by the abstract terminal layer into actual operation. The layer that provides device independence translates virtual opera-tions into the corresponding operations of the appropriate physical terminal. These operations are in turn communicated to the physical device by the *device-driver* layer. When the window system is installed on a different terminal, only the layer that provides device independence needs to be modified; the remainder of the window system can remain unchanged.

In general, the use of abstractions to hide complexity and to provide for portability across different terminal hardware necessitates some compromises. For example, the imaging model of the X Window System [Scheifler and Gettys 1986] depends on the density of pixels on the display. Different bit-mapped displays have different numbers of pixels per inch. Thus, the same software running on two different displays may produce slightly different images. Also, systems such as Sun Microsystem's Sun3 and Digital Equipment Corporation's Decstation 3100 have square pixels, whereas systems such as the Apple Lisa and television monitors have rectangular pixels. As a result, software that produces a circle when run on a Sun3 will produce an ellipse when run on the Apple Lisa.

3.1.2   WINDOW SYSTEM EVENTS

A window system accepts requests for output according to its particular imaging model (Section 3.2 discusses imaging models) and returns results of operator input in the form of events. Although the particular events used are specific to the implementation, they are generally of the following types:

- *Keyboard events.* The operator selects a particular key on the keyboard; it is the responsibility of the client to interpret the individual keystrokes.

- *Location events.* The operator's actions may specify cursor position within some frame of reference. For example, within the X Window System, mouse movements across window boundaries are returned to the client as particular events.

- *Choice events.* Some actions of the operator represent selection of options. These actions, such as pushing a mouse button down (button-down) or releasing a mouse button (button-up), are returned to the client as choice events.

- *Value events.* Some devices, such as potentiometers, generate real values; these values need to be communicated to the client.

- *Timing events.* Time stamps may be used in two ways within a window system. First, they may be used to determine the spacing between two events—to synthesize a double click when the user clicks the mouse button twice in rapid succession. Second, they may be used to ensure that clients operate on associated window system events in the correct order.

Figure 3.1 shows what happens when a client accesses an abstract terminal. The client asks for some event filed in a queue, determines the type of event, and responds accordingly.

Although, from a software perspective, different types of devices are treated identically at the abstract event level, from the operator's perspective they may have different characteristics. For example, a mouse and a trackball are both pointing devices and both generate location events, yet they differ in terms of convenience for the operator.

3.1.3 DEVICE SHARING

The purpose of device sharing is to make available multiple occurrences of the abstract terminal. Each occurrence is accessed (owned) by a different client. For simplicity, in the remainder of this section we will assume that each occurrence of an abstract terminal contains exactly one window. Thus, one of the functions hidden from the client by the window system is the sharing of the single physical device by several processes. Each client appears to be the only client interacting with the terminal. Figure 3.2 shows the configuration.

To illustrate the mechanisms used with single and multiple clients, let us begin with the case in which one client is the sole user of the physical terminal. We will assume that the current cursor position is being displayed on the screen

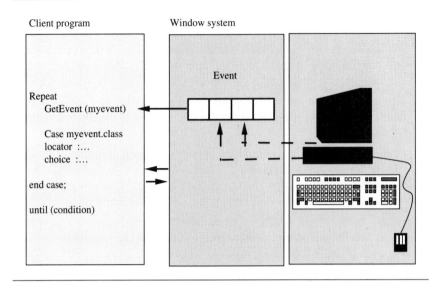

FIGURE 3.1
Principles of input operation of an abstract terminal. The client program is structured to loop through receiving and processing events continually. The window system translates the operator's actions into events for the client program.

and that there is no dedicated hardware to manage the mouse. The following sequence of events occurs when the operator moves the mouse:

1. With each increment of mouse movement, the physical controller generates a message for the device-driver software. (The size of the increments is usually controllable by the device driver.) The device driver calculates the current pixel location of the mouse and reports the result to the window system. The window system generates instructions to move the cursor image to a new position on the screen. It passes those instructions to the device driver, which erases the old mouse cursor bit-map, repaints the destroyed bits at the previous location, and produces the new cursor bit-map.

2. When the operator performs a button-down, an interrupt is generated that is handled by the device driver. The device driver sends an event to the window system, which, in turn, informs the client that a button-down event occurred while the cursor was at a particular location on the screen.

3. When the button is released, the device driver informs the window system of another interrupt. The window system, in turn, informs the client of a button-up event at a particular location.

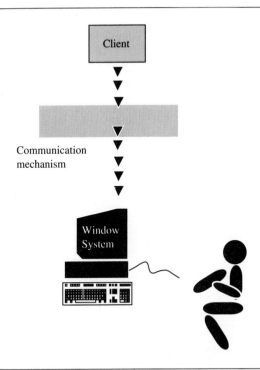

FIGURE 3.2
In a single client system, the abstract terminal managed by the window system
has only one client.

Note that the window system handles the feedback associated with the
movement of the mouse. Note also the level of abstraction reflected in the button
events. The window system does not inform the client of incremental mouse
movements. The location of the cursor is reported to the client only in association
with other information (the state and the identification of the mouse button). On
the other hand, the window system does not deal with objects on the screen or
with interpretation of events. The mapping of the cursor position into a particular
object and the interpretation of the button-down, button-up as a choice event are
handled at a higher level of abstraction than the window system.

Up to this point we have assumed that the physical terminal had one client.
In practice, there almost always are multiple clients. As shown in Figure 3.3,
multiple clients interact with the window system, which then must handle resource sharing. Figure 3.4 represents an actual screen with multiple active clients.

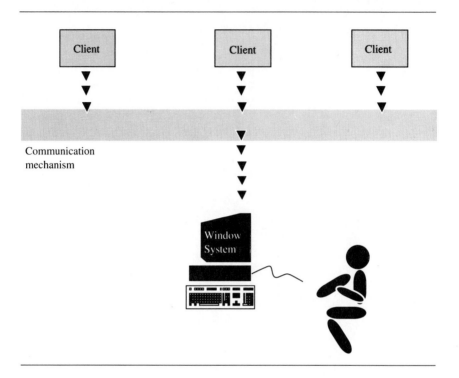

FIGURE 3.3
In a multiple client system, several clients are served by a single occurrence of the
window system.

When there are multiple clients, the window system must perform several
additional tasks. It detects actual cursor position, decides which clients the events
are intended for, maps positions in a coordinate system based on the total display
into positions in a coordinate system based on the client's window, and informs
the client of the events in terms of the client's window. From the point of view of
the client, the information reported by the window system remains unchanged.
Note also that the device driver has no knowledge of the existence of multiple
clients. This knowledge resides solely in the window system.

The concept of *ownership* provides the mechanism for determining which
client receives particular events. A window has an owner (a particular process),
and the window system passes an event to the owner of the window where the
event occurred. Output requests issued by client processes are mapped to the
correct abstract terminal and, consequently, to the window associated with that

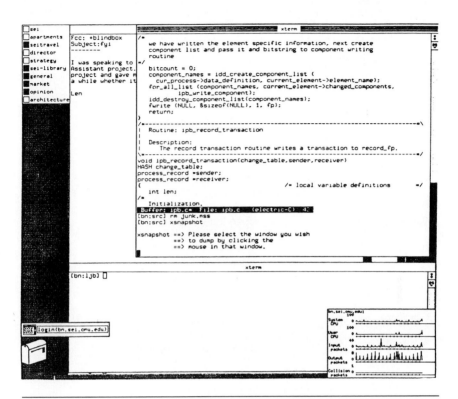

FIGURE 3.4
An actual screen on which multiple windows are simultaneously displayed to the operator. Some of the windows are text windows; others are iconic.

abstract terminal. Any output requests outside the range of the client's window, however, are clipped by the window system. Clipping consists of removing information that would otherwise be drawn outside of the boundaries of the window. Input events are dispatched according to one of two techniques. Either the window system broadcasts an event to all the windows that have expressed interest in this type of event, or the window system sends the event to the *current focus window*. The NeWS window system [SUN 1987] uses the broadcast technique, whereas the X Window System [Scheifler and Gettys 1986] relies on the current focus paradigm. To designate a particular window as the current focus for keyboard events or for any combination of typed events, some client process must issue an appropriate request. The issue of focus is discussed more fully in Section 3.5.1.

3.1.4   EXAMPLE

Figure 3.5 shows a skeleton of code used to cause the X Window System to display "Hello World." This example is intended to demonstrate the level of abstraction of a window system. All the calls are to procedures from a library (Xlib), which actually implements the X Window System protocol necessary to

---

```
/* This is the skeleton of an X window program that produces
        "Hello World" in a window.

   It consists of just the X calls to do this. None of the code to set
   up the parameters for the calls is displayed.   */

   XOpenDisplay;              /*  open the display */

   XLoadQueryFont;            /*  load the correct font with error
                                  return*/

   XCreateSimpleWindow;       /*  create the window */

   XSetStandardProperties;    /*  set the properties to instruct */

   XsetWMHints;               /*  the window manager where
                                    to place the window     */

   XChangeWindowAttribute;    /*  set the window's color map*/

   XCreateGC;                     /* create the graphic context for
                                     text*/

   XSelectInput;                  /* select events of interest, only
                                     expose events */

   XMapWindow;                    /* make the window visible */

   while (not_done) {             /* loop forever processing events */

       XNextEvent;        /*        get expose event */

       XDrawString;       /*        place string on screen */
   }
```

FIGURE 3.5
Hello World skeleton using the X Window System. This example shows the details necessary to write a simple program at the window level.

produce the desired results. A more elaborate example is shown in Appendix A. The program performs the following steps:

- It opens a connection to the display on which the window will appear.

- It instructs the X Window server to load the font necessary for rendering the text. The server returns an indication of whether the font is available. (The error handling for this case is not detailed.)

- It sets the attributes for the window. This includes the height, width, location, border width, and color of the background. Two calls are used: one sends mandatory information to the window system and the other optional information.

- It sets the color map of the window.

- It creates a graphic context that sets the control attributes for bit-map rendition (e.g., logical functions on source and destination pixel values, line and fill styles).

- It specifies which events are of interest. For the purpose of the example, expose events when the window becomes newly visible will be received.

- It makes the window visible. Notice that there is a distinction between creating the window and making it visible. The window must exist before the events it will receive and its color map are specified, but if it were visible before that information was specified, the results would be unpredictable.

- It waits for an expose event to make sure that the window is mapped on the screen. Graphics primitives for nonvisible windows are ignored by the X Window System.

- It draws the text on the window.

In this example, if the window is obscured, the program will take no action. In order to permit redrawing of the content portion of the window, the program should be organized around an infinite loop to acquire the incoming expose events. When the window is exposed, the program should refresh the content portion of that window. Although the program is incomplete, it demonstrates the details with which the client must be concerned, even for very simple cases. This situation is not specific to the X Window System. It is inherent in window systems because of the level of abstraction they provide.

3.2   Imaging Model

The abstract terminal implemented by a window system provides clients with a model to express their output. This model sets the conceptual basis for interactions between the client and the window system. Images to be output are described in terms of the model, and location events are returned in terms of the elements of the model. The following models are in common use:

- *Pixel*. The screen is viewed as a collection of dots that may be turned on or off (or assigned color).

- *Computer Generated Imagery* (*CGI*) [International Organization for Standardization 1986b]. The screen is viewed as a graphics machine that has the ability to interpret elementary graphics requests such as instructions to draw lines and circles in a coordinate space.

- *Graphical Kernel System* (*GKS*) [International Organization for Standardization 1985]. The screen is viewed as a collection of connected segments, each of which is a graphics macro. A graphics macro is an encapsulated sequence of elementary graphics requests.

- *QuickDraw* [Rose et al. 1986]. The screen is viewed as a collection of pixels, regions, and pictures. Regions and pictures are graphics macros.

- *Graphics Device Interface* [Butler 1983]. The screen is viewed as a graphics machine that has the ability to interpret elementary graphics requests. The specification mechanisms are different from CGI.

- *PostScript* [Adobe 1985]. The screen is viewed as a collection of paths and images filtered through the paths.

- *Programmer's Hierarchical Interface to Graphics (PHIGS)* [ISO 1986a]. The screen is viewed as a hierarchical collection of structures.

The pixel model (used in the X Window System), PostScript (used in NeWS and NextStep), and PHIGS will be discussed in more detail. We will also discuss how the imaging model of a window system affects the definition of fonts used to display text. We will start, however, with a brief discussion of how color is managed on bit-mapped terminals.

3.2.1   COLOR

Color terminals may be based on different physical organizations. In this section we describe a common model for color terminals—the red, green, blue (RGB) color model with multiple bit planes.

The physical basis of the model is that each pixel is composed of three phosphors (red, blue, and green). Each phosphor is illuminated with a separate electron beam. The intensity of the illumination and the combination of the phosphors produce the visible color.

Pixels on a black-and-white monitor are either off or on (0 or 1). Thus, each pixel can be represented by one bit, and the collection of pixels can be represented by an m x n rectangle called a plane. The value of m x n depends on the particular terminal, but 1024 is a common value. Since a color monitor has three different phosphors to illuminate, a plane consists of 3 x *m* x *n* bits (one group of *m* x *n* bits for each phosphor).

The number of different values for the intensity of each color depends on the number of planes in the monitor hardware. If the monitor has two planes for color, two bits are dedicated to describing each intensity and four different values of each intensity are possible. The most common color monitors have eight planes, resulting in 256 distinct possible values for each intensity of each color, or a total of approximately 16 million distinct colors.

Clearly, 16 million is too large a number of possible colors for a client to consider. Thus, a *color map* is used to represent the colors possible at any one time. The color map is a much smaller table (256 values is a common size) that yields intensities for red, green, and blue. The intensities are expressed in a number of bits corresponding to the number of planes in the monitor hardware. Often, the color map is accessed by strings that give a name to the generated color. Thus, "yellow" will act as an index to the color map that yields the red, green, and blue intensities that together generate the perceivable color yellow for a particular pixel.

3.2.2 PIXELS AS AN IMAGING MODEL

The most primitive imaging model views the screen as a rectangular collection of pixels. The base coordinate system of the display—both for input and for output— is defined in terms of pixels from an origin. A window in this model is a rectangular area defined, in general, by the *x, y* of the upper left corner and the *x, y* of the lower right corner.

When a window system uses the pixel model, the model is enhanced to improve usability. For example, since it would be too difficult for a client program to specify a line in terms of a sequence of aligned pixels, the window system offers simple graphic operations, such as "draw a line," which translate the starting and ending point coordinates into the correct pixel specification.

The interpretation of input, however, often is the client's responsibility. For example, the X Window System identifies the window (pixel area) within which a choice event occurred, but the client must determine whether the mouse is in the area within which a line is determined to be selected.

3.2.3 POSTSCRIPT

PostScript refers to both an imaging model and a programming language. PostScript is used to describe the appearance of any type of information on a rendition surface (paper or screen). It was originally designed as an output model but has been extended to allow for input.

The PostScript imaging model is based on the stencil/paint paradigm. A stencil is an outline specified by an infinitely thin boundary that is piecewise composed of spline curves. Paint is pure color or texture or an image that is dropped on the drawing surface through the stencil. Figure 3.6 shows paint being dropped through a stencil.

In NeWS, the stencil is the window. This makes it possible for windows to be arbitrary shapes. Location events are determined in terms of windows. Thus, a line is selectable if the stencil is around the line and is interested in a selection event and if the image consists of the line itself. In this case, the window system can determine the selection of the line for the client.

The PostScript language is Turing equivalent. Its syntax is postfix oriented, and the data model has the ability to treat programs as data. This makes it possible to perform any calculation or describe any image in PostScript. Since the NeWS window system includes a PostScript interpreter, one can download a PostScript program (to the window system), which will act on the incoming data. The client thus has the ability to customize actions of the server in a very powerful way, providing the client is willing to describe the desired actions in PostScript.

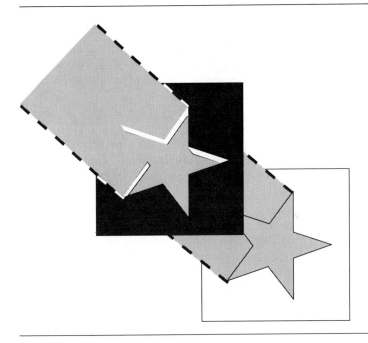

FIGURE 3.6
The PostScript imaging model. The star is the stencil; the paint through the stencil produces an image of the star on the drawing surface.

Figure 3.7 gives an example of a NeWS program that places on the screen a Go game board with several white and black stones. The first portion of the program consists of three PostScript procedures. The "initialize" procedure creates the Go board of 19 horizontal lines and 19 vertical lines. The "black" proce-

---

go.cps

```
cdef initialize (x, y, width, height)
        /can framebuffer width height createcanvas def
        % Make the canvas retained because not ready
        % to handle /Damaged events
        can /Retained true put
        can setcanvas x y movecanvas currentcanvas mapcanvas

        clippath pathbbox pop pop translate
        clippath pathbbox 19 div exch 19 div exch scale pop pop
        -.5 -.5 translate
        1 setgray clippath fill 0 setgray
        1 1 19 { dup 1 moveto dup 19 lineto
                dup 1 exch moveto 19 exch lineto } for
        stroke

        /black { .05 0 360 arc fill  } def
        /white { .5 0 360 arc gsave 1 setgray fill grestore stroke }
cdef black (x,y) x y black
cdef white (x,y) x y white
```

go.c

```
#include "go.h"

main() {
    ps_open_PostScript();
    initialize (500, 100, 200, 200);
    black (7, 5);
    white (7, 6);
    black (8, 6);
    ps_flush_PostScript();
    sleep (30);
    ps_close_PostScript();
}
```

FIGURE 3.7
Sample NeWS program. This program will generate a Go board with several stones. The board is a 19 x 19 grid, and the round stones are either white or black. (Copyright © 1987 Sun Microsystems, Inc. All rights reserved. Reprinted with the permission of Sun Microsystems, Inc.)

dure creates a black circle, and the "white" procedure creates a white circle. These PostScript procedures are merely declared in the NeWS program and passed as data to the window system for execution.

The main program is very simple. It opens the window system to receive PostScript, downloads the initialization of the board, downloads several stones, guarantees that all output is available to the operator, and closes the connection with the window system. This program is strictly output, so there is no demonstration of the event-handling features. All the display-specific features are embedded in the PostScript procedures, which are downloaded. This example demonstrates the compactness of the specification to a window system based on the PostScript model, compared to one based on the pixel model. To create the same image in the X Window System, the client would have had to send:

1. Several requests to the window system to create and initialize a window. (As we saw in Section 3.1.4, this is not trivial.)
2. One request to the window system for each line on the board.
3. One request to the window system for each stone on the board.

Thus, in the X Window System, the communication between the client and the window system for this application is extensive, but each request is easy for the window system to satisfy. To minimize the overhead of transmission, the X Window System bundles requests into transactions. In NeWS, the communication is minimal (only one request to the window system), but satisfying the request requires a window system with a sophisticated interpretation facility.

3.2.4   PHIGS

PHIGS is a graphics standard that is a generalization of the GKS standard. GKS describes a figure as a flat, non-editable segment. In PHIGS, this definition is replaced by the notion of an editable structure. Figure 3.8 shows an example of a structure definition. The request POST_STRUCTURE(A) executes the definition of A. The definition of A is composed of graphics elements included between the requests OPEN_STRUCTURE(A) and CLOSE_STRUCTURE. The element EXECUTE_STRUCTURE behaves just like a procedure call: it saves the current context, deviates to a new context, and then comes back to the calling context. EXECUTE_STRUCTURE(B) saves the current graphics context about A, interprets the definition of B, and, once B has been made part of A, returns to the execution of A. For inputs, PHIGS uses an extension of the GKS notion of logical units to take into account the structural organization. In particular, a PICK returns a path that uniquely denotes the selected element.

In contrast to GKS segments, PHIGS structures can be dynamically modi-

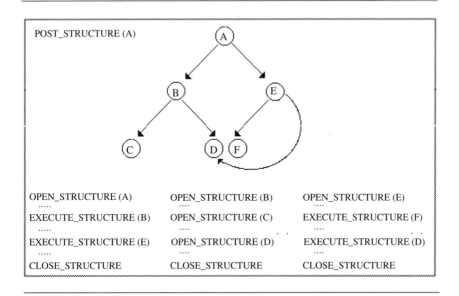

FIGURE 3.8
A PHIGS structure. Structure A is composed of structures B and E, B is composed of structures C and D, and E is composed of structures D and F.

fied. The model for modification is inspired by line text editors. Figure 3.9 illustrates the editing of structure. As with text editors, the recipient must first be opened. OPEN_STRUCTURE(MYHOUSE) opens the structure MYHOUSE; the interpreter places the insertion point for editing at the end of the structure definition and sets itself in input mode. This means that subsequent graphics elements will automatically be added at the end of the current structure. If the client program needs to delete the door element, a DELETE_ELEMENT(MYDOOR) will do the job. The LABEL(MYDOOR) denotes a graphics element symbolically, just as a line number designates a text line in line-based text editors. If one wants to replace the definition of the door, the insertion point can be set at the appropriate location in the structure definition and the replace mode will substitute new graphics elements for the old ones.

3.2.5   FONTS

The imaging model of window systems provides mechanisms for describing arbitrary shapes. Since the presentation of text is so common, window systems maintain special mechanisms for the display of character shapes, or fonts.

Initial Definition of MYHOUSE	Editing MYHOUSE
OPEN_STRUCTURE (MYHOUSE)	OPEN_STRUCTURE (MYHOUSE)
.....	DELETE_ELEMENT (MYWINDOW)
	SET_ELEMENT_POINTER (MYDOOR)
LABEL (MYWINDOW)	SET_EDIT_MODE (REPLACE)
....	
LABEL (MYDOOR)	.....
	.....
....	
CLOSE_STRUCTURE	SET_EDIT_MODE (INSERT)
	CLOSE_STRUCTURE

FIGURE 3.9
A PHIGS structure can be dynamically edited. A structure is opened, edited, and
closed the same way a text document is with a text editor.

A font is a set of typographical characters created with a consistent design.
Characters in a given font have the same general appearance regardless of size
and style (bold, italic, etc.). The size of characters, called font size, is given in
points (1 point equals 1/72 inch). Each font is identified by a name, such as
Geneva or Times. The internal model for representing a font may be pixel-based
or shape-based. Font names and internal models both give rise to portability
problems.

Font names used by one vendor for a window system may be different from
those used by another vendor. Thus, the name used for a particular font in the X
Window System may depend on whether the window system is furnished by
MIT, Hewlett-Packard, or Digital Equipment Corporation. This variation in names
for fonts causes problems for software developers.

The distinction between pixel and shape representations affects portability
across terminals as well as between a terminal and a printer. When a character set
is modeled as a collection of pixels (one bit-map per character), the notion of size
is automatically embedded in the font definition; this modeling technique requires the maintenance of one representation per desired size per font. In order to
save secondary memory space (a 12-point font typically occupies 3K bytes),
however, a font is often stored in a limited number of different sizes and other
sizes are obtained by scaling. Although scaling solves the problem of font-size
unavailability, scaled characters may be unacceptable to typographers or may be
unreadable by the common observer. Also, the pixel model may lead to different
results on terminals with different pixel sizes and resolutions. It may also impede
the ability of printers to produce high-quality texts, as the quality of the printing is
limited by the resolution of the original character bit-maps.

If fonts are maintained as shapes, the appearance of characters is computed for the desired point size and style. Thus, shape-based fonts are more portable across terminals. They also provide better resolution when printed. On the other hand, developing the shapes for each font is complicated and expensive. Also, many font shapes are proprietary, and the licensing arrangements for the fonts often cause difficulties for software developers.

The presentation of text is related not only to the way fonts are managed but also to the imaging model used. For example, producing slanted text is very difficult using the pixel model, regardless of how fonts are maintained, but relatively simple using PostScript. In PostScript, the text is laid out and then the whole line is rotated to produce slanted output. In the pixel model, the window system usually does not have the capability to rotate an image, so the client must calculate the pixel arrangement of the rotated text and provide a bit-map to the window system.

3.3 Resource Management

We have already introduced the idea that a window system is a resource manager for a particular physical terminal. The resources that a physical terminal is assumed to have and that are managed by the window system include:

- High-resolution screen. The assumption is that the screen is bit-mapped.
- Keyboard.
- Pointing device. A multibutton mouse is the most common pointing device, but joysticks, track balls, and various gesturing devices also exist.
- Color map (see 3.2.1).
- Fonts (see 3.2.5).

In the next section we will consider the issues involved in managing a single window owned by a single client. We will then turn to the problems of resource sharing among multiple clients.

3.4 Managing a Single Window

A window is the screen portion of the abstract terminal of a process. It is a drawable surface for that process. Since a window system manages the window, the window is not restricted by the size or shape of the physical screen. Because it is an abstract screen, a window may be bigger than the actual screen. It may be represented by an icon. (For example, in the lower left corner of Figure 3.4 is an icon representing the mailbox used in rural areas of the United States. The icon represents the output of the mail process.)

Windows can have decorations such as title bars and resize boxes. We will now discuss the consequences of resizing a window and then present problems related to the shape of windows.

3.4.1   RESIZING A WINDOW

One of the functions provided by a window system is *resizing*. The operator may indicate to the window system that a particular window is to be resized and then specify the new size. The window system reports these events to the client. The client has two options: (1) displaying only a portion of the desired screen, using the notion of viewport, or (2) resizing the contents to fit the window.

Figure 3.10 illustrates the first option. The client has a collection of information, a portion of which has been sent to the abstract terminal. The information available to the window system represents a *canvas* of information. The part available through the window constitutes a *viewport* onto the canvas. The data are maintained on the canvas in the original scale and proportions specified in the information sent from the client. Scroll bars allow the operator to move around the canvas. Note that the size of the information on the canvas does not change when a resize occurs. Only the portion of the information visible to the operator changes.

The other option in resizing a window is to keep the same information visible to the operator. In this case, the scale of the information must be changed. Pixel replication or sampling techniques are used to expand or shrink the view. Handling aspect ratio changes (changes in the ratio of the sides of the window) becomes a very difficult problem. For example, if a circle is displayed in a window and the resize extends the x direction without modifying the y direction, stretching the image to fit the new window will cause the circle to be displayed as an ellipse.

3.4.2   SHAPE OF WINDOWS

The windows in many systems, such as NextStep, Open Look compliant systems, and Macintosh, are rectangular. This simplifies the management of clipping. On the other hand, rectangular windows may give rise to a number of selection and display problems when used as regions to support graphic objects. For example, as shown in Figure 3.11, two diagonal lines are difficult to separate within rectan-

FIGURE 3.10
The information sent to the abstract terminal represents a canvas of information; the viewport makes a portion of that information available to the operator.

gular regions. In the figure, the top region, implemented as a window with visible borders, overlaps the bottom region. When the cursor is in the shaded area, the window system detects a selection event for the upper line. Thus, the client must maintain both lines within the same region—that is, in the same window—and track the cursor position to determine which line is desired on mouse selection.

In some systems such as NeWS and the X Window System (Version 11, Release 4) it is possible to have arbitrarily shaped windows. In NeWS, the boundary of the window is represented by spline curves and the canvas is clipped by the curves. The term *canvas* is used in NeWS to mean a drawable surface. In the X Window System, the boundary of the window can be represented by a bit-map or by a collection of rectangles.

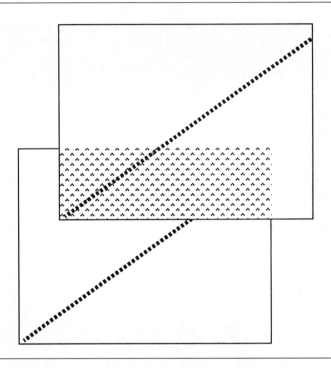

FIGURE 3.11
Two diagonal lines within two different overlapping regions. Since the regions are rectangular, selecting the lines requires selecting the surrounding rectangles. Selection in the shaded area will result in selection of the upper line, which is not necessarily the desired result.

3.5   Managing Multiple Windows

Window systems manage multiple abstract terminals, giving the operator a view of the physical screen such as that displayed in Figure 3.4. Management of the resources of the physical terminal involves managing both the input elements of the terminal and the output. In general, the problem is to allow the operator to differentiate among the various active processes and provide input to the processes as desired. At this point, we will expand our discussion to include instances in which a single client owns a collection of windows.

3.5.1   INPUT MANAGEMENT

Physical input devices generate events of the types discussed in Section 3.1.2. The basic problem for the window system is to direct the various events to the appropriate client process. Since each window is owned by a particular client, this is equivalent to directing the events to the appropriate window. To assist the operator in determining the current state of the window system, two different types of cues are used: the mouse cursor and the text cursor. Each provides the location of one of the types of input devices. Together they determine the client to which an input event is directed.

Mouse Cursor.   The mouse is assumed to have a single position within the physical screen; the *mouse cursor* displays the location of that position to the operator. The shape of the mouse cursor can be changed by the client. This feature allows the client to give the operator a general cue as to the client's activities. See the discussion in Section 2.6.2 about making the system state explicit.

The position of the mouse cursor is maintained at the window system level and is available to the client on request or when a choice event (button up or down) occurs. The client can also move the mouse cursor to a desired position on a particular window.

Choice events are always directed to the window within which the mouse cursor is located. More strictly speaking, choice events are directed to the client that owns the window. When windows overlap, the event may be directed to a window that is invisible below the current window (see Section 3.5.2 for a discussion of window ordering). In certain cases, the overlapping windows are designed to support a single cognitive task (a menu, for example). In such cases, it is the responsibility of the top window to pass the event on to underlying windows.

Text Cursor.   Some windows are created as text windows. This allows them to receive key events. Within these windows is an additional cursor, the text cursor, which indicates current keystroke position.

Current Focus.   Operator events are assigned to the window that is currently the focus of attention. Two models exist for determining the current focus:

1. *Mouse focus*. Operator events are assigned to the window within which the mouse cursor is located.

2. *Click to focus*. The operator must explicitly assign events to a window by selecting that window with a choice event.

It is also possible for a client to explicitly change the input focus independently of any operator-generated events. For example, the client might move the focus to a dialogue box that has just appeared. This feature should be used only in very specific cases, however, since it prevents the operator from engaging in desired opportunistic behavior.

Output Management.   The window system displays multiple abstract screens on the same physical screen. Typically, not all of the active abstract screens will fit on the physical screen simultaneously. Thus, arranging the windows on the physical screen can pose a problem. Figure 3.4 shows seven different active windows. Two of these (the two in the lower left corner) are represented by icons. Three are text windows (the ones in the middle of the screen), and two are graphic windows (in the upper left and lower right corners). This arrangement of the windows obscures portions of some of the active windows. The issues involved in output management are:

- ☐   Window placement—overlapping versus tiling,
- ☐   Management of obscured windows,
- ☐   Hierarchy of windows,
- ☐   Graphic context,
- ☐   Data interchange across windows.

Window Placement—Overlapping.   One strategy for placing windows on the physical screen is to allow them to overlap. With an overlapping window system, the operator can usually specify the location of windows. The client generates a window, and the operator, in conjunction with the window system, has the ability to position, move, and resize the window. The operator can also alter the visibility of windows.

The basis for managing overlapping windows is a current list of active windows. Each window has a size and a physical location. The order in which windows are placed on the physical screen is the reverse of the order in which they appear on the list. The windows on the top of the list are displayed last and, consequently, become the top-level visible windows.

There are four operations available for managing the windows on the list: create, delete, move to top of list, and move to bottom of list. Move to top of list places a particular window in the foreground, whereas move to bottom of list puts a particular window in the background. The operator uses a window system mechanism to invoke these two types of events.

The window system also has a mechanism for iconifying and de-iconifying a window. The iconification may or may not change the position of the window on the screen, but it will usually cause the window to take up less space on the physical screen and thus will make other windows visible.

Window Placement—Tiling.   With a tiled window system, the system—not the operator—is responsible for the size and placement of the individual windows.

The rationale for such systems is as follows:

▫ Screen real estate can be managed more efficiently and more simply by the system than by the operator.

▫ If the operator can see only a portion of a window, that portion should define the client's abstract terminal. When there are no obscured windows, the problems of output to obscured windows do not exist.

With a tiled window system, each client defines the minimum and maximum window size for an abstract terminal [Gosling and Rosenthal 1986; Cohen, Berman, Biggers, and Camaratta 1988]. When less than the minimum size is available, the process is suspended.

Management of Obscured Windows.   Since the window system maintains the illusion that each client is the sole user of the physical device, output may be sent to an abstract terminal regardless of window visibility. A problem arises when a window is newly exposed: the window must be redrawn. There are two techniques (and a compromise) for dealing with the exposure of obscured windows:

1. Generate an "expose" event for the client process. This strategy places the client in charge of redrawing the exposed portion of the window. It simplifies the problem of the window system and saves window system storage.

2. Maintain an abstract terminal in a separate buffer which is then mapped onto the screen. If the window system is to have the ability to redraw each abstract terminal, it must maintain a current copy of each window, whether visible or not. This can be expensive in terms of memory.

3. Maintain separate buffers for a fixed number of abstract terminals. In the X Window System, the client must request this "save under" feature for a particular window. This compromise technique limits the memory requirements and permits specific windows to be redrawn rapidly.

Hierarchy of Windows.   Up to this point, all of the windows have been assumed to be independent. Thus, one window can be repositioned without any effect on the other windows. For some purposes—layout dependency and event propagation—windows should be considered to be related. The relationship among windows is based on the notion of hierarchy.

One use of window hierarchies is in expressing layout constraints: how moving one window will cause subwindows to move or how the position of a window will affect the display of subwindows. Within a hierarchy of windows, children, or subwindows, are positioned relative to a parent window. The children can be moved independently of the parent, but to calculate their position one first determines the position of the parent and then computes their location within the parent. Because the positions of the children are defined relative to that of the parent, the parent and children can move together. The child obscures the portion of the parent in which it resides and is clipped by the boundaries of the parent. Thus, when a child window is moved off the edge of the parent, only a portion of the child remains visible. Following are some examples of the use of window hierarchies:

- ☐ Menus. Menu items may be subwindows all residing within a parent window. When the parent window is positioned, all the menu items are automatically placed relative to the parent window. In addition, the child-parent relationship provides a straightforward mechanism for determining the selected menu item, since events carry the identification of the window where they occurred.

- ☐ Canvas-viewport relationship. An easy mechanism for managing the *canvas-viewport* relationship discussed in Section 3.4.1. is to make one window the child of another. The implementation is slightly counter-intuitive; it relies on the fact that the window system clips a window based on its parent. The viewport and canvas are parent and child windows, respectively. The portion of the canvas that is visible is determined by the clipping mechanism applied to the viewport window. Scrolling is accomplished by moving the canvas rather than the viewport.

A second use of window hierarchies is propagating events. Operator events are directed to the current focus window. If that window has not expressed interest in this particular type of event, the window system redirects the event to the parent window, and so on up the hierarchy. Thus, for example, an operator request to move a window to the bottom of the visibility list would be passed from a child window up the hierarchy until a parent window allowed the visibility change.

The propagation of events is controlled by the client, which specifies the types of events in which windows are interested. One mechanism for simplifying the logic of the window system is to make all windows in a hierarchy children of a special window called the root window and have it consume any unwanted events. Usually the root window corresponds to the background of the display.

The windows in a hierarchy (below the root window) should be owned by a single client, and this client should be responsible for establishing and modifying the hierarchy. It is not desirable to force multiple clients to communicate in order to determine which window should handle a particular event. If the window system returns an event to the owner of the particular window in which the event occurred and that event must be propagated to a parent window, the client should always be the owner of the parent window; the client should not have to engage in interprocess communication to determine the owner of the parent window.

The hierarchy notion is useful for many functions. In some systems, title bars and scroll bars are implemented as child windows of the client window. This approach allows the window system to determine the mouse cursor position, rather than forcing the client to perform the computation. Of course, it is possible for the client to attach its own title bars and scroll bars to windows and define a specific policy.

One factor determining whether child windows are used for auxiliary functions such as menus and title bars is the performance of the window system. When the window system is used for such purposes, several hundred windows may be generated very quickly. If the window system is efficient enough to manage a large number of windows, the window abstraction provides a very attractive solution to the problem of managing related objects on the screen.

Graphic Context.   A graphic context is a data structure that determines aspects of appearance. The graphic context includes graphics attributes such as color maps, character and line styles, and transfer mode between source and destination rendition surfaces. In some window systems, such as Macintosh, each window has an associated graphic context. In other systems, such as the X Window System, graphic contexts are full-fledged resources and can be shared across windows.

Data Interchange Across Windows.   Data interchange across windows relies on a protocol that includes mechanisms for data conversion and data transfer. Data conversion between source and target formats is made possible on an agreement basis. Window systems support a fixed set of predefined types of data, which can be extended by the clients. For example, Macintosh clients can transfer data in at least one of the two standard types: TEXT and PICT. TEXT is a series of ASCII characters, whereas PICT is a sequence of QuickDraw drawing primitives. In addition, clients may define client-specific data formats. In the X Window System, the built-in data types are denoted by names (i.e., X Atoms) such as INTEGER, STRING, PIXMAP, and POSTSCRIPT. They can easily be extended by the clients.

Data transfer is performed via special-purpose operations and buffering mechanisms. In the Macintosh paradigm, the source client writes data into a memory buffer, the *desk scrap* or a *private scrap*. The source client specifies the address of the first byte to be written, the number of bytes, and the data type (i.e., TEXT, PICT, or an application-specific type). To read the information held in the scrap, the recipient application specifies the expected type and a memory location where the contents of the scrap should be copied. If the expected type does not match the type of data stored in the scrap, some information may be lost in the transfer process (see the discussion in Section 2.5.2.).

In the X Window System, data transfer between client processes is based on the notions of selection, owner, and requestor:

☐ A *selection* represents data selected from a window and is attached to a window. Since there may be an arbitrary number of selections, a selection has a unique name (an atom).

☐ The *requestor* of a selection is the client process wishing to obtain the value maintained in the selection. The requestor issues the "XConvertSelection" request and provides the name of the selection, the expected data type, a handle to the buffer containing the data, and the identification of the window to which the handle is attached. This latter parameter is used to notify the requestor that the converted data are available in the buffer.

☐ The *owner* of a selection is the client process possessing the data maintained in the selection. To acquire ownership of a particular selection, a process must issue the "XSetSelectionOwner" primitive and specify the name of the selection as well as the identification of any window that the process owns. The latter parameter is used by the window server to notify the owner that the selection has been requested. On receipt of a SelectionNotify event from the server, the owner converts the content of the selection to the requested data type, places the converted data into the named buffer, and sends the requestor a SelectionNotify event. If the owner does not know how to convert the data, it returns an error indicator in the notify event.

In the Macintosh window system, data conversion is performed by the receiver rather than by the process that currently owns the selection. (In the X Window System, any process can clear previous ownership and become the new owner.). Both the Macintosh and the X Window System use an asynchronous data transfer mechanism. Since the operating system of the Macintosh supports only single tasks, the communication protocol in the Macintosh system is very simple. In the X Window System, owners and requesters must exchange explicit notification events in order to release the various resources used for the transfer.

In general, data transfer mechanisms provided by window systems have been designed to transfer small amounts of data; attempts to transfer very large amounts of data with the standard mechanisms may fail because of lack of memory. For large data exchanges, client programs have to turn to more advanced features, which are more complex to use.

3.6 Multimedia

New input/output technology is continually becoming available. In order to extend existing clients rather than revise them totally, designers must integrate the new technology with existing technology. The best methods for accomplishing this integration have not been determined, but it is clear that they must involve all the levels of user interface software. In this section we discuss two different user interface technologies and attempts at integrating them at the window system level. The two are full motion video and audio.

3.6.1 FULL MOTION VIDEO

The integration of full motion video and bit-mapped graphics has become possible with the development of special video digitizers such as the one produced by Parallax. The Parallax board is an analog-to-digital converter, which digitizes video input fast enough to project it onto a bit-mapped graphics terminal in real time. The board also implements an X Window System protocol. Thus, the video is projected onto a window that can be moved, resized, and hidden, in the same fashion as any other window.

From the client's perspective, a window is either a normal window or a video window. In a normal window, output consists of lines, arcs, and text; input consists of the types of events we have discussed. In a video window, output consists of not only lines, arcs, and text, but also video. Input is the same as for a normal window. Since the video is full motion, the window is being modified continually to reflect the video picture. This requires that the text being projected on top of the video be redrawn whenever the video is redrawn. If the video is enlarged through a zoom facility, the client must specify whether the text is to be enlarged or to remain the same size. Thus, at one level, the issues in resizing windows remain the same with video. At another level, video input has a fixed resolution that zooming will not change. Consequently, the video board must do pixel replication to accomplish the zoom. Unlike most other window systems, a video window system cannot rely on the client to redraw the window in response to a resize command. In a video window system, then, the window system and the client are both involved in various aspects of resizing.

3.6.2 AUDIO

Recently work has been done on integrating audio into a workstation manager. A group from Olivetti [Binding 1990] has constructed a workstation manager that will handle voice using the same concepts as a graphics-based window system. That is, the window system will use a standard window system architecture (Section 3.8.1) and will provide network transparency for the audio servers.

A number of distinctions between audio and graphics make the internals of their window systems fundamentally different. The distinctions relate mainly to the different impact of time on the two media:

◻ Audio is inherently not persistent. When a picture is drawn on a bit-mapped graphics screen, the hardware maintains the picture until some event occurs.

◻ Audio is serial in nature. Audio and visual media differ greatly in the amount of information that can be transferred to an operator in a given amount of time. With graphics, an operator can perceive multiple choices essentially instantaneously. With audio, multiple choices must be presented sequentially.

◻ With audio, task switching is very difficult. In a graphics-based window system, screen space can be managed by use of overlapping windows, and the operator can interrupt a particular window and change its visibility. Providing such a capability with audio would require multiple channels of output, from which the operator would then select. Because of the non-persistent nature of audio, unselected output would not be available for the operator unless it was replayed.

3.7   Human Considerations

Window systems make a distinction between mechanisms and policy. *Mechanisms* provide a means of implementing many different *policies*. For example, it is possible to impose a tiling policy on top of a window system that supports overlapping windows. Psychological considerations arise primarily in areas where window systems impose a policy rather than providing flexible mechanisms. Such considerations include:

◻ Focus issues,

◻ Mouse button usage,

◻ Style of windows, and

◻ Tiling versus overlapping windows.

Following a discussion of these considerations, we will look at the Rooms model [Card and Henderson 1987] which has cognitive motivations and concepts that are of particular relevance to windowing policies.

3.7.1   UNSELECTED WINDOW PROBLEM

We have identified two models for assigning operator event focus: mouse focus and click to focus. Neither model prevents the *unselected window problem,* in which the operator interacts with an undesired window. With both mouse focus systems and click to focus systems, the operator can shift the focus of attention and forget to notify the window system of the change. From the operator's perspective, input is directed to the incorrect client.

One method systems use to minimize this problem is to give the operator cues that indicate which window is currently the focus. In Figure 3.4, the window in the middle right is the current focus. The current focus is indicated in two ways:

1. The title bar for the window in current focus is darkened.

2. The text cursor is displayed as a solid rectangle within the window in current focus and as a hollow rectangle within the other windows.

Even this type of feedback does not eliminate the unselected window problem, however.

3.7.2   BUTTON OVERLOAD PROBLEM

Since the window system performs actions for the client (such as resizing, moving, and scrolling), certain events must be dedicated to specifying these actions. The number of events available for specifying other types of interactions is therefore reduced. For example, if a resize is specified with the right button of the mouse and the client cannot override that specification, the right button is unavailable to the client. Conversely, if the client can override the specification, resize either is unavailable or must be specified in a different fashion, depending on which window is to be resized. This problem is called the *button overload* phenomenon. Clearly, button overloading may lead to lexical inconsistencies between interactive systems.

The choices for the window system, then, are either to not bind its actions to keys, to use obscure keys to control its actions, or to prevent the client from using certain keys. Each option has advantages and disadvantages:

☐   If the window system does not use key bindings, it must designate specific areas such as title bars and scroll bars where window system manipulations can be specified. Any user actions in the reserved areas are interpreted by the window system. Actions outside the reserved areas are directed to the client.

☐   If the window manager uses obscure key bindings, operators may find the bindings difficult to remember and difficult to execute. One window manager for the X Window System, for example, requires the operator to depress the control key, shift, and left buttons simultaneously in order to perform a particular action on windows.

☐   If normal keys are used to control window system tasks, these keys become reserved keys and are unavailable for interactive system tasks.

3.7.3   BEHAVIOR CONSISTENCY PROBLEM

Widespread differences among window systems in appearance and behavior have
led to the efforts at standardization. Apple, for example, has published style
guidelines that all applications for the Macintosh should follow. Apple enforces
its guidelines through a certification process in an attempt to achive consistency
of look and feel. The result is that when an operator operates any Macintosh
application, the window manipulation actions are always identical.

Several other window styles have been defined, such as Open Look from
AT&T and Sun Microsystems. An Open Look window is shown in Figure 3.12.
The Open Look style guidelines give fixed meanings to mouse buttons. Adjustment operations, for example, are always performed using the middle button of a
three-button mouse. The Open Software Foundation has also defined a standard
window style as part of its Motif User Interface Environment. A Motif window is
shown in Figure 3.13. Both windows have an icon indication, a title bar, and a
facility for moving, resizing, and closing.

All these fixed styles are implemented as a portion of a window system.
Consequently, a window system supporting one of the styles implements a particular policy for carrying out window manipulations.

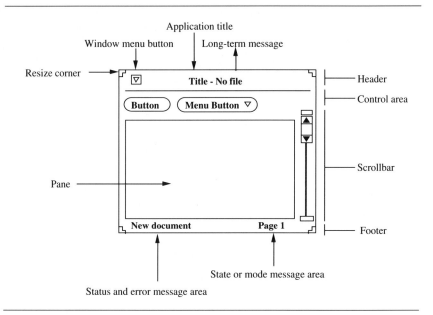

FIGURE 3.12
Open Look Window. The various components of the window are specified by the
Open Look Style Guide. (Copyright © 1989 Sun Microsystems, Inc. All rights re-
served. Reprinted with the permission of Sun Microsystems, Inc. and AT&T.)

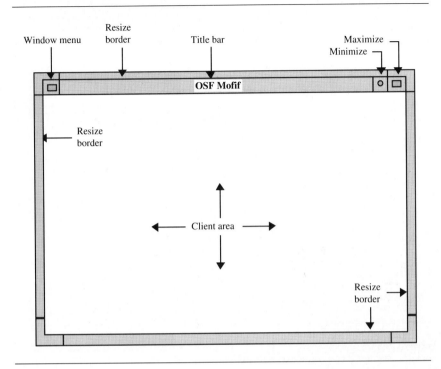

FIGURE 3.13
Motif Window. The various components of the window are specified by the *OSF/Motif Style Guide*. (Courtesy of Open Software Foundation, OSF/Motif™ Style Guide, © 1990. Reprinted by permission of Prentice Hall, Inc. Englewood Cliffs, New Jersey.)

3.7.4 WINDOW TILING

Tiled window systems decide on the size and placement of windows without involving the operator directly. These systems may shift the location and size of a window whenever new windows are created. Such frequent changes can be disconcerting to the operator.

Evidence on the receptiveness of operators to tiled window systems is mixed. It does seem clear that massive and frequent screen reorganizations, unless operator initiated, are undesirable [Bly and Jarret 1986, Cohen, Berman, Biggers, and Camaratta 1988].

3.7.5 THE ROOMS MODEL

The Rooms model is an example of how cognitive studies and information processing can be used to develop better user interface software [Card and Henderson

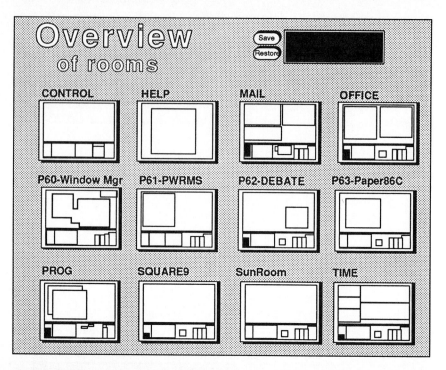

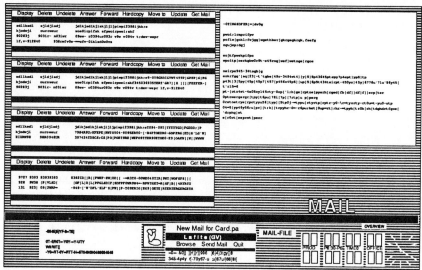

FIGURE 3.14

A Rooms map of space and an expanded window. (Courtesy of ACM, D.A. Henderson, and S.K. Card, "Rooms: the use of multiple virtual workspaces to reduce space contention in a window-based graphical user interface," *Transactions on Graphics*, 5(3), July 1986.)

1987]. It shows that abstraction mechanisms can be appropriately used to manage the visualization of windows.

The first step in the development of Rooms was to analyze the way in which people use windows. The data gathered showed that people use windows in groups. That is, the operator's activity tends to be localized in one group of windows, then transferred to a second group of windows, then localized in that second group, and so on. The pattern of activities supports the hypothesis that an operator performs one task at a time. The windows in which activity is localized are those windows that support the particular task being performed.

The second step in the development of Rooms was to realize that the existing windows could be collected into groups and that these groups could be made the basis for a system. The metaphor of rooms in a building and windows within each room was used as the basis for the user interface. In other words, the aggregation operation was applied to windows and each aggregate was named a room.

In Rooms, shown in Figure 3.14, the operator is provided with a collection of rooms in a building. Within each room, such as the mail room or the project meeting room, windows can be created or destroyed. One particular room is current at any point in time, and all the windows within this room are exposed. Rooms that are not current (in the metaphor, unoccupied rooms) are represented as icons. Thus, when an operator moves from one room to another (changes tasks), the windows in the room being exited become unavailable and the windows in the room being entered become available.

Each room is given a different background so that the operator can tell which room is currently active. An architectural plan of the building is kept available so that the operator can determine how to navigate from one room to another.

Rooms has a number of additional features, but the heart of the system came from the realization that people use windows in a localized manner and thus a system that supported this localization would be used more efficiently. Pre- and post-studies have shown that operators manage about three times as many windows using Rooms as they do with a normal window system. Since operators will manage as many windows as they can comfortably handle, we can conclude that Rooms increased the number of windows with which an operator is comfortable. Rooms is an outstanding example of what can be achieved if designers understand both the cognitive needs of operators and the requirements of software.

3.8 Engineering Considerations

The major engineering issues related to window systems are the following:

☐   The architecture of the window system,

- The style of programming engendered by the fact that window systems are event-based,
- Performance,
- Evaluation.

3.8.1 SOFTWARE ARCHITECTURE

The functionality of a window system can be implemented in a variety of manners. The possible partitionings of the functionality are as follows [Gosling 1986]:

1. Replicate the window system functionality in the address space of each client process.

2. Install the window system functionality in the kernel of the operating system, outside the address spaces of the clients.

3. Have a separate window server process that is outside both the kernel and the client address spaces.

The problem with the first option (replication) is that processes need to explicitly synchronize concurrent access to the screen. The second option (embedding in the kernel) overloads the functionality of the kernel and introduces configuration problems. The technique being used in recent window systems oriented toward networking is the third option: having a separate window server process with its own address space.

The client-server model for window systems has a number of interesting engineering implications for software architecture. These concern the division of functionalities and the problems inherent in networking.

Dividing the Functionalities of a Window System.   A window system has two functional portions: one is terminal specific, managing services for multiple clients, and the other is client specific, managing services for single clients. The communication between the two portions leads to two different architectures.

In the approach taken by the X Window System, the client-specific portion is called the *window manager* and the terminal-specific portion is called the *server*. Figure 3.15 shows the architecture for the X environment. This approach has several advantages:

1. The window manager can communicate with the server as though the window manager were just another client. Thus, the server can deal with clients according to a fixed protocol and does not need to know whether the client is the window manager. It does so by using the facilities provided by the X Lib-X Intrinsics described in Chapter 4.

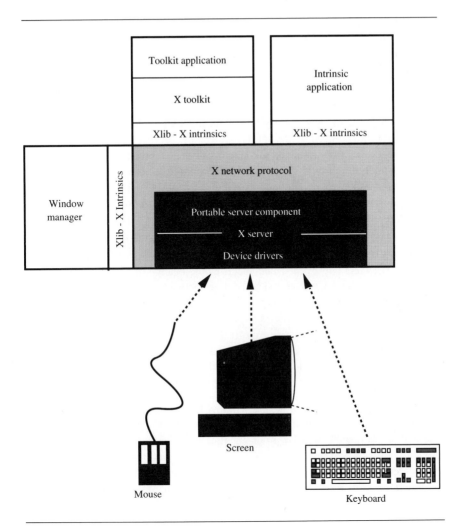

FIGURE 3.15
The client-server architecture. The server, in this case the X server, may have multiple clients; these clients may include a window manager, a client using a toolkit, and a client using the server directly.

2. The server can operate on one node of the network even if its clients are located on different nodes. Terminals that execute the X Window System have appeared on the market. Because these terminals are window manager independent (the window manager is just another client), they can be used with different window managers. Also, since the functionality provided by the window manager is outside the server, X terminals can be constructed with smaller memory and, consequently, can operate more efficiently.

There are several disadvantages to the X Window System approach, however:

1. The actual client may need to communicate with both the window manager and the server. Consequently, the client must know not only the communication protocol used by the server but also the protocol used by the window manager. This complicates the construction of the client. The X Window System community has established a communication protocol between the client and the window manager to which all window managers, in the future, must adhere. The problem is that not only must all window managers adhere to the protocol, but all clients must be aware of the protocol and adhere to it.

2. Operator-generated events may be processed in the wrong order. Suppose the operator wants to switch to another window to modify its contents. The server detects two events: one specifies the change of focus, and the other corresponds to a keystroke. The change focus event is directed to the window manager, whereas the key event is sent to the client process owning the current focus window. On receipt of a change focus event, the window manager issues several requests to the server, including a "change focus request." If the keystroke event arrives at the server before this request does, the current focus window will still be the old one. Consequently, from the operator's perspective, the key event will be directed to the wrong window.

The approach of combining the window manager with the server has been taken by NeWS. The virtue of this approach is that the client need only communicate with the server for window manager functions, using a protocol that it must already know. The disadvantage of this approach is that, for a single operator to interact with multiple styles of windows, the server must contain window manager functions for all of the different styles. In a heterogeneous network, an operator could interact with multiple styles of windows.

Networking.   The use of the operating system's interprocess communication mechanisms allows clients and server to be distributed across local area networks. This is true whether or not the window manager exists separately. Figure 3.16 displays a network that exploits the distinction between clients and servers. A client residing on one workstation can have a server that resides on a different physical workstation. One of the implications of this structure has already been mentioned: it allows nodes of the network to be strictly servers for the window system. Another implication is that it makes possible a heterogeneous network in which the client is on one architecture and the server is on another. As long as both parties adhere to the fixed communication protocol, the instruction sets and data representations used by the parties are irrelevant.

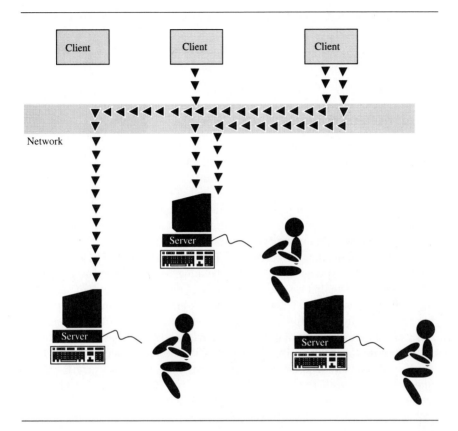

FIGURE 3.16
Network of servers. Each server may serve multiple clients on different nodes of the network.

3.8.2 PROGRAMMING STYLE

Communication with a window system is accomplished through events. Clients, which must be prepared to react to events, should be modeled as cyclic processes executing an event acquisition–event processing main loop. The example shown in Figure 3.1 includes the program skeleton used by every client.

The event model suggests that careful attention be paid to possible side effects of a response to a particular event. Since, in general, any event is possible at any time, any sequencing assumptions in the client program must be explicitly coded. This feature makes programming more difficult than normal programming, in which sequencing is usually controlled by the program and, hence, assumptions can be made about the order of major activities. Many people are uncomfortable with the style of programming associated with event processing. Adhering to this style is important, however, both because operators are unpredictable and because they should feel that they are in control.

3.8.3   PERFORMANCE ISSUES

Several of the resource management issues discussed so far affect performance. In particular, it is important to maintain separate buffers to allow for quick refreshing when a window is exposed. These buffers consume memory very quickly, however. If a system has an inadequate amount of real memory, extensive use of window buffers can result in very high rates of page replacement, with consequent performance problems. Thus, configurations must be established with an adequate amount of real memory.

The communication protocol also affects performance. The client-server model for window systems relies on the operating system's interprocess communication mechanism. In turn, the performance of the interprocess communication mechanism depends on the volume of traffic. Within window systems, the protocol for communication is defined at a higher level of abstraction than bit-maps in order to reduce the volume of traffic. The X Window System has commands such as "draw circle" and "draw line," and graphical communication is handled at that level of abstraction. The NeWS system sends messages that carry PostScript programs. Since PostScript is at a higher level than the X imaging model, PostScript systems will, inherently, have lower communication traffic. This advantage is balanced by the fact that the server on a PostScript system must perform more work.

One possible technique for cutting down the overhead of communication is to bundle transfer requests into transactions. For example, in the X Window System, client requests are accumulated in a queue, the *output buffer*, until some condition occurs. The possible conditions include a call to any routine that requests information from the server (for example, the attributes of a window), requests for acquiring events, and the explicit flush buffer routine. Each transaction encompasses a number of events for a particular client. A consequence of the transaction mechanism is that processing may appear to the operator as a collection of bursts of activity rather than one continuous stream. Whether this is a problem depends on the application, the traffic on the network, and the expectations of the operator. Testing for operator satisfaction is one way of determining whether communication delays cause problems. Visual techniques used in animation, such as wiping the screen clean, smoothly fading from one scene to another, and smoothly moving from one view to the next, may not provide the desired effect.

3.8.4 EVALUATION ISSUES

In general, deciding which window system to use for a particular interactive system is a two-stage process. The first stage is to determine which contenders are technically suitable. The second stage is to choose one of those contenders, taking into consideration both technical and nontechnical factors. The technical adequacy of a particular window system may be evaluated on the basis of the following criteria:

- Does the system separate basic mechanisms from policies? NeWS and the X Window System, for example, support either tiled or overlapping windows. The window system provides the mechanisms; the client has the freedom to choose the policy.

- Does the system adopt the client-server architecture? If it does not, the use of the window system on a network to facilitate sharing of programs and access will not be supported.

- Does the system provide one communication channel per client *process*? If it does, the client is guaranteed to receive events in the right order. If there is one communication channel per *window*, distinguishing the order of events across windows becomes difficult. Having one communication channel per client also saves the client from having to poll all the channels to see if an event has arrived.

- Does the system allow a hierarchy of windows to be defined? When a direct manipulation interface is used, it is important to be able to handle object overlapping. Object overlapping is easily handled within a hierarchy of windows, as movement of the parent will move the entire object.

- Does the window system provide powerful window buffers—that is, the client remains ignorant of whether a particular request is to an off-screen or on-screen surface. If the client has to distinguish between off-screen and on-screen rendition surfaces, the interaction between the client and the window system becomes needlessly complex. Also, a window buffer may act as a cache for pixels and become a performance enhancement mechanism. It also avoids the reinterpretation of graphics requests.

- Does the window system allow clients to regain control in the case of failures? For example, if the client requests an unavailable font, the window system should have a well-defined, consistent method of allowing the client to determine strategy. This facility is important in the building of robust systems.

- What restrictions does the window system impose on portability of clients? Pixel models are device dependent, whereas PostScript is based on distance measurements that are then implemented on a particular device (within its

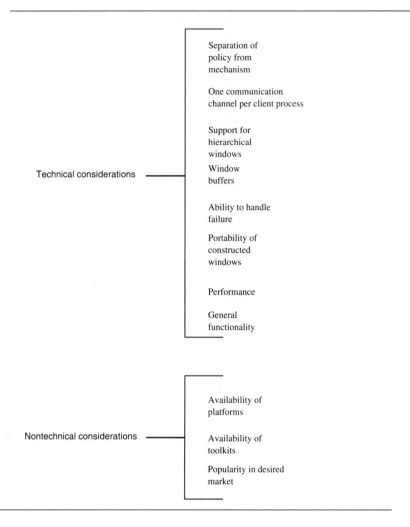

FIGURE 3.17
Technical and nontechnical criteria for evaluating window systems.

tolerance). Consequently, clients of a PostScript-based window system are inherently more portable than clients of a pixel-based window system.

☐   Is the system's performance adequate for the anticipated use?

All these considerations are important in evaluating a window system in the abstract. Other factors also enter into the choice of a particular window system, however. These are:

- □   On what platforms is the window system available? If a particular window system is available only on particular hardware, using that window system implies a host of other choices, which may not be desirable.

- □   Which toolkits are available for the window system? Window systems provide a low level of abstraction for implementing complicated interfaces. Toolkits (see Chapter 4) provide a more desirable programming interface. Yet toolkits are typically implemented on top of a particular window system. Thus, the choice of toolkit will often dictate the choice of window system.

- □   How popular is the window system in the market in which the interactive system will be used? When the interactive system is being developed for sale by a private concern, market considerations are extremely important. Even when this is not the case, the opportunities for acquiring utilities useful for the interactive system are greater if the window system is widely used.

3.9   Window System Used in the Mobile Robot

In choosing a window system for the mobile robot, our first consideration was the types of information available to the user through the window system. The mobile robot has a camera that scans the scene. The information seen through the camera is then processed through several levels of abstraction: edge detection, world modeling, and object recognition. The user interface would make the results of this processing available. Thus, we wanted the user interface to have the ability to display raw television pictures, television pictures overlaid with lines and arcs to indicate the outlines, and television pictures overlaid with indications of the items that had been identified. Any component of the view was to be removable from the current scene, so that the operator could judge the accuracy of the mobile robot's identification.

The requirements that this desired user interface placed on the window system were the ability to display television images, the ability to overlay lines and arcs over these images, and the ability for the operator to interact with portions of the television image and the lines and arcs.

The requirement to display television images could be satisfied in one of two fashions. Either the image could be presented to the window system as a digitized gray scale image, or the analog video signal could be fed directly to the window system and the system itself could manage the digitizing and presentation of the video signal. The technology for having the window system manage the digitizing and presentation of the video signal was available when the decision about a window system was made. The registration (alignment) of overlays posed a problem for existing video/window system technology, however. In order for a line to be placed over a detected edge of a video image, the position of the portion of the image determined to be an edge must be known. This position must have been known initially in order to identify the edge. The view from the camera is continuous, however, and the coordinates of a particular edge change as the camera changes position. It thus becomes the responsibility of the client to maintain the registration as the camera changes position. Such intensive computation was deemed to be unnecessary. Thus, in the designed interface, the operator can see snapshots from the camera and the appropriate overlays, but these snapshots do not move at video rates as the scene under view shifts.

As can be seen from the above discussion, the development of the mobile robot user interface, even in the conceptual stages, followed the iterative process described in Chapter 1 and encountered some of the dangers discussed in that section. An understanding of the task domain and a task decomposition led to a proposed user interface. This proposed interface, in turn, was matched with existing technology, and the expense of developing the proposed interface caused modifications in the design. It is important that the expense of constructing a proposed interface be determined as soon as possible so that alternatives can be explored before commitments are made. In the case of the mobile robot, prototype user interfaces were constructed, but a static prototype would not have shown the problem with registration. Thus, this example illustrates the importance of allowing changes in the design of the user interface at any point in the process.

The expense involved in constructing the originally proposed user interface led to the choice of a more standard user interface, with a display area under the control of the client and a distinct control area that the operator uses to communicate with the client. This style of user interface could be constructed with any of the available window systems.

For the mobile robot, the X Window System was chosen. The choice was heavily influenced by the nontechnical considerations enumerated above. In particular, Suns was to be used as the main computer in the project of which the mobile robot was a portion. This restricted the window system choice to SunView, NeWS, or the X Window System. Since the project had a lifetime of five years, platform portability and the availability of future support were important issues. In 1987, when the decision about a window system was made, the X Window System appeared to be the best choice.

3.10   Future

In the future, some elements discussed in this chapter will remain stable while others evolve further. The elements driving change are the increase in communication bandwidth and the use of new interaction media. The stable elements include the following:

1. Client-server architecture. The localization of device dependencies into a server that provides services over a network to a variety of clients is an element of current networked window systems that will not change. As the speed of information transmission increases, the services that can be provided will evolve, but the basic architecture will not.

   Currently, personal computers do not have well-defined networking and sharing concepts included in the system support. Thus, the window system for the Macintosh, Microsoft Windows, and Presentation Manager do not expose client-server architectures. In the future, as networks of personal computers become more important, the advantages of the client-server architecture for communication will make it the normal architecture for window systems.

2. Bit-mapped graphic terminals. Bit-mapped terminals with a keyboard and pointing device will continue to be an important mechanism for input and output. As the speed of the underlying hardware increases, more and more animation capabilities will be included in the server and the resolution of the display portion will increase, but the basic technology will be with us for quite some time.

More aspects of window systems will change than will remain stable, however. Some of the areas of instability follow.

1. Window managers for bit-mapped graphics. Currently it is unclear whether the best approach for window systems is to include window managers in the server or have them as clients. The introduction of new window management models such as Rooms suggests that separate window managers will evolve in the short term. When the functions provided by window managers stabilize, these functions may be included in a server.

2. Multimedia. Management of individual media will be via a server, as with bit-mapped graphics. The question with multiple media is whether there will be a single server for all media or individual servers for each medium. Having a single server is a very complex solution, but having individual servers leads to synchronization and data exchange problems. The ultimate solution will probably depend on the particular media to be integrated.

3. Artificial reality. One current trend is the use of many media to construct an integrated artificial reality. Prototypes exist for such items as hoods that enable a pilot to maneuver through obstacles and musical instruments that are operated through gestural input. It is not clear whether such techniques will have broad application in general-purpose computation.

4. Natural language interaction—both written and verbal. Natural language processing requires a great deal of domain knowledge. Device-specific

modularization is based on the principle that device management can be abstracted away from domain knowledge. If a speech recognition server must have domain knowledge, abstraction becomes very difficult. Mechanisms for communicating forms of domain knowledge with different semantic content must be developed in order to allow such abstraction.

5. Integration of different media and different modalities. The architectural framework that allows for most efficient integration of multiple media has yet to be determined; this area of research is an active one.

3.11   Summary

In this chapter we discussed issues involved in window systems. In particular, we identified the problems associated with device independence and device sharing, the imaging models used by window systems, and the methods used by window systems for resource management. We also considered window systems from the point of view of cognitive and human factors and pointed out an unusual and interesting window system. We enumerated a number of engineering considerations pertinent to window systems, such as architectural strategies, network and communication techniques, and evaluation issues. We discussed the evaluation problem from the point of view of our mobile robot example and closed with our views on the future.

4

Interaction
Objects

As we saw in Chapter 3, window systems provide their clients with services at a relatively low level of abstraction. The implementation of a sophisticated user interface using this level of services requires a great deal of time and effort. Effort must be spent not only in the development of the user interface but also in its maintenance and refinement. In this chapter we introduce the notion of interaction objects, which provide a more usable, although still not ideal, level of abstraction.

Interaction objects are computer entities that represent syntactic or semantic concepts. In chapter 2, we identified a number of general interaction techniques, such as using menus and forms to extend the memory span of the operator. We also noted the existence of general-purpose syntactic tasks, such as scrolling. These generally useful entities are made available within libraries known as *toolkits*.

In this chapter we will study interaction objects from the following perspectives:

- Interaction objects as abstractions. Section 4.1 discusses the level of abstraction of interaction objects and their appearance both to the client and to the operator.

- Architecture of interaction objects. Section 4.2 shows how an object-oriented paradigm is applied to the construction of interaction objects.

- Composite interaction objects. Section 4.3 is concerned with the composition of interaction objects and with geometry management. Geometry management is a special case of constraint systems, which are also discussed.

◻   Multimedia toolkits. Section 4.4 reviews issues in multimedia toolkits.

◻   Human factors and engineering considerations. Sections 4.5 and 4.6 analyze
the impact of interaction objects on the quality of user interfaces, as well as
engineering concerns with respect to interaction objects.

4.1   Interaction Objects as Abstractions

Interaction objects are software abstractions designed to permit interaction with
the operator. Thus, they have behavior. The actions (or reactions) of interaction
objects have three basic characteristics:

◻   They are observable by both the operator and the client.

◻   They result from computation built into the interaction object.

◻   They are described in terms of properties (also called behavioral attributes),
which act as parameters of the interaction object's perceivable behavior.

In general, the computation that determines the object's action, or behavior,
is hard wired into the interaction object and cannot be changed by observers. In
some cases, the client and, possibly, the operator can specify behavioral attributes,
overriding default values maintained in the computational core of the interaction
object.

Included in an interaction object are techniques for either output, input, or
both. Output provisions of an interaction object define a perceivable behavior in
terms of visual or auditory properties. For example, a button has a specific shape,
may be highlighted, and may produce a sound when pressed. Input provisions
determine the physical actions the operator can perform on the interaction object
through physical devices such as the keyboard and the mouse. For example, an
icon may be moved around with the mouse.

From the point of view of the client, an interaction object is an abstraction
capable of hiding the low-level details of the interaction with the operator. It
transforms the low-level events performed by the operator into higher level events.
For example, double clicking with the left button of the mouse within an interaction
object can be interpreted by this object as a selection. The client is notified of the
selection, but not of the actions the operator used to perform it. For output, the
client is provided with rendition properties but is not aware of the effective
implementation required by the underlying platform. For example, the client may
require an interaction object to be highlighted, depending on the platform highlighting.

Although an interaction object has the ability to interact with an operator and
with a client, it is unable to automatically interact with other interaction objects.

The internal cooperation between the interaction objects of a user interface corresponds to the dialogue control introduced in Chapter 1 (see Figure 1.2). Dialogue control will be discussed in more detail in Chapter 5.

Before discussing interaction objects in general, let us examine a particular interaction object to gain some understanding of the functions provided by interaction objects.

4.1.1 SAMPLE INTERACTION OBJECT

Figure 4.1 shows how the appearance of an Athena toolkit widget changes in response to various mouse actions. (The Athena toolkit is one of the libraries developed for platforms running the X Window System.) In our terminology, a widget is an interaction object. In its initial presentation, the command widget has no highlighting, but has a size, color, border width, and internal text. When the operator moves the mouse into the command widget, the widget's presentation changes—the border changes color to show the operator that the command widget is the current focus of the mouse. When the left mouse button is pressed, the colors of the background and the text are reversed to produce further feedback. When the mouse button is released, the appearance of the command widget reverts to the second state described above, indicating that the mouse is inside the widget. When the mouse is moved outside of the command widget, the appearance reverts to its initial state.

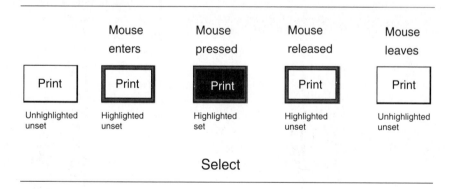

FIGURE 4.1
The appearance of a command widget changes in response to mouse actions. The border changes color to indicate that the widget is the current focus. The background changes color to indicate that the left mouse button has been pushed. After the button is released, the background reverts to its initial appearance. When the mouse is moved out of the widget, the widget reverts to its original appearance.

The response of the widget to the operator and to the client is partially built into the command widget and partially specified by the client and the operator. The computational unit that leads to the observable behavior is built into the command widget and cannot be changed. On the other hand, behavioral attributes used by the computational unit to determine the final appearance of the widget may be specified by the client or the operator.

☐ For output, these attributes include position on the screen, height and width, border width, border color, color of background, and justification of text.

☐ For input, these attributes include the nature of the physical actions the operator must perform on the widget through physical input devices to denote high-level events such as selection. In our example, the client is notified of a "select" event when the operator pushes and releases the left button of the mouse within the command widget.

We will now generalize from the properties of a particular command widget to those of interaction objects in toolkits.

4.1.2   APPEARANCE AND BEHAVIOR OF INTERACTION OBJECTS

The appearance and behavior of interaction objects can be affected by both the operator and the client.

Responses to the Operator.   As discussed in Chapter 2, the designer must choose the interaction objects to suit the operator's tasks. Each interaction object has its own sequence of responses to operator actions and its own appearance.

Figure 4.2 shows several different interaction objects. A table may have a collection of prompts, each with its own area for response, as well as a commit or cancel button. The command widget, for example, might respond in the fashion presented in Section 4.1.1; the menu would highlight the option currently under the mouse cursor. Within a form, each dialogue box may have a prompt and an area for a response. The form also has a commit or cancel button. A slider displays the current setting.

Tables and forms made up of elementary interaction objects are examples of composite objects. Composite interaction objects provide the designer with a higher level of abstraction. They are useful for representing structured semantic concepts, such as functions with their parameters; they are able to maintain both a local thread of dialogue and spatial constraints between the component interaction objects. Problems posed by composite objects will be discussed more fully in Section 4.3.

Whether or not it is composite, each class of interaction object has its own collection of parameters to specify those aspects of appearance controllable by

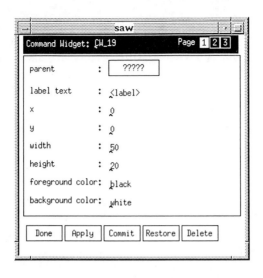

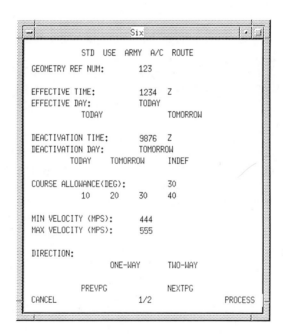

Density: 0 ▬▬▬□═══════ 100   With min/max values

FIGURE 4.2
Sample interaction objects: a table, a form, and a slider.

observers (that is, the operator and the client). In early toolkits, behavioral parameters were accessible only to clients. More recently, they have been made available to the operator in the form of resource files.

A *resource file* is a collection of behavioral parameters. It can be edited by the operator and read at run time by the toolkit when the client requests creation of interaction objects. Since a resource file is read at run time, the source code of the user interface does not have to be compiled when the resource file is modifed. The resource file thus becomes a mechanism for operator customization.

The format and richness of a resource file depend on the toolkit. Resource files range from a sequence of ASCII characters describing behavioral parameters (such as in the X Window System environment) to a sequence of complex structures describing not only behavioral parameters but also the construction of composite interaction objects (such as in the Macintosh toolbox).

Figure 4.3 shows a resource file for a toolkit built on top of the X Toolkit library [MIT 1987]. The resource file allows the setting of arbitrary attributes for widgets declared in a program. The first line, Draw*commands.columns: 1, specifies the number of columns for the composite widget commands used in the program Draw. The second line, Draw*quit.label: Quit, indicates the label for the quit command button used in Draw. The complete Draw program is given in Appendix B.

Figures 4.4, 4.5, and 4.6 show a Macintosh resource file edited with the tool ResEdit. In Figure 4.4, the operator has opened the resource file for Microsoft Word 3.01 and is interested in a dialogue box interaction object. The top-level window, titled Dialog ID = 258 from Word 3.01, shows the operator a general view of dialogue box 258 when used at run time. The operator (of ResEdit) can change the run-time location of the dialogue box by moving it around with the mouse or can get more details about the dialogue box by double clicking on the graphical representation. Figure 4.5 shows the screen after such an action.

In the Macintosh toolbox a dialogue box is built from a list of interaction objects. In Figure 4.5, the interaction objects are the gray rectangle in the middle of the screen and the four buttons near the bottom of the figure. The operator of ResEdit can resize and reposition the various elements through direct manipulation. A double click on one of the components will provide more information about the selected component. Figure 4.6 shows a picture of the screen after a double click on the push button labeled Topics.

The top-level window of Figure 4.6 presents the attributes of Item 1 in the list of interaction objects: components of the dialogue box. Item 1 is currently a push button labeled Topics; it could be replaced by a check box or by a radio control with a different print name. At creation time, it is enabled (that is, it becomes responsive to the operator's actions); it could be disabled. Its location relative to the dialogue box is expressed in pixels; this location could be changed either by moving the item with the mouse in Figure 4.5 or by editing the top, left, bottom, and right fields in Figure 4.6.

```
###################################################
# Draw: Class resource file the simple draw program
###################################################
```

Draw*commands.columns:	1
Draw*quit.label:	Quit
Draw*drawline.label:	Draw Line
Draw*drawrect.label:	Draw Rectangle
Draw*movelineright.label:	Move Line Right
Draw*movelineleft.label:	Move Line Left
Draw*canvas.xRefName:	commands
Draw*canvas.xAddWidth:	True
Draw*canvas.xAttachRight:	True
Draw*canvas.xAttachLeft:	True
Draw*canvas.xAttachBottom:	True
Draw*canvas.xAttachTop:	True
Draw*canvas.xAttachRight:	True

FIGURE 4.3
A sample resource file for a toolkit built using the X Intrinsics library. The syntax is
programname*widgettype.attribute: value. This file makes it possible to set arbitrary
attribute values without recompiling the program.

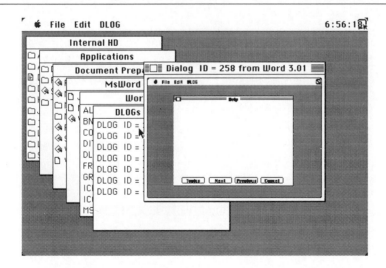

FIGURE 4.4
Macintosh toolbox resource file, a window displaying a dialogue box from Microsoft Word 3.01. The operator can set the position of the dialogue box through
direct manipulation.

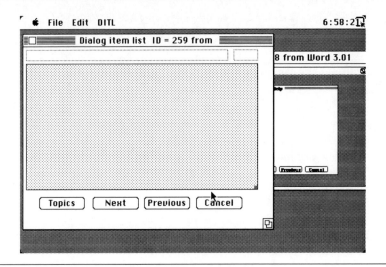

FIGURE 4.5
From the Macintosh toolbox resource file, a window displaying the components of
a dialogue box. The components that can be manipulated include the four buttons
near the bottom of the figure.

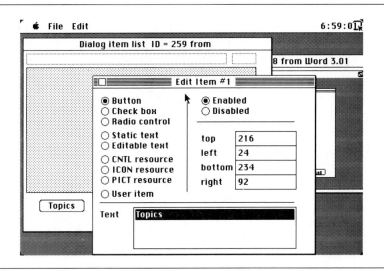

FIGURE 4.6
From the Macintosh toolbox resource file, a window that gives the operator control
over the type of interaction object used in a particular context. The interaction
object is currently a button labeled "Topics," but it could be changed to a check box
or other type of object.

104

In addition to permitting the operator to edit the behavioral attributes of existing interaction objects, ResEdit allows the operator to create and destroy interaction objects through direct manipulation. It is because of the richness of the underlying resource files of the Macintosh toolbox that ResEdit can offer so many options. Resource files based on the X Toolkit Intrinsics, which are limited to the specification of behavioral attributes, do not support such elaborate tools. To fill this gap, User Interface Language (UIL) has been developed for specifying the interaction objects used in an application system [Open Software Foundation 1989]. The compilation of such a specification produces a file similar in functionality to the Macintosh resource files.

Neither UIL nor ResEdit can prevent the operator from fatal errors, such as deleting an interaction object from the resource file. The consequence of such an unintentional action is detectable only at run time, when the client reads the resource file. This situation is unavoidable as long as user interfaces are not developed within integrated environments.

Responses to the Client.   As we saw in the previous section, clients can control some aspects of the presentation of interaction objects. Certain attributes are useful for tuning output rendition, whereas others relate to the interpretation of input events. In addition to modifying input and output behavior, clients must be concerned with creating interaction objects.

Clients create and modify interaction objects through special-purpose primitives. In accordance with the abstract data type model, clients cannot directly modify the data structures themselves. Figure 4.7 illustrates the level of abstraction provided by user interface toolkits. Although this example is expressed in terms of the Athena Widget Toolkit, it demonstrates the activities that clients must perform in order to manipulate interaction objects.

The program places "Hello World" into a command widget and prints a message whenever the operator selects that widget. As in the window system example, the width must be both created and made visible (mapped) (see Figure 3.5). In this case (unlike the window system example), however, all the details for creating the window, setting the graphic context, and so on are handled automatically by the toolkit. Similarly, the acquisition of events, which was explicit in the window example, is performed automatically by XtMainLoop. This primitive cycles infinitely to acquire events and dispatch them to the appropriate interaction objects.

The routine Activate is a *callback procedure*. (A callback procedure is an event-handling technique that will be dealt with in the next section.) The Activate routine is automatically invoked by the toolkit whenever the operator selects the command widget. As shown in the example, it is mentioned by name in the initialization of the widget but is never explicitly called by the client.

As the above example illustrates, the client is responsible for setting and modifying behavioral parameters. It is in charge of defining the relationships

```
/*
 * This is a sample Athena Widget program which places
 * "Hello World" in a command widget and then
 * prints a message when it is selected by the mouse.
 */

/*
 * This is the procedure that is called by the toolkit
 * whenever the widget is selected.
 */

void Activate ()
{
    printf( "button was activated.\n" );
}


void main(argc, argv)
    unsigned int argc;
    char **argv;
{

/*
 * declare the arguments which will be sent to the toolkit.
 */

    static XtCallbackRec callbacks[] = {
      { Activate, NULL },
      { NULL, NULL },
    };

    static Arg args[] = {
      { XtNcallback, (XtArgVal)callbacks },
      { XtNlabel, (XtArgVal)"Hello World"},
    };

    toplevel = XtInitialize( NULL, "Demo", NULL, 0,
                  &argc, argv );

    XtCreateManagedWidget( "command", commandWidgetClass,
                  toplevel,
                  args, XtNumber(args) );

    XtRealizeWidget(toplevel);

    XtMainLoop();
}
```

FIGURE 4.7
Using the Athena Widget Toolkit, the program places "Hello World" into a command widget, registers parameters including the callback routine, and then calls a routine to handle events.

among interaction objects and of processing input events. Event handling is by far the most complicated aspect of the client's responsibilities.

The command widget presented in section 4.1.1 recognizes a predefined event: the select event. Each event indicates a specific sequence of operator actions. For example, the select event corresponds to the following ordered set of conditions: "mouse inside command widget," "left button down," and "left button up."

The flexibility of interaction objects, in terms of behavioral parameters including events, affects the types of interfaces that can be constructed. For example, if the command widget reports only the select event, the only types of interfaces that can be constructed involving the command widget are various types of fixed format interfaces. On the other hand, if the command widget can generate events such as move or resize, it is possible to produce interfaces that permit more dynamic direct manipulation.

The client can handle events through one of two methods. The choice of method depends on the particular toolkit.

1. The client polls to see which events are available and which are of interest to each interaction object. This technique is used in the Macintosh toolbox [Rose et al. 1986].

2. The client associates routines with the interaction object for each possible event. When an event occurs, the associated routine is automatically invoked. This technique, called *callback*, is used in many different toolkits, such as the X Toolkit Intrinsics.

Figure 4.8 gives a segment of a client program that uses the Macintosh toolbox. The program assumes that a window contains a collection of interaction objects. In the Macintosh documentation, interaction objects are called controls. The segment shows the logic necessary to handle events within the Macintosh toolbox.

The client contains a main loop that retrieves the next event. The event type, which is obtained by the main loop (in the example, a mouse event), contains neither the identification of the window nor the interaction object related to the event. Consequently, the toolkit is asked to determine the window and the portion of the window where the event occurred. In the example, the event is related to the content portion of the window (that is, it is not related to the borders). From there, the client asks the toolkit to identify the control that caused the event and the control type.

The point of this example is to show the level of abstraction the toolkit provides by assisting the client in dispatching low-level events. At the window level, the client must maintain the various data structures and traversal routines for those data structures. At the toolkit level, this function is handled for the client. If the toolkit automatically tagged events with the object within which they occurred, the client would not have to perform the traversal through the various types of toolkit entities.

```
/*
 * Loop for ever on event acquisition
 */
while (go) {

/*
 * Get next event of any type and process it according to its type
 */
        if (GetNextEvent(everyEvent, myevent))
            switch (myevent->what) {
                case keyDown : ..... break;
                case mouseUp :
                case mouseDown:
/*
 * Find window and get a high level description of mouse location.
 */
                wheremouse = FindWindow(myevent->where,
                &whichwindow);
                switch (wheremouse) {
                    case inDesk:
                    /*
                     * in top level window
                     */
                    ..... ; break;

                        case inMenuBar:
                     /*
                     * in menu bar
                     */
                    ......; break;

                    case inGrow: case inDrag:
                    /*
                    *in window borders to manipulate the window
                    */
                    ...... ; break;

                        case inContent:
                        /*
                        * in the content part of the window.
                        * switch from global mouse coordinates to
                        * coordinates relative to the window
                        */
                        localwhere = &myevent->where;
                        GlobalToLocal (&localwhere);
```

FIGURE 4.8
Acquisition of events with the Macintosh toolbox. The program is informed whenever an event occurs and then must query the toolbox to determine which interaction object caused the event.

```
whereincontrol = FindControl (localwhere,
                    &whichwindow, &whichcontrol);

/*
test whether the event happened in a control.
if so,findout where in the control.
*/
if (whichcontrol != NIL) {
switch (whereincontrol) {
case inButton:
/*
* toolkit perform the lexical feedback
* until the end user releases the mouse
  * button.
*/
    if (TrackControl(whichcontrol,
            localwhere, ...) )
    ....... ;
    break;
    ... ; } /* end switch (whereincontrol) */

    /* end if (whichcontrol != NIL) */

} /* end switch (wheremouse) */

} /* end switch (myevent->what) */

} /* end while (go) */
```

FIGURE 4.8
(continued)

Some toolkits allow the client to define its own set of events in terms of lower level primitives. For example, toolkits constructed on top of the X Toolkit Intrinsics library can define higher level events, called actions, in terms of regular expressions. These expressions are based on primitive events such as mouse button1 up, key pressed, and drag. The client defines its own higher level actions by specifying the action definition in a translation table. The interaction object then interprets the translation table to determine which action to generate and which procedure to call to interpret the action. Figure 4.9 illustrates the technique for defining two new actions: "beep" and "quit."

As shown in Figure 4.9, the definition of a new action involves six steps:

1. Define the name of the action and associate it with a procedure, which acts as the interpreter of the action. In our example, the declaration and the

```
XtTranslations mytranstable;

/*
 * Procedure to ring the terminal bell.
 */

static void beep (w, event, params, numparams)

        Widget w;
        Xevent *event;
        String *params;
        int   numparams;
{
        XBell (XtDisplay(w), 50);
}

/*
 * Procedure to exit from the program.
 */

static void quit (w, event, params, numparams)

        Widget w;
        Xevent *event;
        String *params;
        int   numparams;
{
        exit (0);
}

/*
 *  Define the action table by associating:
 *     - action "beep" with procedure beep,
 *     - action "quit" with procedure quit.
 */

static XtActionsRec myactionstable [] = {
   { "beep", beep },
   { "quit", quit },
};

/*
 * Override translations which create a newline
 * in widget w (w will be created further).
```

FIGURE 4.9
Definition of a new action (a high-level event) using the X Toolkit Intrinsics. The program defines the actions "beep" and "quit" and modifies the translation table of the toolkit to call the correct procedures when the operator presses the return key, Control-J, or Control-Q.

```
 * Associate the sequence Ctrl Q to action quit.
 */

static char mytranslations [] =
    "<Key> Return:     beep() \n\
    Ctrl<Key>J:       beep() \n\
    Ctrl<Key>Q:       quit()";

/*
 * Add the actions defined in myactionstable.
 */
XtAddActions (myactionstable, XtNumber(myactionstable));

/*
 * Compile the translations into transtable.
 */
mytranstable = XtParseTranslationTable (mytranslations);

/*
 *  Create widget w
 */
w = XtCreateManagedWidget (.....);

/*
 * Install transtable into widget w.
 */
XtOverrideTranslations (w, mytranstable);
```

FIGURE 4.9
(continued)

association are expressed with the array myactionstable. Actions "beep" and "quit" are associated with procedures beep and quit, respectively.

2. Write the action interpreter. An action interpreter is a procedure whose formal parameters must successively denote the widget concerned with the action at run time, the X Window System event that caused the interpreter to be invoked, an array of strings containing any arguments specified in the translations, and the length of this array. In our example, procedure beep rings the terminal bell, and procedure quit exits from the program.

3. Define the translation table that expresses the mapping between low-level events caused by the operator and the new action. In our example, this is performed with the array mytranslations. Action beep is a high-level event defined by either of two low-level events: the Return key pressed or Control-J pressed. Action quit is defined by the low-level event Control-Q pressed.

In this example, the specification of the translation table is performed by the client. An alternative is to define the translation table in a resource file (as discussed in Section 4.1.2). The resource file approach is more appropriate when customization is to be performed by the operator.

4.   Register the new action with the primitive XtAddActions.

5.   Compile the translation table with the primitive XtParseTranslationTable. In our example, the result is saved in mytranstable.

6.   Install the compiled translation table in a widget. The X Toolkit Intrinsics provide two types of installation: extension, which merges a list of translations with a new list of translations, and override, which replaces existing translations with the new translation list. In our example, XtOverrideTranslations has been used to replace the default translations of widget w with mytranstable. With the override, if the class that widget w belongs to accepts carriage returns, the instance w does not any more: any time the Return key is pressed, the computer will beep.

In summary, toolkits' handling of events can differ in two ways: (1) the method used (polling or callback), and (2) whether or not an abstraction mechanism is provided for defining high-level events.

4.1.3   RELATIONSHIP BETWEEN INTERACTION OBJECTS AND THE UNDERLYING WINDOW SYSTEM

As shown in Figure 1.2, interaction objects are built on top of a window system. The relationships between an interaction object and the underlying window system may be examined from two points of view: from the perspective of their own clients and from the perspective of the interaction object as a client of the window system.

Interface to the Client.   A window system presents to the client an interface that clearly separates input and output. The base object is a window, and the output to the window is specified in terms of a particular imaging model. The input from the window is expressed in terms of events which are at a level close to the physical level of events. The control structure of the client must be structured to respond to these low-level events.

An interaction object presents to the client an interface that combines input and output. The base object is one of a collection of object classes defined in the toolkit. Output to the object is specified in terms of parameters of the object class. Input from the object is either event-based (as in window systems, although at a higher level) or specified as one of the parameters of the object. In either case, the object itself determines its behavior, modified only by the parameters specified by the client.

Interaction Objects as Clients of the Window System.   An interaction object acts as a client of the window system; the window system reports all relevant changes in either cursor or mouse state to the interaction object. The interaction object recognizes mouse positions and mouse button states and sets its appearance accordingly. As with any abstraction mechanism, the fact that the interaction object maintains its own state reduces the flexibility of the client but simplifies the programming task.

The feasibility of constructing interaction objects from the underlying window abstractions depends on the expense of managing multiple windows. Consider, for example, the construction of the command widget shown in Figure 4.1. Two possibilities may be examined:

1. The command widget could be constructed with an underlying window representing the border of the command widget and a child window containing the label. This approach has the advantage of causing the window system to move both portions together. When the interaction object is moved, the underlying window is moved too, and the window system maintains the child in the proper position with respect to its parent. It also has the advantage of simplifying the changing of the color of the border during highlighting. The color of the underlying window is changed without affecting the color of the child window. It has the disadvantage of requiring two windows. If windows are expensive to create and maintain, the use of two windows introduces additional overhead.

2. The command widget could be constructed with a single underlying window with a collection of images, four of which represent the border and one of which represents the text. This approach has the advantage that only one window must be managed, but the disadvantage that the color of the four border segments must be changed independently.

In summary, using windows as the basis for the implementation of interaction objects has the advantage of permitting reuse of features provided by the window system, such as change of exposure and event acquisition. However, windows may be expensive to create and manage. In the Macintosh toolbox, interaction objects are not windows but rectangles related to some window. Similarly, the Open Software Foundation (OSF) [1989] has introduced the notion of *gadget,* a sort of "lightweight" window.

4.2   Interaction Object Architecture

In general, toolkit architectures are inspired by the object-oriented paradigm. In this section we briefly present the principles of this approach and show how these principles apply to the design of user interface toolkits. We then look at the benefits and drawbacks of such toolkits. Although the object-oriented paradigm is widely used, other approaches must be considered when a toolkit is designed.

4.2.1   PRINCIPLES OF THE OBJECT-ORIENTED PARADIGM

An object-oriented architecture is characterized by two features:

1.   Encapsulation of both behavior and data into classes,

2.   Subclassing with inheritance.

A *class* is a description common to a collection of objects. It defines a template from which objects can be instantiated at run time. *Objects* are also referred to as *class instances*. An object is some data (usually called attributes or variables) and a set of procedures (also referred to as methods). Attributes are encapsulated: they cannot be modified by direct reference. Access to an attribute is acquired by invoking a method of the object.

In general, instances of a class share the methods defined in the class but have their own copy of the attribute values. Some object-oriented languages, such as LOOPS [Bobrow and Stefik 1981], make a distinction between instance attributes and class attributes. Instance attributes are local to each instance, whereas class attributes are common to all instances. Instance attributes can be seen as the local memory of a process, whereas class attributes define a memory common to multiple processes. In the next section we will see that the X Toolkit Intrinsics exploits this distinction.

Classes may have subclasses. Each subclass inherits procedures and data from its parent and adds data and behavior. Inherited items may be overridden by the subclass. For example, the method Draw defined in class Shape is automatically inherited by Rectangle, a subclass of Shape. However, Rectangle can redefine the implementation of Draw. Thus, subclassing provides the basis for specializing existing code without modifying the original code. If a class C does not satisfy some requirements, one can define a new class C' as a subclass of C to extend and override parts that do not fit the current situation. The existing class C is not (and must not be) modified. An instance of class C' owns those methods from C which were not overridden, as well as the methods from C' which were added.

Classes and subclasses define a hierarchy. *Single inheritance* requires each class (except the root class) to have exactly one parent. *Multiple inheritance* allows a class to have multiple parents; hence, each class can inherit from multiple classes. Single inheritance can be represented as a tree, multiple inheritance as an acyclically oriented graph. Some classes in the hierarchy are never instantiated; these classes are called *metaclasses*.

A metaclass can be seen as a "convenience" class. It is useful for encapsulating a collection of data and behavior that cannot exist by itself in the domain but that is common to multiple distinct classes. For example, the notion of shape, which includes attributes that any graphical entity must possess (location, color, filling), can be represented as the metaclass Shape. Subclasses of Shape, such as Rectangle and Triangle, then automatically inherit the attributes of location, color, and filling.

These general principles apply to the implementation of all toolkits. We next look at a particular toolkit, the X Toolkit Intrinsics, and how it uses an object-oriented architecture to organize its widgets into classes.

4.2.2   ARCHITECTURE OF THE X TOOLKIT INTRINSICS

Although the X Toolkit Intrinsics is implemented in C rather than a language with object-oriented constructs, it defines an object-oriented architectural model, provides a built-in mechanism for inheritance, and conveys programming rules for defining new classes. The X Toolkit Intrinsics implements several basic widget classes. A widget is an instance of a widget class.

As shown in Figure 4.10, the Core widget class is the root of the hierarchy. It contains attributes that are inherited by all other classes. Some of these attributes are common to all widgets, whereas others are local.

- ☐ Class attributes of the Core class include information such as the superclass name, the class name, and methods for resize and destroy operations. These attributes are gathered in a record of type CoreClassPart created for each widget class and common to all instances of that class.
- ☐ Instance attributes of the Core class include information such as identification of the parent widget and of a window, location, and size on the screen. These attributes are gathered in a record of type CorePart created for each widget instance.

Since all widgets are implemented as windows in the X Window System, one can view the attributes and methods of a window as part of a widget definition. The methods of the Core widget class consist of the procedures necessary to create and manipulate windows and events, such as create, resize, and expose. Such methods, common to any widget, are referenced in the class attributes part. On the other hand, the particular location, size, and window identification, which are specific to each widget, are instance attributes.

As shown in Figure 4.10, below the Core class the hierarchy divides into two groups: the Primitive and the Composite widget classes. The Primitive widget class is never instantiated. It serves as the basis for the definition of simple widget classes such as labels, buttons, and arrows. It includes simple attributes such as a foreground color.

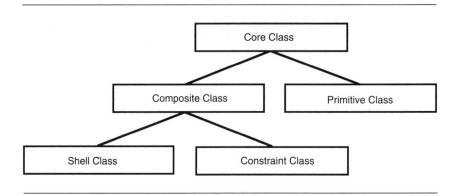

FIGURE 4.10
The hierarchy of basic widgets provided by the X Toolkit Intrinsics. The Core class
has two subclasses (Composite and Primitive), and Composite in turn has two
subclasses (Shell and Constraint).

The X Toolkit Intrinsics offers two subclasses for the Composite class: the
Shell widget class and the Constraint widget class. The purpose of Shell widgets
is to provide an interface between the window manager and its siblings. The
Constraint class is a metaclass whose primary role is to manage the spatial relationships of the siblings (minimum and maximum size, relative location). Constraints and composition will be discussed further in Section 4.3.

The Composite widget class is also a metaclass for defining widget classes
whose instances are containers for other widgets. It includes methods for managing a set of children, such as destroying or mapping the children when the parent
composite widget is destroyed or mapped to the screen.

The method for defining a new class relies on the distinction between class
attributes and instance attributes already described for the Core class. This distinction exists for any widget class. Figure 4.11 illustrates the method for defining
the class MyTree as a subclass of the Constraint class. A widget of class MyTree
is composed of two records:

1. Type MyTreeClassRec is common to all instances of class MyTree. The type
   MyTreeClassRec is built from the concatenation of the class attributes inherited from the superclasses. Since MyTree is a subclass of Constraint, it
   includes the class attributes of classes Core, Composite, and Constraint.

2. Type MyTreePartRec is unique to each instance. The type MyTreePartRec
   is defined as the concatenation of the instance attributes of superclasses
   Core, Composite, and Constraint.

One record for the class MyTree

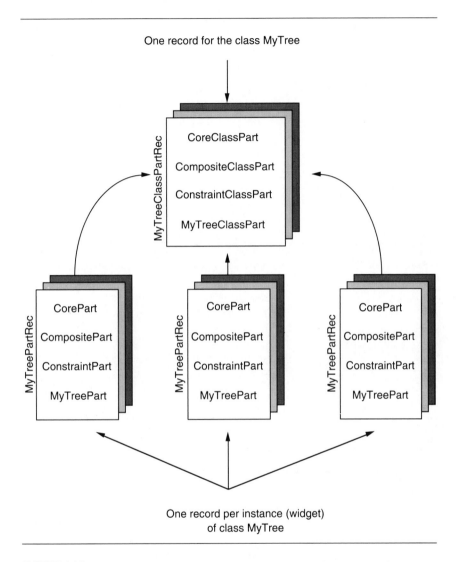

One record per instance (widget)
of class MyTree

FIGURE 4.11
The definition of a new class based on the X Toolkit Intrinsics. The class MyTree is
added as a subclass of the Constraint class.

At run time, only one record of type MyTreeClassRec is instantiated, whereas one
record of type MyTreePartRec is instantiated for each newly created widget of
class MyTree.

The rules described above have been applied to the construction of several X
Window toolkits, including HP widgets, Motif, and Athena widgets. Thus, for

example, the command widget shown in Figure 4.1 includes local data that contain the attributes set by the client. It also contains local data that maintain the current state of the widget and the details necessary for interaction with the underlying window system. In addition to the attributes, the command widget contains the procedures for manipulating the local data. Each instance of the command widget has its own set of local data, but all instances share the procedures for manipulating the data. Now the power of the object-oriented approach becomes apparent.

4.2.3   THE BENEFITS OF THE OBJECT-ORIENTED APPROACH

One driving principle of the object-oriented paradigm is reusability. Reusability increases programming productivity and reliability. Object-oriented languages combine reusability and reliability through the subclassing mechanism. Subclassing offers a way to adapt existing abstractions to a particular situation without modifying the original code.

Subclassing is particularly helpful in the domain of user interfaces, since adaptation to the operator's needs is unavoidable. Another benefit of the object-oriented model is that it allows an object to be seen as an agent, rather than as a passive set of data.

Subclassing.   In the domain of toolkits, subclassing allows the programmer to specialize and inherit from "ready to use" functionalities. For example, in the X Window System environment, the implementor of a new subclass of the Core widget class can ignore all attributes dealing with the underlying window, as they are automatically inherited.

Consider the command widget, which is a subclass of the Label widget class, which in turn is a subclass of the Core widget class. The label widget has the same behavior as the command widget, except that no user interaction can occur within it. Thus, the command widget specializes the label widget by adding procedures to deal with the events of button down, button up, and mouse entry into the underlying window.

One important aspect of inheritance is polymorphism. Polymorphism enables clients to invoke a method without being aware of the class that effectively realizes the method: the definition of an object is distributed across the class hierarchy. For example, a client can send a destroy request to any widget, provided the widget class includes or inherits the definition of a destroy method. In the X Toolkit Intrinsics, procedure destroy is referenced in the Core class; it might be redefined lower in the hierarchy. The client does not need to know where in the hierarchy the implementation of destroy occurs.

Objects and Agents.   Another driving principle in object-oriented design is encapsulation, which stipulates that the behavior of the object can be affected only through the use of methods. For example, if an object is to be relocated on a screen, it must have a move method. The object can then be instructed to move itself to the desired position. Note the style of programming introduced by this strong use of encapsulation: an object is not moved (since the data that represent its current position are hidden from external view)—rather, it is instructed to *move itself* to some location. The object is not a passive collection of data but an agent able to decide about its state. In Chapter 5 we will see how this notion of agent can be used to model interaction objects as effective communicators with the operator.

In summary, object-oriented architectures, when applied to toolkits, begin with the most general aspects of interaction objects and specialize to particular interaction objects. Inheritance is a key technique for reusability: when a new interaction object is introduced, it can be defined as a combination and a specialization of existing classes, rather than as a new entity built from scratch.

4.2.4   THE DRAWBACKS OF THE OBJECT-ORIENTED APPROACH

Using an object-oriented model has some drawbacks.

- □   Defining or reusing the class hierarchy is difficult.
- □   There are no clear semantics for multiple inheritance.
- □   Computational distribution is difficult to master.
- □   There is sometimes no clear object-oriented model.

Defining and Reusing a Class Hierarchy.   Constructing a hierarchy of classes in an object-oriented system is not a trivial problem. There may be multiple independent hierarchies, but the root class of a particular hierarchy should contain the features common to all its subclasses. If this set is too small, not much is inherited by the subclasses and the power is lost. If this set is too large, modularity is in danger.

Although object-oriented environments claim reusability, it is very hard for the newcomer to determine what to reuse. Browsers, such as file browsers, offer a way to explore environments but they do not support the task of searching the hierarchy to find which classes solve a particular problem or provide a particular service.

Resolving the Semantics for Multiple Inheritance.   In addition to defining the appropriate granularity of object classes, designers have to deal with the semantic ambiguity of multiple inheritance. Conflicts may arise when several superclasses implement methods with identical names. In the absence of clear semantics for multiple inheritance, the ambiguity is currently resolved in an ad-hoc fashion at the implementation level.

Managing Computational Distribution.   The use of callbacks to implement core functionality leads to situations where core application functionality is performed in a callback routine. In application systems with a large core functionality and a small user interface portion, knowledge of a particular portion of the core functionality is likely to be spread through several routines. When the same piece of application semantics is maintained in several places, performing any modification involving the semantics can be difficult.

For example, consider the case of modifying an environment in the mobile robot example. The modification occurs through the movement of a wall. The movement of the wall results in a callback to a procedure that knows it is being called by an instance tied to a particular wall in a particular environment.

Now suppose that the same wall is simultaneously modified through a different view or by the robot. A separate procedure is called to modify the same environmental data structure. Thus, the knowledge of that data structure must occur in two places within the system. Consequently, a configuration management problem is inherent in modifications to the data structures. Although this type of decentralization is not implied in the use of object-oriented architectures, care needs to be taken in the structuring of any functionality that is outside the domain of the toolkit.

Reconciling the Object-Oriented Model with the Application Programmer's Interface.   It is not always obvious from the client side whether or not the interaction objects available from a library were constructed according to the object-oriented paradigm. In some systems, the client program must know that it exists inside a class structure. In such a system, such as Interviews [Linton, Vlissides, and Calder 1989], the total application is a collection of classes, and the client is composed partially of subclasses of existing interaction objects, partially of functions called as a result of user interaction, and partially of independent classes. Communication between a client program and an interaction object is in the form of messages between the various objects.

In other systems, such as those based on X Intrinsics, the client program does not need to know that the interaction objects are constructed in an object-oriented fashion. In these systems, interaction objects are packaged as a procedure library that the client program calls to provide desired services.

Despite their drawbacks, object-oriented architectures for user interface toolkits have proven to be extremely powerful and flexible and are widely used.

4.2.5   NON-OBJECT-ORIENTED CONSTRUCTION METHODS

The alternative to object-oriented construction is to develop each interaction object completely, with its own appearance and behavior. Thus, each object stands alone, without reference to other objects. Since there is no hierarchy, each interaction object can then be modified without concern for any other interaction objects. The existence and structure of each interaction object is hidden not only from the client but also from other interaction objects. Data sharing is made explicit through global data structures rather than implicit through subclassing.

4.3   Composite Objects

If all interaction objects are simple objects, it becomes the responsibility of the client to manage the relationships between them. In a great many cases, multiple interaction objects can be combined to form composite objects, which appear to the operator as a single object. An example might be a menu, which is a collection of individual buttons but appears to the operator as a single entity.

If the toolkit assumes responsibility for managing the interrelationships among some of its objects, a great deal of new power is introduced. In this section the following facets of composite objects will be discussed:

- Composition without any additional functionality.
- Management of the geometry of composite interaction objects.
- Use of constraints to express relationships between interaction objects. (Garnet and abstract imaging machines are presented as examples of constraint-based systems.)

4.3.1   SIMPLE COMPOSITION

If an interaction object is declared to be a *composite object*, it can have children. The composite parent-child hierarchy is not the same as the subclassing hierarchy discussed in the previous section. A Motif bulletin board widget, for example, has children that are not specializations of the bulletin board class. These children can be buttons or scroll bars or other objects from other widget classes.

Composite objects allow the creation of a run-time hierarchy in which the position of a child is specified relative to the position of the parent. If the parent is moved, the child is automatically moved. This run-time hierarchy of widgets is based on the underlying hierarchy of windows from which the widgets are constructed.

The simplest type of composite object is a recipient with no interactions of its own. Such objects are called *containers*. A container has size, position, and, most importantly, children with which the operator interacts.

Figure 4.12 shows a container. Although the object in the figure appears to be a menu, it is implemented as an underlying container and a collection of command buttons. Each command button has its own callback procedure for selection. The container provides geometric coherence—that is, the menu is made

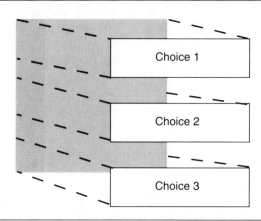

FIGURE 4.12
A container with several command buttons. To the operator this composite object appears to be a menu.

visible by making the container visible and the menu is moved by moving the container. This means that the client can create various types of menus (pop up, tear off, pull down) with a minimum amount of specification.

Putting objects on top of an underlying container leads to many other types of interaction objects. Tables, forms, and dialogue boxes can all be created by composing objects on top of a single underlying container. The table, menu, form and dialogue boxes of Figure 4.2 illustrate some of the types of objects that can be constructed using this mechanism.

Containers can be children of other containers. Thus, for example, a dialogue box can be moved on a form. When composite objects are being used, the client must determine the object with which the operator is interacting. Suppose that in the data entry form in Figure 4.2b, the dialogue boxes and the whole underlying form are movable. When the operator positions the mouse over a dialogue box and issues a move command, the client must determine whether that move command is intended for the dialogue box or for the underlying form. It is at this point that the principles of clear interface design discussed in Chapter 2 become important. The issue is not so much that the client determines which components get moved as that the client and the operator must have the same model of how movement is performed.

Feedback is one mechanism for indicating the results of a particular action to the operator. Low-level feedback is typically the responsibility of interaction objects. In the case of composite objects, the mouse is considered to be within the visible simple object. If the operator issues to that object a command, such as a move, that the object is not interested in, the object passes that command to its parent. When a level in the hierarchy is reached that is interested in the command, feedback is issued to indicate to the operator the effects of the action. Again, it is important that the client and the operator have the same model of which component of a compound object (or the whole object) is being manipulated by a particular action. This principle applies equally to the manipulation of the object and the termination of operator interaction with the object.

4.3.2 GEOMETRY MANAGEMENT

The previous section discussed the positioning of objects relative to a parent. Another consideration that affects the relationship between objects is size. Some toolkits, such as X Toolkit Intrinsics and Andrew [Morris et al. 1986], have automatic geometry management of children by their parent. The basic idea is that the parent is responsible for both the size and the position of its children. The parent determines the size of its children, and then the children are responsible for living within this size. If the child is in turn the parent of embedded objects, it informs the embedded objects of their new size, and so on.

Sometimes the child and its parent negotiate. The child may give a minimum size below which it is not reasonably visible—for example, a text field may specify a size at which it becomes unreadable. In some cases, an object will totally change its presentation as a result of a size adjustment. If a text field is too small, it may change itself into some iconic form to indicate that text exists in a certain place. In any case, the parent is the final arbiter of the size of its children. A child cannot know what additional siblings the parent has and what constraints the parent is currently enforcing.

Geometry management is a very powerful concept which frees the client from responsibility for placing objects. Figure 4.13 shows a form made up of eight objects and the same form with eleven objects. From the client's point of view, the only difference in the specification of the form is in the number of children to be created.

When geometry management is combined with the use of object-oriented architectures, which encapsulate both data and behavior, very sophisticated objects can be constructed. Consider two objects. The first object is a text object, which has associated with it a text field and an editor. Since the object knows how to display the text based on the space it has available, the object can have its size changed by its parent.

The second object is a graphics object. Again, the object has both its data and an editor; therefore, it is able to adjust its presentation based on its current size. If the graphics object is a child of the text object, the operator sees an editor that intermixes text and graphics. The important concept is that the two different

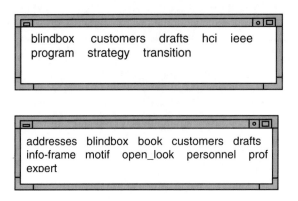

FIGURE 4.13
Athena widget geometry management for a form containing (a) 8 and (b) 11 children. The form automatically positions the children and changes its size to accommodate them.

types of objects (and their associated editors) need only be concerned with the space taken by a child object, not with the fact that a child is a particular type.

The Andrew toolkit includes a document editor that exploits these concepts. It allows text, graphics, and formulas to be intermixed. The operator can expand a particular graphic for editing and then reduce it again to fit it into the space allotted within the document. Figure 4.14 displays a document with embedded text and graphics and shows the objects associated with each.

4.3.3   CONSTRAINTS

Geometry management is a special case of the use of constraint systems. A constraint is an equation or a system of equations that expresses a relationship between its elements. As a simple example, consider $F = 32 + (9/5)\,C$, which is a formula for converting temperature from Celsius to Farenheit. As such, it imposes a relationship between the two representations of temperature. If there is a representation of C in the system, when it changes, the corresponding representation of F will be changed. Also, if a representation of F changes, the corresponding representation of C will also be changed. The relationships may be those of equality, as in the example, or of inequality.

Various types of constraint systems are found in a variety of applications. In the field of user interfaces, only equality constraints have been used thus far. There are two types of equality constraints: two way and one way. Two-way constraints impose relationships on all the elements in a system of equations. In

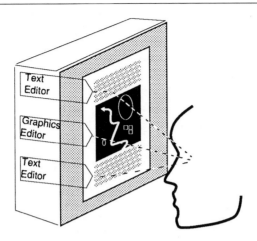

FIGURE 4.14
Document with text and graphics as objects, and the editors associated with each.

the temperature example, if C changes, then F will be changed. Similarly, if F changes, then C will be recomputed. In a one-way evaluation system, F is changed if C changes. If one wants C to change when F changes, one has to express C in terms of F.

Constraints are used in the user interface field in two ways. First, they are used to specify the relationship between interaction objects. For example, the geometry management discussed in the previous section could be formulated as a collection of spatial constraints between parent and child interaction objects. The second application of constraints is to specify relationships between a domain concept and an interaction object. For example, the position of a slider used to represent the speed of the mobile robot could be constrained to the domain concept of speed. In the remainder of this section we will discuss two-way constraints, one-way constraints, and constraint evaluation techniques.

Two-Way Constraints.   Two-way constraints provide the most natural way to specify relationships between two interaction objects or between an interaction object and a domain concept. To illustrate this mechanism, we will build on the temperature example.

Suppose the domain maintains a concept of temperature in Celsius displayed to the operator by means of a slider. (A slider is an interaction object whose value is displayed via a bar; see Figure 4.2c.) The operator can also manipulate the slider to specify a value. A two-way constraint tying the value of the slider to the domain temperature might be:

slider.value = domain.temperature.

Note that this specification is declarative in nature; that is, a constraint specifies a relationship to be maintained, regardless of other activities in the system. It does not specify how the relationship is to be maintained. It is the responsibility of the constraint system manager to guarantee that whenever slider.value is changed, domain.temperature is also modified, and vice versa.

Complex cases may arise. Suppose, for example, that the domain maintains the temperature in Celsius and that the user interface wishes to present this temperature in Fahrenheit. Then the constraint formula between the slider and the temperature becomes:

slider.value = 32 + 9/5 domain.temperature.

When domain.temperature is changed, the calculation of slider.value is straightforward, but when slider.value is modified, the system must automatically calculate domain. temperature. A linear equation such as this one can easily be solved, but uniquely solving a general system of equations may be difficult or even impossible.

We now consider how the type of geometry management discussed in Section 4.3.2 might be handled with a system of constraints. The geometric constraints for a container with five children, for example, might be expressed as a system of inequalities that described the minimum size of the children as a function of the length of the text within them and the fact that they should not overlap. Three problems arise in treating a complicated problem with two-way constraints:

1. There is not a unique solution. Thus, a constraint system must be satisfied with any solution.

2. Sometimes there is no solution and at least one of the constraints must be violated. Choosing which constraint to violate is very difficult for a general constraint solver.

3. Fundamentally and most importantly, there are no known efficient algorithms for solving a general system of constraints. Thus, the response would be unacceptably slow.

Two-way constraints were first introduced in the user interface field by ThingLab [Borning 1986a, Borning 1986b]. Most recently, a system named CONSTRAINTS [Vander Zanden 1989] has used a clever incremental evaluation algorithm to solve linear systems of constraints.

One-Way Constraints.   One-way constraints are easy to evaluate. Many two-way constraints can be respecified as a collection of one-way constraints. The temperature calculation, for example, can be specified as both

slider.value = 32 + (9/5) domain.temperature

and

domain.temperature = 5 (slider.value - 32) / 9.

Since only independent variables can be modified with one-way constraints, nonlinear types of constraints can be easily specified.

One-way constraints have two limitations: the specifier must state the second function explicitly, and some way must be devised to limit the side effects of computations. The second difficulty can be illustrated with the temperature example. The constraint on slider.value will, in general, be re-evaluated whenever domain.temperature is modified. But once slider.value is modified, the other constraint is triggered. Consequently, an infinite loop results. This is one of the evaluation issues discussed in the next section.

An early use of one-way constraints in the description of user interfaces can be seen in Bass [1985]. More modern usages will be presented in Sections 4.3.4 on Garnet and 4.3.5 on abstract imaging.

Evaluation of One-Way Constraints.   Issues in the evaluation of one-way constraints include detecting infinite loops and choosing the time for evaluating constraints.

As shown in the previous section, it is possible to create infinite loops of one-way constraints. This is not a problem with two-way constraints, since the system treats the constraints as a system and simultaneously solves for all the unknowns. One technique for dealing with the infinite loop problem is to explicitly state which equations are a portion of the constraint system (or, sometimes, which equations are not). Thus, in the temperature example, the evaluation of domain.temperature could be invoked only when the operator performed an action, not as a portion of the constraint system. On the other hand, the evaluation of slider.value as a result of modifications of domain.temperature would be a portion of the constraint system. Thus, the operator could modify slider.value without generating an infinite loop.

Even if the number of equations included in the constraint system is reduced, infinite loops can still arise. A conservative technique for identifying infinite loops is to detect cycles in a compile-time dependency graph—a graph displaying values that depend on other values. If there is no cycle in this graph, then no infinite loop can arise as a result of the constraint system. This technique is conservative because a cycle in the compile-time graph may not necessarily indicate a run-time infinite loop; some of the evaluations may be data dependent, such as those in an if statement.

A second technique is to identify loops at run time. The easiest method is to have a threshold for the number of times a single constraint can be evaluated. Passing this threshold indicates an infinite loop. The threshold can be set either arbitrarily or as a result of some compile-time analysis, although it is not possible to precisely determine when an infinite loop occurs.

Once an infinite loop is detected, the options are to notify the operator and terminate the execution or to retain the last values assigned and continue the execution.

A constraint can be evaluated either when dependent variables are modified (eager evaluation) or when the value of the dependent variable is required for another calculation (lazy evaluation). Eager evaluation has the advantage that values are always available when they are needed, without any bookkeeping to determine which values are up to date and which need to be recalculated. Lazy evaluation has the advantage that only those values which are needed are calculated. There is no evidence in the user interface domain that one technique is superior to the other.

4.3.4   GARNET

Garnet is a recent system that takes an innovative approach to the production of interaction objects [Myers 1989b]. In Garnet, interaction objects are categorized into a few different types of interactors. Actual interaction objects are produced from an interactor type through the specification of parameters. The interaction objects are then constrained to certain behavior. A large number of different interaction objects can be constructed from a fairly small number of interactors. The parameter specification is made possible through a special-purpose language. Types of interactors include menu-interactors and select-and-change-interactors.

- A *menu-interactor* consists of a list of choices and a particular geometry for those choices. Feedback occurs when the cursor is positioned over a particular choice. When a selection has been made, the presentation can be left as originally specified or modified. The specification of a menu consists of a specification of its geometry, cursor feedback, a definition of selection, and selection feedback. These parameters give only a flavor of what is necessary to totally specify a menu.

- A *select-and-change-interactor* is used to move or change the size of an object (or of a set of objects). Feedback is specified to reflect the movement or size change, or the object itself is changed to reflect the mouse movement. If feedback is chosen, the object jumps to the mouse position on completion of the action. Again, it is possible to specify what mouse or keyboard actions cause the movement or size change.

4.3.5   ABSTRACT IMAGING

Geometry management provides a means for dealing with the geometry of an independent collection of objects but not a means for dealing with objects that have structural (rather than geometric) relationships. Abstract imaging allows the

```
┌─────────────────────────────────────────────────────────────┐
│                                                             │
│    If   {Cond}   Then   {Stmt}   Else   {Stmt}   endif      │
│                                                             │
└─────────────────────────────────────────────────────────────┘
```

FIGURE 4.15
An if statement displayed in a wide window.

client to describe an image at a high level of abstraction. The abstract imaging system then actually builds the presentation from the high-level description.

For example, consider the problem of automatically formatting program segments in a syntax-directed editor. The elements of the segments have a syntactic relationship, and the presentation should display this relationship. Figures 4.15 and 4.16 illustrate two ways a single if statement might be presented, depending on the shape of the available screen space. The automatic choice of presentation would be based on an abstract imaging model. The model we will discuss is that of the box.

The *box* was first used in TEX [Knuth 1979] for output rendition. Since then, the box concept has been extended by a number of tools [Mikelsons 1981, Coutaz 1984, Coutaz 1984, Alhers and Dwelly1986, Quint 1987] to apply to input as well: each box provides a location for presentation as well as a focus for input.

The box is a directed graph structure. The graph corresponds to a syntactic description of the client data to be rendered. Associated with each node of the graph are attributes that can be used to express spatial relationships (such as alignment and indentation), visual effects (such as highlighting and coloring),

```
┌────────────────────────────┐
│  If  {Cond}                │
│                            │
│        Then  {Stmt}        │
│                            │
│        Else  {Stmt}        │
│                            │
│  endif                     │
└────────────────────────────┘
```

FIGURE 4.16
The same if statement displayed in a narrow window.

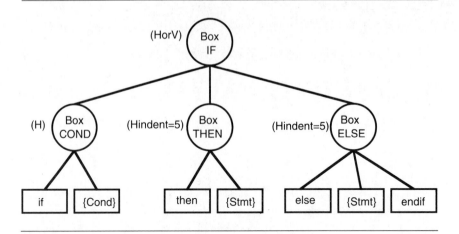

FIGURE 4.17
The box tree for the if statement in Figures 4.15 and 4.16. The root instructs the formatter to first attempt a horizontal layout. The next level gives the indentation instructions.

polymorphism (such as elision), and, possibly, links to client data. Figure 4.17 displays the tree structure for the simple case of the if statement displayed in Figures 4.15 and 4.16. The formatting attribute HorV in Figure 4.17 instructs the renderer to try to display the subtrees horizontally before displaying them vertically. The attribute H concatenates the subtrees horizontally, and Hindent specifies the value of the horizontal indentation if one has to be performed.

Leaves are recipients of client-dependent information and contain only typed knowledge (e.g., image, text). A leaf wraps an imaginary rectangle around the information. The presentation of the information in a leaf is then adjusted by the abstract image renderer according to the formatting attributes and the surface used for rendition (e.g., a window).

In abstract imaging, presentation is independent of the semantics of the client data: boxes have no knowledge about their content. This idea also underlies dialogue control systems, presented in Chapter 5.

4.4   Multimedia

Chapter 3 discussed some early efforts at developing multimedia window systems. At the toolkit level, very little work has been done on mixing media [Hodges,

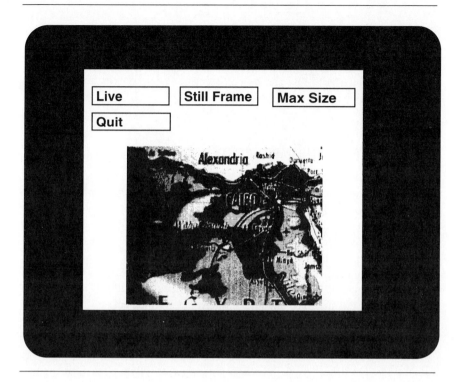

FIGURE 4.18
Video widget from the Parallax graphics board. The picture is from a video source, and the buttons are normal command widgets.

Sasnett, and Ackerman 1989]. Most notable is work on constructing interaction objects to manage the Parallax graphics board, which displays full-motion video. Figure 4.18 displays a video picture of a map, together with some control buttons. The control buttons represent normal X widgets, and the video is digitized by the Parallax graphics board.

Integration of media at the toolkit level requires that each interaction object be able to support multiple media technologies. This feature has desirable performance possibilities, but it means that each interaction object must be aware of, and take advantage of, each of the modalities. When the technologies are substantially different—for example, audio and graphics—the interaction objects could become quite difficult to generate. At the moment, integrated multimedia from a software point of view is very much a research issue.

4.5   Human Considerations

Toolkits impose policies. Because of these policies, use of a toolkit restricts the types of user interfaces that can be constructed. When toolkits are combined, feedback and consistency must be considered.

4.5.1   RESTRICTIONS IMPOSED BY TOOLKITS

The distinction between design and implementation becomes obvious at the toolkit level. Not all the user interfaces that superficially seem easy to implement are in fact easy to realize. The construction of a user interface is facilitated when the selected toolkit contains a suitable collection of interaction objects. On the other hand, if the design of the user interface calls for the creation of new interaction objects, the implementation may become a hard and a time-consuming task.

For example, consider Figure 4.19. This interface consists of a collection of rectangles connected by diagonal lines. If the selected toolkit does not allow for diagonal lines, this interface becomes expensive to implement.

Figure 4.20 shows a different interface with similar functionality. In this case, the diagonal lines were replaced by horizontal and vertical lines. This rendering is cheaper to implement with the Athena Widget toolkit. Because widgets,

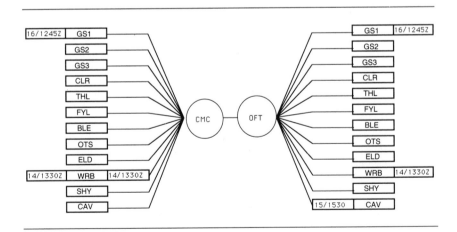

FIGURE 4.19
A user interface in which the diagonal lines were drawn by a specially constructed line widget.

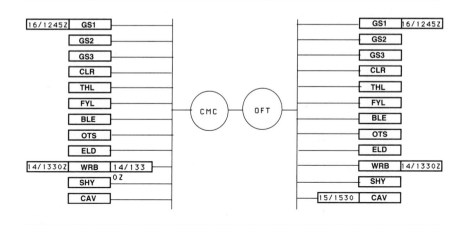

FIGURE 4.20
A different rendition of Figure 4.19 constructed entirely with the Athena Widget toolkit. The diagonal lines were replaced by horizontal and vertical lines.

based on windows, are rectangular entities with sides parallel to the screen, the Athena widget set has no interaction object to support diagonal lines.

From the perspective of a human factors specialist, the two figures may not be interchangeable. Figure 4.19 suggests that each rectangular box has a connection to the larger box in the center. Figure 4.20 suggests that each rectangular box feeds into a common connection with the larger box in the center. Is this distinction important? The answer depends on the task domain and on the operator. What is unquestionable is that, given the use of the Athena widget set, Figure 4.20 is less expensive to implement. The key point is that the user interface designer must take implementation considerations into account in order to produce a design that can be easily implemented within the constraints of a particular toolkit.

4.5.2   COMBINING DIFFERENT TOOLKITS

Different toolkits have different collections of interaction objects. Consequently, it may be appealing to be able to combine interaction objects from multiple toolkits. When combining different toolkits, the designer must take into account (1) their distinct styles and (2) possible feedback problems, which may arise when toolkits based on different media are combined.

Different Styles.   In order to achieve a desired functionality, it may be necessary to use interaction objects from different toolkits. Because different toolkits embody different conventions about interaction techniques and general appearance, mixing interaction objects from different toolkits may lead to an interface that is confusing to the operator.

Since more complicated interaction objects (such as the Andrew editor) embody a large collection of interactions, combining them can lead to an interface in which there are multiple different editors, each with a different user interface. On the other hand, since different toolkits provide different functions, it may be necessary to combine interaction objects from several toolkits in order to produce one desired interface. This problem is basically unsolvable at the toolkit level. User Interface Management Systems (discussed in Chapter 6) offer promise of techniques for providing consistent interfaces across multiple toolkits.

Feedback Problems with Different Media.   When toolkits based on different media (such as gesturing and graphics) are combined in one application system, one immediate problem is managing feedback. In a totally graphic system, when an interaction object is selected, feedback is given to the operator to indicate the state of the interaction object. The production of this feedback is the responsibility of the toolkit, since the interaction object embodies a notion of selection and feedback.

In a mixed media system, either a single interaction object must understand both media in order to provide feedback or feedback becomes the responsibility of the client. If a single interaction object manages two different types of media, the interaction object becomes very complicated because of the cross-communication.

For example, consider the problem of selecting a graphic button. When a mouse is used to perform the selection, the underlying window system, which manages the mouse cursor, can readily determine whether the mouse is inside the graphic button. When a gesturing system is used to do the selection, one of the levels of abstraction in the user interface must identify the current position of the finger. Thus, either the underlying window system manages the gesturing system (and thus interaction objects manage the gesturing system as well as the graphics system) or the client must indicate to the graphic system when it is the current focus of a finger.

If multiple media are integrated at the toolkit level, the interaction objects in that toolkit must all understand the implications of any action in any one of the media.

4.6   Engineering Considerations

The toolkit world is currently very dynamic. Standardized toolkits, although of limited functionality, are becoming available. Efforts are under way to standardize the application programmer's interface, and yet software development using toolkits must proceed. In this section we discuss the standardization and customization of toolkits, the application programming interface, and the evaluation of toolkits.

4.6.1   STANDARDIZATION

Efforts are under way to standardize the look and feel of toolkits, as well as the application programming interface. The look of a toolkit is the visual appearance of the interaction objects within the toolkit. The feel of a toolkit is the behavior of the particular interaction objects. Look and feel are such a crucial aspect of toolkits that they have been the subject of litigation [Samuelson 1989].

Look and Feel.   Toolkits provide a collection of interaction objects; each object could conceivably have its own look and feel. As was discussed in Section 2.6.1, however, consistency is one of the important characteristics of a user interface.

In Section 3.7.3 we briefly discussed Motif and Open Look. Both of these user interface specifications include window managers as well as toolkits. From the functional point of view, there is little difference between the two specifications. Both have a collection of interaction objects that provide menus, forms, and textual input and output. The two specifications, however, are very different visually.

The Open Look specification emphasizes the use of different borders and spacing to provide cues to the function of different collections of interaction objects. In Figure 4.21, portions of two different menus are displayed. The Edit

FIGURE 4.21
Open Look menus. The Edit button is a portion of a linear menu. When the button is selected, the pull-down menu appears.

button is a portion of a linear menu. When the button is chosen, the Cut/Copy/ Paste menu is pulled down. A border and a shadow box indicate that this menu is a pull-down menu.

In Figure 4.22, two different selections are displayed. The space between the choices in Figure 4.22b provides a cue that the selections are not exclusive. The style guide for Open Look indicates under which circumstances various features are to be used. No style enforcement mechanism is available at the toolkit level.

Figure 4.23 displays a Motif interaction object. Motif objects emphasize various types of three-dimensional appearances. Notice how some buttons appear to be indented and others seem to stick out from the screen. These looks provide visual cues about the functions of the buttons. Pop-up menus, for example, always appear to stick up.

Open Look and Motif both assume that they are operating on a bit-mapped graphics terminal. The problem they attack, then, is ensuring consistency across different applications on the same type of terminal. A more general problem is attacked by IBM's System's Application Architecture (SAA): applications may operate within environments ranging from mainframes to personal computers and using terminals ranging from character based to bit-mapped graphics. The problem is not only to ensure consistency across applications, but also to allow a single application to run across different platform types.

SAA is a general framework for solving the problem of consistency. It is composed of three components: Common Communications Support (CCS), Common User Access (CUA), and Common Programming Interface (CPI). CUA defines the look and feel of a user interface across a variety of terminal types. It discusses, for example, how to simulate pull-down menus and dragging on character terminals. CUA is still evolving. IBM is a member of OSF and thus may use Motif for its CUA look and feel. IBM has also licensed NextStep and could use that for its look and feel. IBM has a look and feel for its current offerings that is neither Motif nor NextStep.

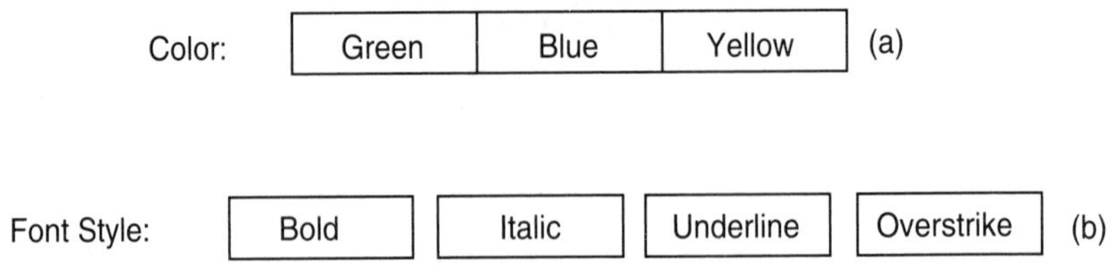

Color: | Green | Blue | Yellow | (a)

Font Style: | Bold | | Italic | | Underline | | Overstrike | (b)

FIGURE 4.22
Open Look menus. The connected boxes in (a) provide a cue that the selections are exclusive, whereas the spacing in (b) shows that the selections are not exclusive.

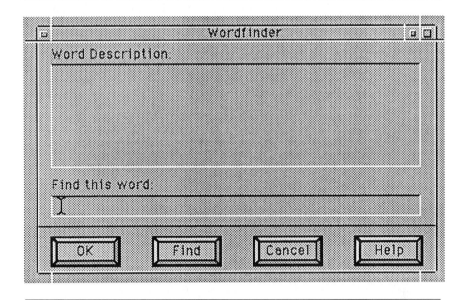

FIGURE 4.23
An example of a Motif interaction object. Note the three-dimensional appearance
of the components.

The important lesson to be learned from CUA is that the problems of defining a consistent look and feel are much more complicated than those resolved by
a single terminal type approach. The Macintosh Desktop, OSF/Motif, and Open
Look all can assume a fixed terminal type for their style guides. Ensuring consistency across differing terminal types adds another dimension to the problem of
look and feel.

X Toolkit Intrinsics.   The X Consortium has developed a standard library, the X
Toolkit Intrinsics, for specifying toolkits. This library conveys a model upon
which toolkits can be built, but it does not enforce any particular look and feel.
The Intrinsics are a collection of procedures that interact with the X Window
System and thus embody its philosophy of geometry management and resource
specification.

Figure 4.7 shows how toolkits are developed on top of the Intrinsics. Although the program uses an Athena command widget, calls are directed to the X
Toolkit Intrinsics. (Procedure names prefixed with "Xt" denote functions provided by the Intrinsics library.) In particular, parameters to
XtCreateManagedWidget include a symbolic name (command) and the widget
class (commandWidgetClass) of the widget to be created. The name and the

widget class are used as indexes into a resource table, which determines the look and some of the feel of the widget. This use of resources to tailor the appearance and behavior of a widget is a special case of customization.

4.6.2 CUSTOMIZATION

A large number of activities of interaction objects can be parameterized to provide flexibility to the clients. Parameters can be specified in an external file, which is read in at run time. By making it possible to adjust parameters without modifying source code, this technique allows some of the appearance of an interface to be customized quite easily.

For example, although the fields of the form in Figure 2.16 are displayed in English, French could have been used just as easily. Multilingual user interfaces can be supported with little effort by providing one file per language. In the case of the mobile robot, a language for display is specified at initialization time, and the appropriate file is then used when interaction objects are created. Dynamic switching between languages poses problems, however, because all the displayed information must be translated. For instance, messages still visible in a text window must be translated when the display language is varied.

In general, parameters that may be changed frequently are best specified externally to the program, most easily in a file. Of course, such parameters should have default values so that they can be omitted when they are irrelevant to the particular execution of the application system. In constructing a system, it is best to err on the side of too many parameters rather than too few. The use of resource files as discussed in Section 4.1.2 is one application of the use of external files to set parameters for a run-time system.

4.6.3 APPLICATION PROGRAMMING INTERFACE

Efforts are under way to standardize the application programming interface (API) for toolkits. In the particular context of toolkits, an API defines the protocol by which the client accesses the services of a particular toolkit.

The developer of application software is concerned about the API of the toolkit, since the application software is developed either to use a single toolkit or to allow for multiple toolkits. In the first case, the developer is concerned about having to change toolkits because of market considerations. In the second case, the developer is concerned about the expense of supporting multiple toolkits.

Toolkits are available that support multiple underlying toolkits based on a single API. Two models exist for implementing such a toolkit:

1. Support only the interaction object functionalities that are available in *all* of the supported toolkits (the intersection of functionalities). This approach has

the obvious problem of limiting the types of user interfaces that can be constructed.

2.   Support any of the interaction object functionalities that are available in any of the supported toolkits (the union of functionalities). Functionalities present in one toolkit but not in others are simulated for the others.

One problem with having a common API for multiple toolkits is that inconsistent style issues cannot be dealt with by mapping an interaction object in one toolkit to an equivalent object in another. For example, the *Open Look Style Guide* suggests that menus in the control area be pull-down menus. The *OSF Style Guide* allows single buttons in the menu bar (controlling the same functionality). The software developer must decide whether to use pull-down menus or single buttons for certain functions and a common API will only serve to implement that choice on a particular toolkit. A common API will not map from multiple choices to one choice automatically.

One component of IBM's Systems Application Architecture is the Common Programming Interface (CPI). CPI is intended to allow for a common API across various terminal types. Thus, CPI cannot make many assumptions about the services available from the terminal. CPI has the same problems as a uniform API for look and feel across toolkits. Either it can capture the least common denominator (the intersection approach) or it can simulate functionality (the union approach). Within CPI, the client specifies the minimum terminal configuration, and the user interface is then defined based on the terminal configuration. Different applications running on a bit-mapped graphics terminal thus may have different user interface styles because one application specified a minimum terminal configuration of a character-based terminal and another specified a minimum terminal configuration of a bit-mapped graphics terminal.

A uniform API would increase the portability of user interfaces across toolkits. In a domain whose technology is evolving rapidly, however, it is risky to create a standard based on the current state of the art, which is almost certain to become obsolete in the next few years. One promising way to cope with this problem is to exploit the incremental development approach supported by the object-oriented paradigm.

Object-oriented environments allow new functionalities to be defined without endangering existing ones. The difficulty resides in the definition of an appropriate basic platform. In the X Window System community, the X Toolkit Intrinsics provides such a common basis. For example, in toolkits based on the Intrinsics, the client can customize the meaning of mouse and keyboard events. This customization involves constructing a sequence of events under which specified procedures will be called. The specification of the sequence of events is identical for all the widgets constructed using the X Toolkit Intrinsics. Thus, from the point of view of the client, customization of any of the toolkit objects relies on the same process.

4.6.4   EVALUATION CRITERIA

The evaluation of toolkits reveals the same trade-offs between technical and nontechnical criteria that we saw in the evaluation of window systems.

Technical Criteria.   Technical criteria include consistency in behavior and appearance, object-oriented design, power of interaction objects, support for customization, and performance.

1. Consistency in behavior and appearance. The toolkit's various components should act in a similar fashion and utilize a common style. For example, the same mouse button should be used to move all toolkit elements, and the same type of feedback should be provided for all the elements (for example, an outline to make concrete a movement of an object).

2. Object-oriented design. Clearly, we are using first-generation toolkits. Evolution is inevitable. The object-oriented paradigm, which supports iterative design through the ability to add new specializations without affecting existing ones, should therefore serve as the driving principle for constructing toolkits. All toolkits will evolve through the addition of new classes of interaction objects. Toolkits that are constructed in an object-oriented fashion will be able to evolve more smoothly than those that are not.

3. Power of interaction objects. As we saw in Section 4.1.2., the power of the interaction objects available in the toolkit has a strong impact on the types of interfaces that can be built. The power of a toolkit has multiple facets, including level of abstraction, imaging model, and support for direct manipulation.

   The level of abstraction refers to the variety and richness of interaction objects. Toolkits that provide sophisticated editors, for example, enable the implementation of application systems with sophisticated editing capabilities.

   The imaging model determines the graphical capabilities of the toolkit. Some toolkits support arbitrary graphical images within interaction objects, some allow bit-maps, and some just allow text. Clearly, for a sophisticated interface, the ability to present arbitrary graphical images within an interaction object is important.

   Direct manipulation has been identified as a useful concept by cognitive psychologists. However, implementing direct manipulation interfaces is not easy. Mouse tracking requires drawing the outline of an object at the current location of the mouse, then erasing the outline and repainting the bits destroyed by the object at the previous location, and performing the sequence again in real time.

   Powerful features within the toolkit should be optional. The Athena Widget toolkit, for example, requires that geometry management be used whenever widgets are combined. The geometry manager will rearrange the contents of a display, often arbitrarily. It therefore becomes very difficult to construct an interface for a package such as MacDraw. In such a package, the operator specifies the location and size of components. If the toolkit arbitrarily rearranges the location and size, the operator cannot specify them.

4. Support for customization. Customization should be made accessible to the client as well as to the operator. The notion of a resource enables customization. A different approach is that chosen by NeWS, which allows clients to perform customization by downloading PostScript code.

5. Performance. The performance of a toolkit can become an issue. Several different aspects of performance should be examined. First, the time needed to create a new interaction object should be examined. Creation can be a relatively lengthy, and hence expensive, operation if a new window must be created to support each new interaction object

   Second, the time needed to manage large numbers of interaction objects should be examined. Some forms may require that several thousand interaction objects exist simultaneously. (This is sometimes a result of the difficulty of creating and destroying an interaction object.) A large number of interaction objects may severely lengthen response times.

   Finally, the space required by the toolkit should be examined. Window systems tend to be heavy consumers of memory, and toolkits may also consume large amounts of memory. When a toolkit is being evaluated, the implications on the main memory requirement for the supporting platform should be considered.

Nontechnical Criteria.   The nontechnical portion of the evaluation involves considerations similar to those associated with window systems:

- Broadness of use of the toolkit, both within industry and within the community for which the product is targeted.
- Number of window systems that support the particular toolkit.
- Support for the toolkit. The level of sophistication required for the installation and use of vendor-supplied toolkits is different from that required for the installation and use of public domain and special-purpose toolkits.

4.7   Mobile Robot Example

For the user interface of the mobile robot, existing toolkits posed the same problem as existing window systems—that is, implementing the desired interface was the responsibility of the client and hence would be expensive.

Recall from Chapter 3 that the desired interface for the mobile robot was to display to the operator information about the scene that was being constructed. This information was to be displayed at different levels of abstraction. Such an interface requires a very flexible notion of selection object. The selection object should have arbitrary shape and should be constructed of lines and arcs automatically registered with the underlying video image. At the time the window system was chosen, arbitrary shapes for interaction objects were not available in standard toolkits. Consequently, the constructed user interface was less elaborate than that originally desired.

The interface for the mobile robot (as shown in the figures in Chapter 2) was constructed using the Hewlett Packard Toolkit, which is a public domain toolkit available with the X Window System. Some of the considerations that led to the choice of this toolkit were as follows:

- The toolkit is available for the X Window System. Since the X Window System had been chosen as the base window system, the availability of the toolkit for the X Window System was a critical factor.

- The toolkit is based on the X Toolkit Intrinsics. Even if the HP toolkit is superseded by other toolkits (which is likely), the Intrinsics have been adopted by the X Consortium as the basis for any future endorsed toolkits. Thus, converting from the HP toolkit to another one should be relatively simple.

- The toolkit has interaction objects that perform geometry management as well as ones that do not. Thus, the choice of this toolkit did not predetermine whether geometry management would be used.

4.8 Future

Several trends are apparent within the development of interaction objects:

1. Interaction objects will continue to be developed using the object-oriented paradigm. Challenges will include deciding on the correct classes for interaction objects and extending the concepts of how interaction objects should interact. The latter is related to the problem of dialogue control discussed in Chapter 5.

2. New and richer interaction objects will emerge. These interaction objects will be specialized for particular domains, such as document processing. The use of visual abstractions, such as those used in Rooms to aggregate windows, will be developed within the general context of interaction objects.

3. Multimedia interaction objects will emerge for pairs of media. Currently, simple versions of such objects are available for video and graphics. Sound/ video and sound/graphics are other pairs of media for which interaction

objects can be expected. Some media are too distinct to be managed by a single interaction object.

4. Animated interaction objects will become available. Currently available interaction objects change state only in response to client action or operator action. An animated object would have a built-in mechanism for state changes; for example, the interaction object might change state with the passage of time. Interaction with such objects will depend on the particular state in which the interaction occurs.

4.9 Summary

In this chapter we described interaction objects and discussed the issues related to the construction and use of toolkits. We looked at examples of interaction objects and presented their behavior from both the operator's and the application programmer's point of view.

We then explained the use of the object-oriented paradigm in the construction of toolkits and enumerated the benefits and the drawbacks of this approach. We explored composite objects constructed using object-oriented techniques, and we considered different techniques for dealing with composite objects, such as geometry management and constraint management.

We examined the impact of toolkits on the operator, engineering issues related to the use of toolkits, and the characteristics to be considered in evaluating toolkits.

5

Dialogue
Control

Chapters 3 and 4 were concerned with the software tools and the techniques that establish the foundations for the development of user interfaces. As illustrated in Figure 1.2, this platform includes a window system for device independence and for device sharing and a user interface toolkit for interaction objects.

Window systems and toolkits are necessary components of user interface software, but they do not, by themselves, ensure that an interactive system provides either a high-quality or a low-cost user interface. For the types of user interfaces discussed in Chapter 2 to be provided in a cost-efficient manner, another level of run-time abstraction is necessary. This layer, called the *dialogue controller*, provides the following:

□ Appropriate architectural structure for supporting incremental development,

□ Mapping and transformation between the functional core of an application and interaction objects, and

□ Control of the dynamic behavior of an interface.

The concept of a dialogue controller is used in several types of run-time support: ad-hoc run-time kernels, application skeletons, and user interface generators. These and other terms are defined in Section 5.1.

As a mediator between the functional core and the interactive objects, a dialogue controller must satisfy a number of requirements. These are identified in Section 5.2.

Dialogue control may also be studied from a theoretical perspective. Various models of dialogue control are presented in Section 5.3.

In Section 5.4 we switch to a more practical concern—the implementation of dialogue controllers. Such implementation should be performed within the framework of an architectural model. We present two approaches to the construction of dialogue control and compare them in light of the requirements discussed in Section 5.2.

The chapter closes with a discussion of human issues, engineering issues, and open questions in the area.

5.1   Definitions

The term *user interface management system* (UIMS) is widely used to cover a number of different services. It is used both to refer to an architecture emphasizing separation between the user interface and the functional core and to refer to the tools used to specify and execute the user interface. The term originated at a workshop in Seeheim, Germany [Pfaff 1985] and was chosen to emphasize the similarity of a UIMS to a database management system. We will use the term UIMS to designate a collection of services for the specification, design, evaluation, and run-time support of user interfaces. In this chapter we are concerned with those run-time services of a UIMS , which provide for dialogue control. The other services of a UIMS will be the topic of Chapter 6.

In Chapter 1 we identified the functional core of an interactive system as a collection of objects (the semantic objects) that maintain application domain knowledge but no presentation knowledge. In this chapter we will use the term *presentation* or *presentation component* to refer to the services provided by the toolkit and window system layers of the interactive application.

We will now look at the forms a dialogue controller may assume. A dialogue controller may be part of a run-time kernel without addition context, it may be part of an application skeleton, or it may be used as the run-time support for a user interface generator.

5.1.1   DIALOGUE CONTROLLER

A dialogue controller is essentially the run-time kernel of a user interface. As illustrated in Figure 5.1, it is the arbitrator that controls the relationships between the functional core and the presentation component. The dialogue controller of a user interface is responsible for:

- Maintaining a correspondence between semantic objects and interaction objects,

□ Maintaining relationships among interaction objects,

□ Maintaining a dynamic representation of the state of the dialogue between the functional core and the presentation component, and

□ Defining two communication protocols, one suitable for the modeling techniques of the functional core, and the second adequate for the presentation component.

The correspondence between the semantic objects processed by the functional core and the interaction objects of the presentation component can be from one semantic object to multiple interaction objects or from multiple semantic objects to a single interaction object. The dialogue controller also manages media dependencies, since the functional core is media independent but interaction objects are media dependent.

Often, multiple operator interactions are required to generate a single command to the functional core. The arbitrator collects the components for the command and decides when it is appropriate to issue the command to the functional

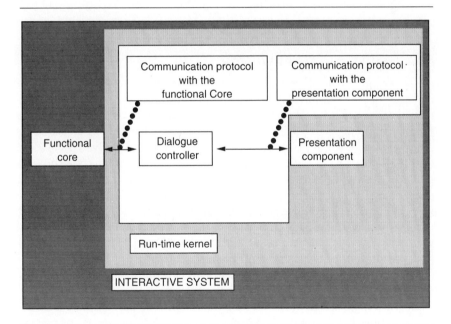

FIGURE 5.1
The dialogue controller as a portion of the run-time kernel of the user interface. The run-time kernel consists of the dialogue controller and the presentation component. The dialogue controller includes the communication protocol with both the functional core and the presentation component.

core. It is for this reason that the arbitrator is described as a dialogue controller. We will elaborate on the notion of dialogue in Section 5.2.

The functional core and the presentation component define two perspectives of the same application domain. In the functional core, objects are data structures needed to perform domain-specific computations or provide media-independent user interface services. In the presentation component, objects are interaction objects driven by a need to appropriately and easily convey the functioning of the interactive system. Since they have different purposes, the functional core and the presentation component use different representation techniques. Therefore, the dialogue controller needs to handle a communication protocol for each of its partners.

The dialogue controller and its protocols are often developed for a particular interactive system and with the help of services provided by a particular user interface toolkit. As we discussed in Chapter 4, however, user interface toolkits convey a programming style and require that the programmer comply with a fixed set of rules in order to use the services successfully. There is a subset of the dialogue controller that is independent of the functional core but necessary to the implementation of any user interface. This application skeleton can be reused with different functional cores.

5.1.2   APPLICATION SKELETONS

An *application skeleton,* or application framework, is the reusable portion of a dialogue controller. It provides the user interface software designer with a package that implements much of the user interface. An application skeleton provides the overall architecture of the interactive system, as well as the building blocks of the user interface toolkit, prior to the implementation of the interactive system.

In this case, as shown in Figure 5.2, the task of the user interface software designer consists of extending the skeleton, filling holes in the skeleton, and overloading parts that do not match the requirements identified at the user interface design stage. Opportunities to extend and overload are two major benefits of the object-oriented paradigm. It is not surprising, then, that application frameworks such as MacApp [Schmucker 1986], Aïda [Ilog 1989] and ApEx [Coutaz 1987a] have been developed using the object-oriented model.

The use of constraint and geometry managers within toolkits (Section 4.3) is an example of embedding a form of dialogue control in an application framework. The toolkit acts as the application framework, and the constraint manager is responsible for managing the relationships among some of the interaction objects.

Although application frameworks implement much of the user interface, they require the user interface software designer to modify and extend existing

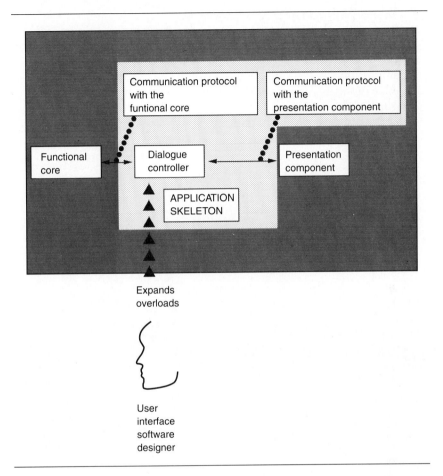

FIGURE 5.2
Application frameworks. The application skeleton consists of those portions of the dialogue controller which are application independent. The user interface software designer must complete the run-time kernel by providing the application-specific portions.

code. Programming is a time-consuming task which lengthens the design-imple-ment-test cycle, and thus it may impede or even discourage the iterative refine-ment of the user interface. User interface generators tend to support rapid prototyping more effectively.

5.1.3   USER INTERFACE GENERATORS

When the dialogue controller is used as the run-time support of an automatically generated user interface, it becomes part of a *user interface generator*. As shown in Figure 5.3, user interface generators produce a user interface from a high-level description of the user interface. User interface generators will be discussed in more detail in Chapter 6.

In this chapter we focus on dialogue controllers as run-time kernels. We need now to identify the requirements for such kernels.

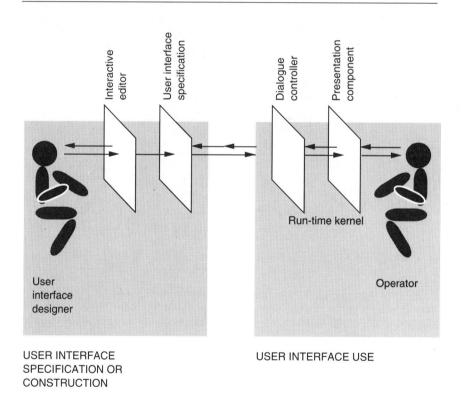

USER INTERFACE
SPECIFICATION OR
CONSTRUCTION

USER INTERFACE USE

FIGURE 5.3
User interface generators. The user interface designer specifies the user interface, using either a special-purpose language or a graphical editor. The run-time kernel is then generated from the specification.

5.2   Requirements for Dialogue Controllers

At a very abstract level, dialogue control defines the policy between the partners of a conversation for taking turns in the generation of utterances. In real life, a conversation among multiple participants is either directed by a leader or distributed among the partners, depending on the characteristics of the task and the participants. In general, control of dialogue switches between these two extremes. As shown in Figure 5.4, utterances are interleaved between partners and may overlap over time. A similar schema should apply to computer-human interaction.

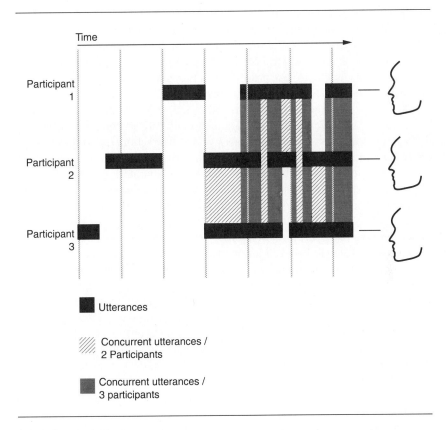

FIGURE 5.4
Emission of utterances over time in real life. During some time periods, only one participant is speaking; during others, two or three participants are speaking simultaneously.

Section 5.2.1 analyzes the requirements for interleaving among the components of an interactive system. The requirements for communication between the functional core and the dialogue controller are discussed in Section 5.2.2. The communication is defined in a protocol called the application programmer's interface (API) to the dialogue controller. In Chapter 2 we discussed the utility of general services such as help, undo-redo, and defaults. The breadth and the quality of such facilities depend on the dialogue controller, as well as on the functional core. This shared responsibility for general services is considered in Section 5.2.3.

5.2.1   REQUIREMENTS FOR INTERLEAVING

In computer-human interaction, participants may be identified at various levels of abstraction. As shown in Figure 5.5, one perspective defines the operator and the interactive system as two participants. Within the interactive system, the functional core, the dialogue controller, and the presentation components are cooperative participants which make possible the interaction with the operator. Refining one step further (as in Section 5.4.2), we may view the presentation component as a set of agents which act as partners in realizing the user interface.

The successive refinement of participants into subparticipants suggests that dialogue control is distributed at various levels of abstraction. It also suggests that the overall control of a dialogue is determined by the policies defined at each level of abstraction. We will next consider desirable policies at the three levels identified so far: between the operator and the interactive system, among the three main components of the interactive system, and inside the presentation component.

Policy Between the Operator and the Interactive System.   In Chapter 2, we observed that a dialogue between an operator and an interactive system may be either user-driven or system-driven. The better style to use depends on the nature of the system as well as on the model designers have of the operator. The two styles differ in the number of semantically valid inputs available to the operator at any point in time. If this number is always one, the operator is led from subtask to subtask, without the power to make any decisions at the task level. If this number is greater than one, the operator is able to dynamically update a task plan in the way best suited to his or her needs. The operator may initiate several subtasks and accomplish them in parallel. Since a task (or a subtask) may involve domain-dependent computation, such parallelism can require modeling multiple threads of dialogue in the functional core.

Multiple threads of dialogue often occur in systems that provide extensive verifications and suggestions about the task domain. For example, a syntax editor may check that a variable referenced in the body of a procedure is properly

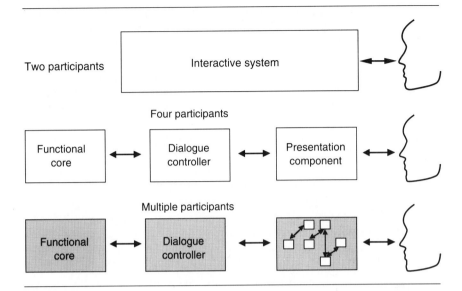

FIGURE 5.5
The levels of partners in an interactive system. (a) At the top level of abstraction there are only two participants: the operator and the interactive system. (b) At the next level there are four: the operator, the presentation component, the dialogue controller, and the functional core. (c) At deeper levels, there are multiple participants, depending on the degree of decomposition of the software.

declared. In the mobile robot example, the system checks that routes do not cross walls. A system can be designed so that, when a semantic error occurs, the functional core rejects the operator's action and requires immediate correction; alternatively, it may accept the operator's action and maintain a model of the error. In the first case, the operator has to enter a planning phase to correct the error and restart the subtask from scratch; there is no such notion as a pending task. In the second case, the functional core accepts partially accomplished subtasks by remembering semantic errors. By doing so, it maintains multiple threads of task accomplishment.

Clearly, a functional core that has only one thread of input is easier to implement, but it imposes on the operator a task decomposition that may not be natural. For example, in an early version of the mobile robot, the functional core refused to accept inconsistent environments. In particular, when the operator moved a route that would intersect a wall, the action would be rejected. The operator had to move the wall (or a set of walls) in an order that maintained semantic validity. Experiments have shown that this lack of error modeling is unnecessarily constraining: an environment needs to be semantically valid only when a mission is being specified or executed. This is an example of the general problem, discussed in Section 2.6.2, of timing error feedback.

The collaboration between an interactive system and the operator is thus constrained at the semantic level by the design of the functional core. The next two sections show how the dialogue controller should support such design decisions.

Policy among the Components of the Interactive System.   One classification of control flow within an interactive system is based on whether the control is external, internal, or mixed [Tanner and Buxton 1983]. The control is internal when it resides in the functional core; that is, interaction is driven by computational considerations, and the dialogue controller is modeled as a presentation server. The control is external when it is maintained in the dialogue controller; the interaction is driven by the operator's input events, and the functional core is viewed as a semantic server. The control is mixed when it is handled sometimes by the functional core and other times by the dialogue controller.

In general, mixed control is most appropriate. Mixed control allows the functional core and the dialogue controller to be equal partners. Server models, implicit in internal and external control, bias the balance of the interaction. With such models, the interaction is driven either by the functional core or by the operator. Such systematic behavior is in contradiction to the principles discussed in Section 2.5.3.

A mixed control model allows control to shift, depending on the circumstances of an interaction. For example, during the specification of the mobile robot's environments and missions, the interaction is typically user-driven. At this stage, the presentation component is the main controller of the interactive system. It acquires the events that express the operator's actions, and the functional core is invoked for semantic checking. On the other hand, during mission execution, the functional core is typically in charge of the interaction. At this stage the operator is essentially an observer, although action that affects the progress of the mission is allowed. The consequence for the interactive system is that, although the functional core performs relevant computations and sends messages to the dialogue controller to express the current state of the robot, the presentation component must listen to and process the operator's inputs. Only a mixed model of control permits control to flow back and forth to the most relevant participant.

The internal and external locations of control are special constrained cases of a more general view in which the components of an interactive system are equal participants. In addition, the internal-external approaches suggest a sequential model of computation, which may be convenient for simple interactive systems but makes it hard to support the principle of direct manipulation.

In direct-manipulation user interfaces, an input expression may evolve in parallel with an output expression in order to provide immediate and meaningful feedback. In particular, during the specification of a command, inputs and outputs may be interleaved. "Rubber banding" is a common example. Another example is found in the Macintosh Desktop Finder. In Finder, moving an icon across the screen constitutes a partial input expression until the mouse button is released. The operator's action denotes the command name (for example, copy) and a file name (for example, the file being pointed at) but the destination file name is missing. Although the command is only partially specified, the system is able to provide the operator with two complementary forms of immediate feedback: lexical feedback (an icon outline following the mouse cursor) and semantic feedback (a reverse video of icons representing valid recipients).

The above examples indicate that direct manipulation user interfaces require high-bandwidth interleaved communication between the dialogue controller and the functional core during the elaboration of input expressions.

Policy Inside the Presentation Component.   The presentation component, which expresses the state of the functional core to the operator, should be able to map the multithread facilities (if any) supported in the functional core. Thus, multiple interaction objects should be simultaneously available to the operator and manipulable in any order. In addition to reflecting the internal multithread structure of the functional core, the presentation component may also support interleaving between presentation objects.

Interleaving inside the presentation component allows the operator to act on a presentation object (for example, specify several fields in a form), then manipulate other presentation objects, and later come back to the original one. Clearly, this facility supports opportunistic planning. It also has some software implications, which will be discussed in Section 5.4.

The Macintosh dialogue box provides an example of lack of interleaving. A dialogue box is a presentation object that forces the operator to act on it before any action can take place in any other presentation object. Figures 5.6 and 5.7 show the dialogue boxes for the Print and Page Setup commands, respectively. When a document is to be printed, the size of the paper is an important parameter. You may observe that the box in Figure 5.6 does not contain this variable. In order to check the current setting for paper format before pushing the OK button of the Print dialogue box, the operator has to issue the Page Setup command, but to do so the operator must first cancel the Print command.

The preceding example shows how interleaving between presentation objects facilitates task accomplishment. In particular, such interleaving allows the operator to access variables of interest that designers have decided not (or forgotten) to present in the current task.

In summary, interleaving supports dialogue flexibility at several levels. At the action level, interleaving between the presentation objects and the operator permits the operator to switch focus from presentation object to presentation object at will. At the command level, interleaving between the components of an

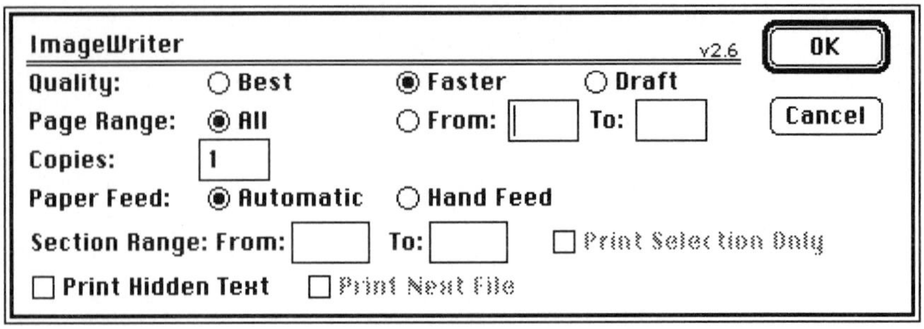

```
┌─────────────────────────────────────────────────────────────┐
│ ImageWriter                                    v2.6  ╭──────╮ │
│                                                      │  OK  │ │
│ Quality:       ○ Best      ● Faster    ○ Draft       ╰──────╯ │
│ Page Range:    ● All       ○ From: │  │ To: │  │   ╭────────╮ │
│ Copies:        │ 1 │                               │ Cancel │ │
│ Paper Feed:    ● Automatic  ○ Hand Feed            ╰────────╯ │
│ Section Range: From: │   │  To: │   │   ☐ Print Selection Only│
│ ☐ Print Hidden Text    ☐ Print Next File                     │
└─────────────────────────────────────────────────────────────┘
```

FIGURE 5.6
The dialogue box for the Macintosh Print command. Notice that if the page size is incorrect, there is no way of modifying it without canceling the command. (Courtesy of Microsoft Word © 1984–1990 Microsoft Corporation. Reprinted by permission.)

interactive system and the operator allows immediate and domain-dependent informative feedback to be provided. At the task level, interleaving between the functional core and the operator makes it possible for several threads of reasoning to be carried out in parallel.

Now we will consider the protocol between the dialogue controller and the functional core.

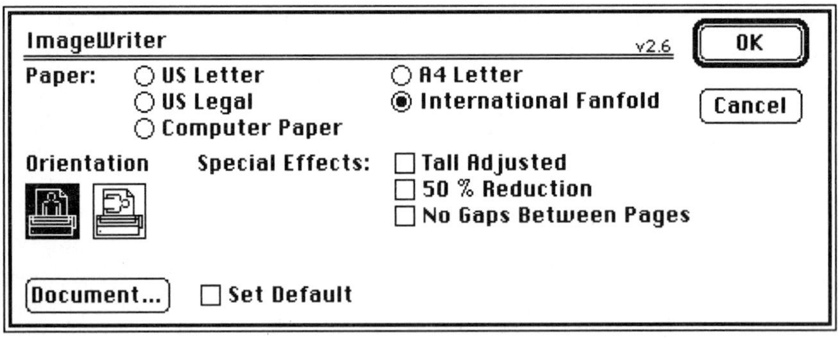

```
┌─────────────────────────────────────────────────────────────┐
│ ImageWriter                                    v2.6  ╭──────╮ │
│                                                      │  OK  │ │
│ Paper:   ○ US Letter       ○ A4 Letter               ╰──────╯ │
│          ○ US Legal        ● International Fanfold ╭────────╮ │
│          ○ Computer Paper                          │ Cancel │ │
│ Orientation  Special Effects:  ☐ Tall Adjusted     ╰────────╯ │
│  ▣ ▣                           ☐ 50 % Reduction               │
│                                ☐ No Gaps Between Pages        │
│ ╭──────────╮  ☐ Set Default                                   │
│ │ Document…│                                                  │
│ ╰──────────╯                                                  │
└─────────────────────────────────────────────────────────────┘
```

FIGURE 5.7
The dialogue box for the Macintosh Page Setup command. (Courtesy of Microsoft Word © 1984–1990 Microsoft Corporation. Reprinted by permission.)

5.2.2   REQUIREMENTS FOR THE PROTOCOL WITH THE FUNCTIONAL CORE: API

The protocol between the functional core and the dialogue controller is implemented by an interface called the application programmer's interface (API). Designing and implementating an API involves answering four types of questions:

1. What is the correct level of abstraction for the data being transferred? Data may range from low lexical level, such as pixels, to high semantic level, such as records.

2. What component owns the data to be transferred? The data may be owned by either the functional core or the dialogue controller, or may be shared between them.

3. How are the data described? The data that cross the interface can be described implicitly or explicitly.

4. How are the data accessed? The data can be accessed either procedurally or declaratively.

We will now discuss each of these issues in more detail.

Level of Abstraction of Data Transferred.   The separation between the functional core and the user interface is motivated by the software engineering principle of separation of concerns. The concerns of the functional core are different from those of the dialogue controller, so they should be implemented in different modules. This separation supports iterative refinement of the user interface. Isolating the concerns of the functional core and the dialogue controller leads to the requirement that the functional core be *media independent*; that is, data exchanged with the dialogue controller should not contain any reference to the media used for presentation. This requirement is satisfied only if the data transferred through the API is expressed in terms of the semantic concepts of the functional core.

Data exchanged between the functional core and the dialogue controller should be expressed at the level of abstraction defined by the functional core. For example, a functional core that uses a real number to model temperature should communicate with the dialogue controller in terms of real numbers; it should not have any knowledge about the presentation of the value to the operator.

The fact that the API is media independent does not mean that the functional core has no responsibility for interaction. The API should allow the functional core to express to the operator changes in the state of semantic concepts relevant to the current task. For example, the state may include a boolean to indicate that the notion of temperature is not currently modifiable by the operator. Such a condition may be determined by the functional core on the basis of domain-dependent information. The dialogue controller is then in charge of translating the fact that the concept is unavailable in presentation form. For example, the user might not be able to move the thermometer, which presents the notion of temperature, toward a source of heat.

As another example, consider the selection of a file for a move operation and the highlighting of currently legal receptors for that file. The dialogue controller communicates to the functional core the fact that a particular file has been selected. It hides the fact that the selection has been accomplished by a mouse click. The functional core then indicates legal receptors, but it does not know how this legality is presented to the operator. The dialogue controller highlights the icons that represent legal receptors, and will move the icon representing the selected file only if the receptor is legal.

The notion of multiple views allows the operator to observe and manipulate a concept through several perspectives. The advantages with regard to task accomplishment were discussed in Section 2.5.1. The problem for the dialogue controller is to guarantee consistency between the perspectives. For example, if the operator of the mobile robot system moves a wall in an environment, the same wall, visible in another window, should also move (unless this is not desired). In any case, the focus of attention of the operator is a unique conceptual object (a particular wall), whereas the dialogue controller has to deal with at least two presentation objects (one per perspective).

Since the data crossing the interface consists of objects at the semantic level of the functional core, maintaining the consistency of multiple views is the responsibility of the dialogue controller. In the mobile robot example, for instance, there is only one semantic concept of a particular wall (the functional core perspective) and only that one concept crosses the interface. Providing two presentations of that concept to the operator is the responsibility of the dialogue controller.

Ownership of Data Transferred.   The level of abstraction at which data are transferred between the functional core and the dialogue controller is independent of the ownership of the data. There are basically two models for data ownership:

1. The data objects that represent the communication are *shared* by the dialogue controller and the functional core.

2. The data objects that represent the communication exist *on one side* of the interface, either as part of the functional core or within the dialogue controller.

Data sharing requires a synchronization mechanism for controlling conflicting accesses by multiple agents. In the particular case of an API, the functional core and the dialogue controller exchange data by requesting values of shared data items and permission to modify them. The primitives for access control are made available by a special-purpose component.

In practice, in nondistributed systems, the special-purpose component is split between the dialogue controller and the functional core. As a result, the dialogue controller and the functional core have equal ability to access and modify shared data. In a distributed system, however, there may be a separate physical component with which the functional core and the dialogue controller must negotiate. In recent distributed object-oriented systems such as Guide [Krakowiak et al. 1990], object sharing is automatically handled and thus is transparent to the client.

If the data transferred between the functional core and the dialogue controller are not shared but owned by one side, that side is responsible for controlling access and synchronization.

Although in some sense ownership of data does not automatically confer special rights to the data, whether the data are owned or shared tends to affect the design of the API. Consequently, it is important to make an explicit decision about ownership.

Description of Data Transferred.   The data that cross the interface can be described either *explicitly,* in a separate declaration of structure, type, preconditions, and postconditions, or *implicitly,* as an enumeration of parameters of procedures that modify the data in the interface. For example, an explicit description of the interface data for the mobile robot would include data structures, such as environments, missions, and walls, which implement the semantic concepts. A precondition to the specification of a mission would be the existence of at least one environment, and a postcondition to the creation of an environment would be incrementing the number of available environments.

There are a number of advantages to maintaining an explicit interface:

1. An explicit interface facilitates change of the interactive system. An external specification of the interface provides a contract between the functional core software designer and the user interface software designer. When changes occur in the API, it is easy to locate the portions of each piece of software affected by the changes.

2. An explicit interface provides hooks for semantic delegation. Semantic delegation involves having semantic checking performed by the user interface rather than by the functional core. One of the advantages of this technique is the enhancement of system functionality (see Section 5.4.2.4). When data in the interface are specified explicitly, it is easier to determine what semantic knowledge is accessible to the dialogue controller. For example, in the mobile robot system, the preconditions and postconditions on mission specification allow the dialogue controller to dynamically determine when to let the operator construct a mission.

3. An explicit interface facilitates the automatic generation of user interfaces. In systems such as Mickey [Olsen 1989], MacIda UIMS [Petoud and Pigneur 1990], and ITS [Bennett et al. 1989], default presentation objects can be

elaborated automatically from the definition of the data structures exported by the functional core. For example, a record structure may be presented by the system as a dialogue box, an enumerated type may be linked to a list of radio buttons, and a function may be mapped to a menu item.

Maintaining an explicit interface is a step with which many software engineers are unfamiliar, but it yields large benefits throughout the life cycle of a system.

Access to Data Transferred.   There are two basic techniques for expressing data access: the declarative model, as in Mickey [Olsen 1989], and the procedural paradigm, as in ApEx [Coutaz 1987a]. Serpent [Bass et al. 1990] provides a mixture of these two models. Generally speaking, a declarative expression speci-fies "the what" (the desired result), whereas a procedural expression describes "the how" (the computation leading to the result). Examples of procedural lan-guages are C and Ada. Examples of declarative languages are formalisms used in expert systems, such as OPS83 [Forgy 1984], and query languages used in data-base systems, such as SQL and Sequel [Date 1981].

The declarative approach provides a syntax to describe how the data are interrelated and is usually implemented with a constraint mechanism to enforce dependencies. The relationship among the data items can be viewed as a set of rules.

The procedural approach defines the API as an abstract machine whose instruction set allows the functional core to dynamically express changes relevant to the external world and vice versa. For example, this instruction set would include operations such as the following:

☐ "Write mydata" and "Read mydata" would signal, respectively, that the data structure "mydata" (for example, temperature) had a new value or needed a new value.

☐ "Invalidate mydata" would indicate that "mydata" should not be modified or invoked until a "Validate mydata" was issued.

☐ "Create mydata" would express the creation of an instance of a concept with the initial value "mydata," and "Destroy mydata" would signal its destruction.

The advantages of a declarative API are simplicity and power of expression. A declarative language avoids the problems of determining the mechanisms by which a particular desired result is to be achieved. The mechanisms are provided automatically by the system.

The advantage of a procedural API is the precision it allows in modifica-tions. One can directly specify the precise changes and type of access desired instead of relying on generalized system-level abstractions to do exactly the correct action.

The disadvantage of a declarative API is that it may prevent the designer from accessing details that would be useful to express highly dynamic events. This is a general problem common to specification languages: they are either too high level or too low level. If they are too high level, they may hide details that one would like to control; if they are too low level, they require too much effort to express an action. For example, consider the creation and destruction of objects. An error detected by the functional core results in the creation of a semantic object that describes the reasons for the failure. The job of the dialogue controller is to create an object specializing in the presentation of errors. In this case, the difficulty is to statically specify in the dialogue controller the conditions that will provoke, at run time, a failure caused by the functional core only.

High-quality semantic feedback is achieved more easily with the procedural approach, but configuration management is by far better supported by a declarative language. High-quality semantic feedback often requires precision and speed in data modification, and that is the positive aspect of a procedural API. Configuration management requires that interdependencies among data items be maintained so that the side effects of a modification can be propagated. Automatic propagation is one of the services that the declarative approach provides. A mixture of the two approaches appears to be preferable. The difficulty is to achieve an appropriate balance between the two techniques.

In summary, the API should:

☐ Perform data transfer at the level of abstraction defined by the functional core,

☐ Embed a clear model for data ownership (whether data are shared or owned by a particular side), and

☐ Provide a formalism to explicitly describe the data transferred, whether it be procedural, declarative, or a mixture of the two.

In practice, declarative accessing of data is used most often (although not necessarily) with a shared data model and with the explicit declaration of the data. The procedural approach is used most often when the objects that define the interface are viewed as being owned by one side of the interface. In this case there is rarely explicit description of the data that cross the interface.

Having described the protocol that governs the exchange of data with the functional core, we can now focus on particular types of information for the support of general services.

5.2.3 SUPPORT FOR GENERAL SERVICES

Section 2.5.2 discussed general services such as undo-redo, cut-copy-paste, and help. These services involve both the functional core and the dialogue controller.

Undo-Redo.   Undo and redo facilities, which respectively undo and redo the effect of the last command, rely on the existence of a history. A history is a mechanism for remembering the most recent commands. In this discussion, a command should be interpreted as an operator action that results in a change in the state of the interactive system. As discussed earlier, the interactive system includes a number of participants. Its state is therefore defined as the union of the states of the various participants: the semantic partner (the functional core) and the syntactic and lexical partners (the dialogue controller and the presentation objects).

Undoing a semantic action (such as undoing the creation of a wall in the mobile robot example) relies on the services of the functional core. Undoing a syntactic action (such as resizing, scrolling, or moving a window) relies on the services of the presentation objects. These services should be implemented according to the design criteria presented in Chapter 2. More difficult is the definition of a semantics and a breadth for undo-redo that matches the operator's expectation and intention.

The semantics of undo-redo depends on the maximum size of the stack of saved commands maintained by the history. The stack size may be limited to one (as in the Macintosh environment) or parameterized (as in the Unix shell). As a result, the two successive Macintosh undos results in no change in the original state, whereas each activation of the Unix shell redo executes the current command on the top of the stack and, thus, two successive redos will execute the prior command twice more.

The breadth of undo-redo depends on the extent of the history mechanism. The history may be viewed as a global service, may be distributed across the interactive system, or may be available as a combination of both. In the first case the last command is the absolute last action of the operator, whereas in the distributed basis the undoable command is relative to the current presentation object.

The Macintosh implementation of Microsoft Word is an example of a mixture of global and local histories: semantic commands are global to the interactive system, whereas syntactic commands are local to interaction objects. Microsoft-Word allows the operator to open several documents simultaneously. The last undoable semantic command is made available as an item in the Edit pop-up menu. If, for example, the user pastes some information in the first document, the menu item makes explicit the nature of the undoable function: Undo Paste. If the operator switches to a second document, the undoable command is still Undo Paste, although the paste action does not concern the current document. On the other hand, windows, which are interaction objects, remember their previous size. As a result, it is possible to undo a window size modification at the window level.

In summary, undo-redo facilities involve three levels of abstraction:

1. The presentation component maintains local histories and reverse functions specific to presentation objects.

2. The dialogue controller maintains a global history or a local history for commands with semantic side effects.

3. The functional core implements the reverse functions.

Cut-Copy-Paste.   Cutting, copying, and pasting of information may occur either inside a single use of an interactive system, between multiple usages of the same interactive system, or between different interactive systems. As discussed in Section 3.3.2, window systems define a format (or a set of formats) for data transfer. For example, the Macintosh toolbox supports a wide range of formats, since it allows application programmers to define their own protocol. The cut-and-paste facilities provided by windowing systems, however, do not address the more difficult aspects of the transfer of data.

The difficult portion is the interpretation of incoming data by the recipient. In most current implementations, the recipient is the functional core. The problem with this approach is that the level of abstraction of the data transferred through the cut-and-paste buffer generally does not match the level of abstraction of the data structures used for computation in the functional core. In particular, the formalism used to express the content of the cut-and-paste buffer relies heavily on layout considerations (see the abstract image machines and the various graphics machines in Chapter 4). As a result, the functional core must maintain a translation process to convert from a layout specification to a functional specification. This responsibility should lie, instead, within the dialogue controller, which acts as the mediator between the functional core and the presentation.

Delivering data at a level of abstraction usable by the functional core is an important step toward presentation independence. The incoming data, however, must be checked by the functional core for semantic validity. One important and as yet unsolved problem is finding a general mechanism for type checking and type recasting. For example, in a structured document editor, the operator may cut a section from one document and paste it back into a second document at a location where only subsections are expected. Clearly, the functional core should be able to recast the incoming section as a subsection.

In summary, cut-and-paste facilities involve three levels of abstraction:

1. The presentation component gets data through the cut-and-paste services.

2. The dialogue controller translates between the format used in the transfer protocol and the format of the functional core's internal data structures.

3. The functional core performs type checking and type recasting.

Window systems provide the basic mechanism for data transfer at the presentation level. At the other two levels, the dialogue controller and the functional core, there are currently no general techniques available.

Help.   Like histories, help facilities may be available globally or locally. The goal of help is to provide the operator with useful support. This goal is hard to achieve for three reasons:

1. It requires defining a model of the functioning of the interactive system and a model of the operator. Typically the system model is useful for providing procedural knowledge; given a question about how to do a particular thing, the help system is able to suggest a plan of action. The operator model is useful for devising the form of the answer, especially the level of detail to be provided.

2. It requires access to the state of the interactive system which, by definition, is distributed across multiple participants. State knowledge is helpful for elaborating answers relevant to the current situation.

3. It involves the definition of a query language. All the issues involved in the definition of a language (naturalness, coverage, syntax, and so on) must be solved for the query language.

The three requirements listed above are aimed at providing the operator with dynamic help with complex queries. Dynamic help reflects the current state of the system and must be continually updated. For example, presenting a list of current environments in the mobile robot requires that the functional core make that list available. Although dynamic and tuned help is strongly desirable, static help is much easier to implement.

No computation is needed for static help, but close attention should be paid to the content of the help messages [Borenstein 1985]. In the case of the mobile robot, a static message was defined for every class of presentation object. Such a message can be invoked through the help operation, which is attached to every instance of the presentation object. This simple solution does not require the definition of a new language: the help operation is just another available operation. It does not require the implementation of any new mechanism: messages are gathered in editable resource files.

The elementary static help of the mobile robot could be enhanced by adding a hypertext facility [Conklin 1987]. Instead of being independent, messages would include links to concepts presented in different messages. The help facility would thus allow the operator to navigate from help message to help message, without necessarily invoking the help operation. A problem with this approach is that it involves semantic information rather than static information. For example, the system could tell the operator which options were available given the current state of the functional core. All these concepts of help are important, but the implementation of help can become a very expensive portion of the total interactive system. Consequently, help facilities are not as available as one might wish.

In summary, full-fledged help for effective problem solving is desirable but requires the definition of a query language and the development of an automatic planner based on a knowledge base. Simple static help may be provided at minimal cost by assigning help information to every presentation object in the interactive system. We now turn to a discussion of the models used to describe dialogue.

5.3   Abstract Basis of Dialogue Control

A number of different models have been devised to describe (and hence specify) operator interactions. These models are:

1. Formal grammar models, in particular Backus-Naur Form (BNF),
2. Finite-state machines, usually augmented, and
3. Production or event systems.

Any implementation of these models includes two portions. First is a language for describing interactions in terms of the model. A program in this language becomes a specification of the behavior of the dialogue controller. Second is the run-time interpretation of the specification. One implementation decision is whether to compile the specification language into a lower level description or to directly interpret it.

5.3.1   FORMAL GRAMMAR MODELS

Formal grammar models draw on the analogy between computer-human interaction and an ordinary conversation between individuals. A successful conversation relies on use of a common language, which may be described with a formal grammar. Similarly, BNF may be used to specify the interaction between the operator and the interactive system. Each nonterminal in BNF has an associated action routine that describes the presentation and the actions associated with the presentation. A legal interaction is one that can be parsed through BNF. Early user interface generators such as SYNGRAPH [Olsen and Dempsey 1983] used BNF to specify user interactions.

BNF, by its nature, conveys an explicit sequence of events. This imposes a particular style on the interface or requires a tremendous effort by the designer to specify each possible ordering. The mobile robot system, for example, allows different parameter orderings and task switching. The operator can edit the fields in a form in any order and can use direct manipulation to switch from moving a

wall to requesting and editing a form about another semantic object, then resume
the action on the wall. This type of behavior would require a very large BNF
grammar to allow for all possible variations of operator input order.

Since all actions in BNF must be explicitly stated, certain desirable features
(such as allowing the operator to enter parameters in any order or to change the
current task while in the middle of a task) are difficult to specify. An additional
problem of this specification technique is lack of support for levels of abstraction.
The specification of a selection of an object (for example, "cursor over object"
and "button click") is one level of abstraction; the specification of the ordering of
parameters to a command is a higher level. Levels of abstractions can be expressed
with nonterminals. The nesting of nonterminals is hard to decipher by examination, however, and BNF becomes too obscure for a specifier to understand easily.

5.3.2   TRANSITION NETWORKS

An alternative to BNF as a specification model is based on the theory of finite-
state automata. A finite-state automaton is represented as a directed graph, or a
transition network, whose nodes denote states and whose vertices express the
conditions that lead from state to state. In the domain of computer-human interaction, vertices are labeled with lexical items to model legal actions of the operator,
and nodes are named to denote interaction states. Like BNF, transition networks
do not distinguish between levels of abstraction, and thus a specification based on
a transition network becomes difficult to code and decipher. Consequently, transition networks have been augmented to support richer descriptions.

Recursive transition networks replace the flat organization of the classic
transition diagram with a structured representation: vertices (or nodes) may be
labeled with names denoting subgraphs. Thus, a dialogue may be decomposed
into subdialogues. For supporting context-sensitive interactions, vertices can also
contain registers and boolean functions. Boolean functions, which may reference
register values, determine the conditions for traversing vertices.

Jacob's system [Jacob 1984] and Rapid/USE [Wasserman 1985] are examples
of user interface generators based on the finite-state machine paradigm. Finite-
state machines suffer from the same sequencing problems as BNF. As a consequence, they are inadequate for expressing interleaving and parallelism. Statecharts
[Harel 1987] are an extension of finite-state machines that allow for the expression
of parallelism.

5.3.3   PRODUCTION SYSTEMS

Production systems are collections of rules of the form *if* "conditions" *then* "action." Rules whose condition part is satisfied by the current state of the system are

fired. When a rule is fired, the action part is executed. Since the rules rely only on the current state of the system, there is no inherent sequencing in the rules. Thus, different orders of parameters and commands can be easily allowed for: *if* "all parameters and command have been specified" *then* " perform action." This rule will be fired whenever all the parameters and the command have been provided, regardless of ordering.

The nature of condition and action parts of a rule varies from system to system. The production model used in Serpent will be described in Chapter 6. In event response systems (ERS) [Hill 1987a, Hill 1987b], a condition includes a conjunction of boolean flags and, possibly, a reference to an event. Flags model the state of the interaction, and events are used to communicate information to the functional core, to presentation objects. or with interaction devices. Events are data structures maintained in a unique queue. A condition part is satisfied when its flags are true and when the referenced event (if any) is first in the queue. When a condition part is satisfied, the event is removed from the queue, the flags turn to false, and the action part is executed. The action part may include sending events and setting flags and event fields.

Production models have been used recently in an attempt to specify the parallelism that operators seem to require. Systems based on production rules suffer from several problems, however. Since control is not explicitly transferred within the specification of the dialogue, the system must monitor a large data space in order to decide which rules to fire. This monitoring of a large data space may lead to performance problems. Recently, the development of more efficient production systems [Forgy 1984] has reduced the magnitude of this drawback.

A second problem associated with the use of production models is lack of explicit transfer of control. Programmers are taught to think in terms of sequential algorithms, whereas the data-driven nature of production models requires a heavily parallel method of thinking. This problem can be overcome with training, and if production rule systems prove to be suitably useful, programmers will be taught earlier to think in terms of parallel solutions to problems.

A third problem with production rules is lack of encapsulation for the expression of levels of abstraction. The multiagent model presented in the next section constitutes an attempt to combine the parallelism conveyed by the production model with the encapsulation mechanism embedded in the object-oriented paradigm.

5.4 Architectural Models

Chapters 1, 3, and 4 considered the logical basis of interactive systems and identified and discussed various levels of abstraction. The issue we will discuss in

this section is how these logical components are organized into a software architecture. One extreme is to treat the levels of abstraction as layers in a software
architecture. This approach was the basis of early attempts at building interactive
support systems. Another extreme is to decentralize the logical levels. This approach is the basis of multiagent models. We will discuss both of these extremes
in this section.

5.4.1   MONOLITHIC SEQUENTIAL ARCHITECTURES

A monolithic approach to architectural decomposition of an interactive system
treats the logical levels of Figure 1.2 as physical layers. The usual way of doing
this is to group the logical levels of window systems and interaction objects into a
presentation layer and to consider the dialogue control logical level as the dialogue controller layer. This architecture was first identified at Seeheim [Pfaff
1985].

From this perspective came a linguistic approach that identified the notions
of semantics, syntax, and lexicon with the three components of an interactive
system: the functional core implements the semantics, the dialogue controller
deals with syntactic issues, and the presentation layer is in charge of the lexical
aspects of the interaction. The advantage of this view is that the notions of
semantics, syntax, and lexicon are well understood by computer scientists.
Therefore, it is a useful framework for teaching design of interactive systems. In
addition, it was tempting for computer scientists to transfer their knowledge from
automatic compiler generation to automatic user interface generation. The result
has been the emergence of a wide variety of "rapid prototyping tools" based on
BNF and finite-state machines. The problem is that compiler technology, which
relies on a sequential analysis of predictable input expressions, does not focus on
interactivity.

The sequential linguistic model of interaction does not support the opportunistic problem-solving strategy of the operator, and it provides poor semantic
feedback unless the software implementer violates the principle of separation of
concerns between the functional core and the dialogue controller. In addition,
first-generation systems based on this architecture made a distinction between the
language used by the operator to specify input expressions and the language used
by the interactive system to produce output expressions. As a result of this di-
chotomy, outputs could not be reused as input data. In other words, cut-and-paste
facilities were totally discarded. A second consequence of this distinction was the
functional asymmetry of dialogue controllers that were only able to support input.
In such cases, the functional core was in charge of producing output expressions,
and half of the interaction was removed from the control of the dialogue controller.

Systems based on finite-state machines also failed to support basic principles
from cognitive psychology. In such systems, the flexibility of the interaction
depends on the completeness of the automata, which theoretically should model

all the possible mental paths of the operator. In practice, this technique is too cumbersome. As a result, operators of systems based on this technology are often stuck in a state until they satisfy some invisible condition built into the automata.

These observations have encouraged computer scientists to investigate different architectural models. One is a highly parallel modular organization built around the notion of agents. Multiagent models separate concepts and presentation techniques at every level of abstraction. In doing so, they distribute the separation of concerns among cooperating agents. They differ, however, in the way they implement distribution and cooperation.

5.4.2 MULTIAGENT ARCHITECTURES

The multiagent model is based on the functioning of stimulus-response systems. Such systems are organized as a collection of agents that react to a given set of external phenomena (stimuli) and that, in turn, produce new stimuli.

Definition.   The multiagent model structures an interactive system into a collection of specialized agents that produce and react to events. An *agent* is a complete information processing system: it includes event receivers and event transmitters, a memory to maintain a state, and a processor that cyclically processes input events, updates its own state, and may produce events or change its interest in input event classes. Agents communicate with other agents, including the operator. Agents that communicate directly with the operator are called presentation objects, interactors, or interactive objects. Such agents should be viewed as partners of the operator: they listen to the operator, they possess a convenient expertise, and they provide adequate feedback.

Benefits.   The multiagent model, which stresses a highly parallel modular organization, distributes the state of the interaction among a collection of cooperating units. Modularity, parallelism, and distribution are convenient mechanisms for supporting all of the following:

- *Iterative design.* An agent defines the unit for modularity. It is thus possible to modify the unit's behavior without affecting the rest of the system.
- *Distributed applications.* An agent defines the unit for processing. It is thus possible to execute the unit on a processor different from the processor on which the unit was created. It is also possible to use instances of a class of agents to present a concept on several workstations. This property is essential to the implementation of groupware (systems that provide a shared environment for supporting cooperative work).
- *Multithread dialogues.* An agent can be associated with each thread of the operator's activity. Since a state is locally maintained by the agent, the interaction between the user and the agent can be suspended and resumed at

the operator's will. When a thread of activity is too complex or too rich to be represented by a single agent, it can represented by a collection of cooperating agents.

In addition to the fact that it satisfies the need for better user interfaces, another advantage of the multiagent model is that it can be easily be implemented in terms of object-oriented languages. An object class defines a category of agents, where class operators and attributes model the instruction set and the state of an agent, respectively, and where an event class denotes a method. An object and an agent are both highly specialized processing units, and both decide their own state: a state is not manipulated by others, but results from processing triggered by others. The subclassing mechanism provided by object-oriented languages can be usefully exploited to modify a user interface without changing the existing code.

A number of multiagent models and tools have been developed along the lines of the object-oriented and event-processing paradigms. The model-view-controller (MVC) [Goldberg 1984, Krasner and Pope 1988] and PAC [Coutaz 1987b, Coutaz 1988] are multiagent models. Interviews [Linton, Vlissides, and Calder 1989] and Aïda [Ilog 1989] are toolkits based on such a model, whereas GWUIMS [Sibert, Hurley, and Bleser 1986], Serpent [Bass et al. 1990] and Sassafras [Hill 1987b] are run-time kernels and user interface generators organized according to a multiagent model. In no case do these models and tools deny the principle of separation of the functional core from the user interface. In fact, they go further, applying the separation at various levels of abstraction and distributing the responsibility of the dialogue among a set of cooperating agents. As of today, none of these models or tools has emerged as a definite solution. The next section analyzes one such model: PAC.

PAC, a Multiagent Model.   As shown in Figure 5.8, PAC recursively structures an interactive system as a hierarchy of agents. An agent defines a competence at some level of abstraction. It is a three-facet logical cluster that includes a presentation, an abstraction and a control. At any level of abstraction:

1. A presentation is a perceivable behavior,

2. An abstraction is the functional core, which implements some expertise in a media-independent way, and

3. A control links an abstraction to a presentation, controls the behavior of the two perspectives it serves, remembers a local state for supporting multithread dialogue, and maintains relationships with other agents.

PAC differs from the older model-view-controller model (MVC) in the way it divides up various functionalities. A model in the MVC model corresponds to a PAC abstraction: both represent a competence that is media independent. In MVC a view is responsible for outputs and a control handles inputs [Krasner and

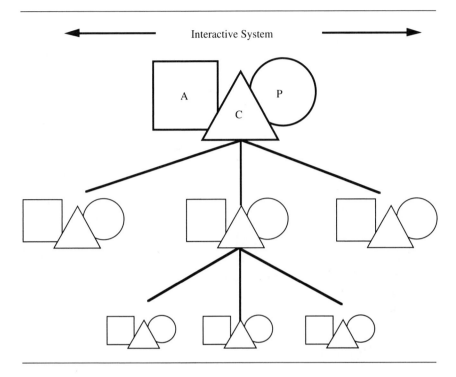

FIGURE 5.8
An interactive system modeled as a collection of agents, which in turn are made up of other agents. P stands for presentation, A for abstraction, and C for control.

Pope 1988]. Thus, the combination of an MVC view and an MVC control corresponds to a PAC presentation. The PAC control, which mediates between the media-independent functional core and the media-dependent perspective of an agent, has no direct correspondence in MVC. It can, however, be considered as a particular class of model. Figure 5.9 shows how the two models relate.

PAC conveys a hierarchy that can be usefully exploited for defining levels of refinements or relationships. We now describe the interpretation of such a hierarchy from the top to the bottom levels.

1. *The Top Level of the Hierarchy.* At the top level of the hierarchy, the abstraction corresponds to the functional core of the interactive system. For example, in the mobile robot system, this abstraction is the rule-based intelligent supervisor shown in Figure 1.4. At this level of abstraction, rules express procedural knowledge, and working memory elements model cartographic knowledge. For instance, any wall, place, or route in an environment is represented as a

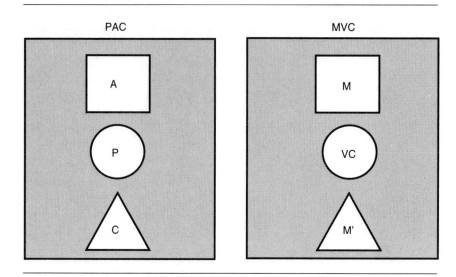

FIGURE 5.9
A comparison of PAC and MVC models. The abstraction A of PAC is represented by the model M of MVC, and the presentation P of PAC is represented by the view and controller VC of MVC. The control C of PAC has no direct correspondence but could be represented as a particular model class M'.

memory element on which rules can "reason." Such memory elements have no knowledge about their graphic counterparts on the screen. They are not aware of the existence of the graphic representations. They are and must be presentation independent.

The top-level control has a role similar to that of the dialogue controller introduced in Figure 5.1. It bridges the gap between the functional core and the perceivable world in the following ways:

- It provides mechanisms for indirection and translation between the functional core and the user interface. For example, in the mobile robot system, the top-level control dynamically maintains a mapping table correlating the identity of the working memory elements with the identity of their corresponding PAC agents. Walls and routes handled in the user interface part of the interactive system are referenced with PAC IDs, but in the top-level abstraction they are known by memory element IDs. Switching between reference domains is one task of the top-level control. The virtue of this indirection is that it allows the abstraction to remain ignorant of the details of the presentation.

❑ It maintains the state of the interaction at a high level of abstraction—that is, at the level of abstraction defined by the functional core. For example, it remembers (or checks) whether a function (or a set of functions) of the functional core is invalid, and it remembers the parameters that have already been specified for a function. In a shortcut, it is the abstract machine that implements the protocol between the functional core and the user interface. In the mobile robot system, the protocol includes requests such as "move this wall," "create a wall," and "delete this wall." Such requests may result from the operator's actions or may be issued by the top-level abstraction.

❑ It implements a protocol to control the hierarchy of PAC agents. In the mobile robot system, this protocol is semantically very similar to that maintained for the functional core. The main difference is that the protocol with the functional core involves memory element IDs, whereas the protocol with the PAC agents involves PAC IDs.

The top-level presentation may be interpreted in different ways, depending on the tools used for implementation. One desirable, but unfortunately not yet widely available, way of modeling the top-level presentation is as a general geometry manager. Such a geometry manager, as used in Garnet [Myers 1989b] or the box mechanism [Herrmann and Hill 1990], is in charge of maintaining the spatial relationships between the presentation parts of the various subagents.

2. *The Bottom Level of the Hierarchy.* At the bottom of the hierarchy, elementary PAC agents define the unitary partners of the operator. They are the smallest units on which an operator can act. For example, in the mobile robot system, walls and places are made real on the screen in the form of elementary PAC agents. Figure 5.10 shows one of them.

The presentation of a PAC wall agent produces a shape (that of a wall) with a designated pick point (a hot spot) that the operator can select with the mouse. Mouse events are caught by the hot spot and processed by the presentation to provide local feedback. Local feedback includes showing the list of operations available for the wall in a pop-up menu, performing rubber banding when the wall is resized, and tracking the shape of the wall when the wall is moved around with the mouse. In addition to painting the screen images and providing local feedback, the presentation of a wall maintains a state for graphical purposes. Such a state includes the coordinates of the wall relative to the rendering surface (for example, a window), the wall's length (expressed in terms of pixels), the thickness of the line that draws the wall, and the shape of the icon that identifies the hot spot.

The abstraction part of a wall agent models the notion of wall as used in the real world without any reference to its graphical counterpart. By "real world" we mean the domain modeled for the mobile robot. In this world, the length and thickness of walls are expressed in terms of meters, not pixels, and locations are

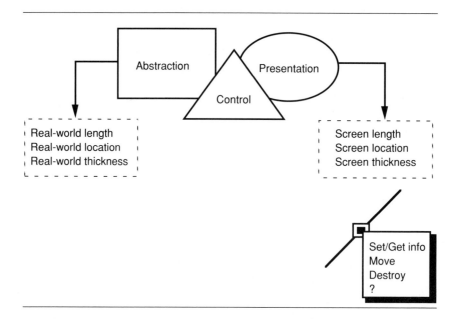

FIGURE 5.10
A PAC wall agent. The abstraction uses a real-world coordinate system, and the presentation uses a screen coordinate system to actually draw the line representing the wall.

relative to a global world coordinate system, which is convenient for architects but not for a window system.

The control part of a wall agent is the local chief for the three-facet cluster: it maintains consistency between the presentation and abstraction parts, it remembers a state useful for multithreading, and it participates with other agents in data exchanges.

▫ To maintain consistency, the control performs translations between the formalisms used in the two perspectives. For example, it converts meters into pixels and vice versa; it also performs transformations between the abstract and the graphical coordinate systems.

▫ To remember a state for multithreading, the control behaves like a local syntax analyzer—that is, a local finite-state machine. Moving a wall, for example, requires two actions: selecting the operator in a pop-up menu and specifying the new location. Each action is a lexical unit that may be leaved with actions on other agents. Therefore, the control part of a wall must maintain a local state of its interaction with the operator.

☐ To bring about consistency in data exchanges, the control must participate in messages sent to and received from other agents. The control part of a wall agent may be notified that an operation is not currently available—for example, that the "move" operation is not accessible to the operator. The role of the control part is to communicate the invalidity of the operation to the presentation part, which in turn will dim the "move" item in the pop-up menu.

3. *The Intermediate Levels of the Hierarchy.* Intermediate PAC agents are used to represent combinations of relationships and levels of abstraction. One common relationship is that of composition. A composed PAC agent defines a new abstraction, whose behavior results from both the behavior of its components and the new characteristics and constraints that are added. For example, in the mobile robot system, the window that displays the notion of environment is an agent composed of wall agents, route agents, and so on, on top of which are new constraints and facilities for supporting syntactic tasks such as visibility, scaling, and scrolling.

Figure 5.8 shows an idealized, informal, and intuitive view of a PAC organization. Experience with previous applications of the PAC model has shown that it is generally easy for the software designer to identify the top-level components and the low-level agents. The nature and role of the intermediate agents are not so easily identified. The next section provides a set of heuristic rules that may help in the process of building software architectures for interactive systems.

Software Design Rules.   The following rules are driven by software reusability considerations. They result from the application of the PAC model to the design of several applications. Most of them, however, are general enough to be considered in the development of any agent-based software architecture. We will illustrate the application of these rules with the mobile robot system. Figure 5.11 shows the software architecture of our reference example and will be used in the description of the software rules.

The fundamental principle driving the design of interactive software architectures is to separate abstraction and presentation issues at every level of abstraction. Rule 1 indicates how to enhance reusability of an abstraction and its related presentation.

A second principle is to support iterative design. Our hypothesis is that agent-based software architectures satisfy this requirement, since an agent is the unit for modification. Rule 2 specifies how to facilitate agent substitution.

A third principle is to organize the agents of a user interface in order to satisfy human needs for multithread dialogues, multiple views of the same se-

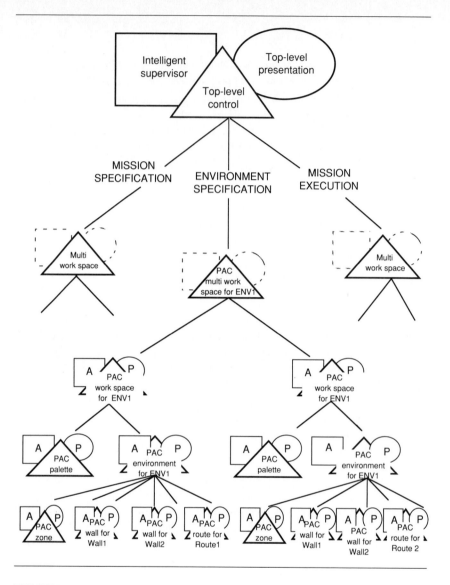

FIGURE 5.11
The PAC architecture of the mobile robot system. At the bottom of the hierarchy, unitary agents such as zones, walls, and routes are grouped to form an environment agent. Since an environment may be opened several times, a multi work space agent controls the visual consistency between the multiple views of an environment. The top-level control mediates between the presentation PAC agents and the functional core (the top-level abstraction).

176

mantic concepts, and informative feedback about errors. Rules 3 and 4 indicate how to introduce intermediate agents that support such requirements. Rule 5 suggests a way to model the notion of semantic error.

Rule 6 is concerned with the problem of distributing domain knowledge across the levels of abstraction of an interactive system.

Rule 1. *Use* indirection *to enhance reusability of an abstraction and its related presentation.*

Indirection between an abstraction and a presentation means that the code of an abstraction does not contain any explicit reference to items defined in the presentation and vice versa. The benefit of indirection is straightforward: one component can be linked to another one without any change in the implementation, and the behavior of one component can be modified without any modification of the surrounding components. Ideally, indirection should be applied at every level of abstraction.

In the mobile robot system, working memory elements of the top-level abstraction do not include any attribute to designate the graphic agents through which they are presented to the operator. Conversely, the PAC agents do not point at memory elements. At the lowest level of abstraction, the abstract items of PAC agents such as walls do not depend on rendition attributes. Thus, one can change the pictures of walls without modifying their abstract representation.

Indirection requires the existence of a mechanism for linkage. Links may be static or dynamic, multiple or simple. A static link defines a fixed mapping between an abstraction and a presentation. Dynamic linkage allows for redefinition, creation, and deletion of associations. Multiple linkage supports $1:n$ correspondences between an abstraction and a set of presentations.

Dynamic linkage is mandatory in systems where concept instances may be created and deleted dynamically. In the mobile robot system, the user may add a new wall to an environment by creating an agent, an instance of the class PAC wall. The creation of such an agent is handled by a hierarchy of agents and is signaled to the top-level control. This control saves the identity of the PAC wall agent, notes the existence of an unresolved reference, and translates the event into the formalism of the top-level abstraction (the intelligent supervisor). The linkage will be complete when the intelligent supervisor returns the identity of the newly created memory element.

Multiple linkage provides the foundation for multiple views. As shown in Figure 2.8, an environment, which is a semantic concept, may be viewed simultaneously in multiple windows. In the PAC architecture shown in Figure 5.11, such windows are modeled as PAC agents, instances of a class called PAC environment. Since an environment is a composite item, a memory element modeling a wall may have multiple PAC wall agents associated with it (one per window). In Figure 5.11, the semantic concept ENV1 maintained in the intelligent supervisor has been opened twice by the operator. As a result, two PAC environment agents have been created, and memory elements such as Wall1, Wall2, and Route1 of ENV1 are each made visible by two PAC agents.

Although indirection is a well-known mechanism in computer science, it is still not widely applied in the domain of interactive software. Tools such as user interface generators convey indirection between the functional core and the user interface. It is not clear, however, that they all support the mechanism inside the user interface per se. In the absence of such support, the software designer must be careful to provide a link mechanism that supports indirection. The PAC model suggests that such a mechanism should be implemented in the control portion.

Because of the existence of a control, the presentation and its related abstraction need never communicate directly with each other; each can communicate with the control in its own formalism. In particular, any reference to an abstract user interface entity made by the top-level abstraction is automatically translated by the control into a reference to a PAC agent, and conversely, any reference to a PAC agent is translated into a reference to an abstract user interface entity. In the mobile robot system, the translation is used not only for mapping two different views of the same abstract entity but also for mapping between two different implementation languages: OPS5 for the top-level abstraction and C for the user interface. A control is the location for making all of the necessary transformations between the Abstraction and the presentation.

Rule 2. *Use symbolic references to enhance reusability at the agent level.*

Symbolic referencing, another form of indirection, relies on dynamic binding. In the domain of object-oriented language, symbolic references may include names such as: MyFather, MyFirstBrother, MyBoss, or MySiblings, whose effective denotation is dynamically determined at run time. Symbolic references provide a way to code an agent without any knowledge about actual cooperating agents. By making it easy to substitute agents, symbolic referencing supports iterative design. For example, PAC wall and PAC route agents refer symbolically to a PAC environment as their Father. Therefore, the agents can be reused as parts of any other type of superagent.

Note that, whereas rule 1 stresses reusability for the abstraction and presentation facets, rule 2 stresses reusability at the agent level.

Rule 3. *Use an agent to cement actions distributed over multiple agents into a higher abstraction.*

Often the specification of a command involves actions distributed over multiple agents. This is particularly true of CAD interactive systems in which a palette (which is an agent) is used to display the possible options and a window (which is yet another agent) is used as a scratch area for creating and editing an artifact (for example, a document in a text editor). The same situation occurs in the specification of environments in the mobile robot system.

The creation of a route implies selecting the route icon in the palette, then drawing the route in the scratch area. The combination of the two actions has a meaning—creating a route—but the palette and the scratch area are not aware of each other. They would otherwise be dependent on each other, and then the first one would not be reusable without the second. Multithread dialogue authorizes logically connected actions to be interleaved with "foreign" actions. As a consequence, there are conflicting needs to maintain "mutual ignorance" between two agents, to remember logically connected actions, and to combine these actions into a higher abstraction (a command). The multiagent framework provides a natural way of satisfying such requirements: introducing an intermediate agent to serve as a cement. Figure 5.12 shows the general solution, based on the mobile robot system.

In Figure 5.11, a palette is implemented as an instance of the class PAC palette and a scratch area is an instance of the class PAC environment. The

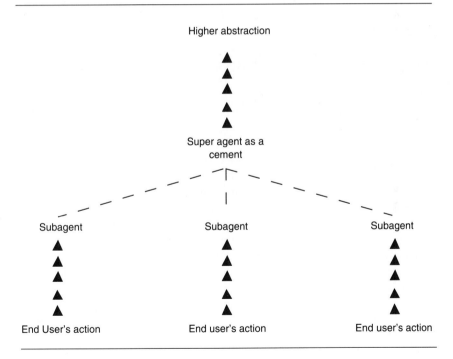

FIGURE 5.12
Use of an agent to cement distributed actions into a higher abstraction. Each subagent performs a single action; the superagent manages the connections between the subagents.

cement agent is an instance of the class PAC Workspace. Any relevant action of the operator on a palette agent—for example, a mouse click on the route icon—has immediate local feedback on the presentation of the palette—for example, a reverse video of the icon. This feedback is provided locally by the presentation part of the palette. The palette agent abstracts the operator's action and notifies the cement agent with a message of the form "the operator is interested in creating *this* type of concept." The cement agent then informs the environment agent that subsequent mouse clicks happening in its free space should be interpreted as the creation of an instance of "*this* type of concept." Once the operator has performed the expected actions, the cement agent is able to create an abstraction "creation of a concept of *this* type." Note that, in order to satisfy rule 1, *this* is expressed in terms of PAC IDs. The conversion into functional core IDs is performed by the top-level control.

The cement agent behaves like a syntax analyzer, which controls the local automata maintained by its subagents. Input for syntax analysis may come in any order from multiple sources. If, in addition, the cement agent is able to handle the construction of several commands simultaneously, it provides an easy way to implement multithread dialogues.

Rule 4. *Use an agent to maintain visual consistency among multiple views.*

In Chapter 2 we discussed the usefulness of multiple views of semantic concepts. One semantic concept of general interest is the focus of attention. In a document preparation system, the focus of attention is a document. In the mobile robot system, one focus of attention is an environment. The challenge in maintaining multiple views of the same concept is to ensure visual consistency. Any action on one view should be reported in the other views.

According to rule 2, which stresses mutual ignorance to enhance reusability, agents that implement the views of a semantic concept should not know each other. As shown in Figure 5.13, a multiple views agent is introduced to express the logical link. Any action with a visual side effect on a view is reported to the multiple views agent, which broadcasts the update to the other siblings.

In the mobile robot system, the multi work space agent is in charge of the various work spaces an operator may open to create and edit an environment. As mentioned above, a work space agent includes a palette and a scratch area where the environment is effectively built. Each work space defines a context—that is, a way of working. For example, in one work space the current mode of creation is "wall," whereas in a second one the creation mode is set to "route." Routes may be invisible in one work space but visible in another (see Figure 2.8). Therefore, a work space defines a view.

When the operator opens an environment, a work space agent is created under the control of its associated multi work space agent. Any operator's action with a semantic side effect detected by a work space agent is reported to the multi work space agent, which in turn notifies the other siblings of the modification. It

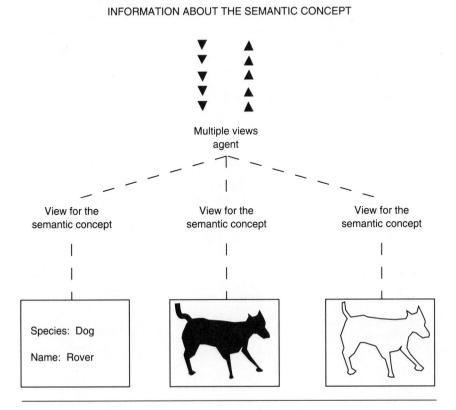

INFORMATION ABOUT THE SEMANTIC CONCEPT

Multiple views
agent

View for the
semantic concept

View for the
semantic concept

View for the
semantic concept

Species: Dog

Name: Rover

FIGURE 5.13
Use of an agent to maintain visual consistency among multiple views. Each subagent
has a particular competence for rendering the notion of dog, and each communicates with the superagent that manages the multiple views.

is up to these siblings to take the modification into account. For example, the
notification of the creation of a route in a work space where routes are invisible
will have no perceivable effect but will be remembered.

Rule 5. *Use an agent to present error messages.*

Error messages often are implemented as static character strings scattered across
the code of the system. As a result, semantic feedback is poor quality and the
message cannot be modified without recompiling the code. An alternative is to
explicitly model the notion of error in the top-level abstraction and to feed agents
specializing in error rendition.

Figure 5.14 illustrates one way to present error messages. This method requires the top-level abstraction to generate the appropriate information. The intelligent supervisor models errors as tuples whose first item identifies the error category (for example, critical or tolerable) and whose remaining items describe the precise cause of the problem in terms of memory elements. The abstract representation of an error is then used as input to an agent that automatically generates a message expressed in a natural language (in the robot system, either

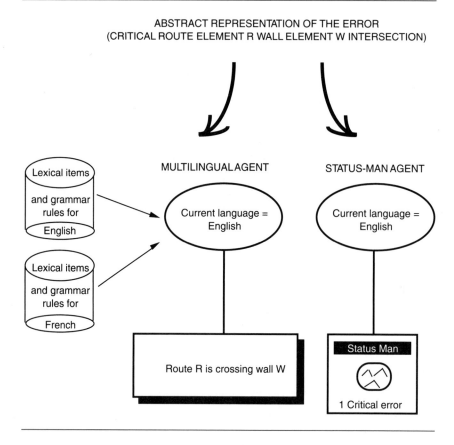

FIGURE 5.14
Use of agents to present error messages. The top-level agent generates the error message in an abstract form. The lower level agents interpret the error, depending on the current language. The textual agent and the Status Man are two different presentations of the same abstract error.

English or French, depending on the user's preference). It can also be used as input for the Status Man agent mentioned in Chapter 2. Within the framework of the PAC model, the Status Man is modeled by having an abstraction that counts the symbolic messages issued by the top-level abstraction, a presentation that shows a smiling, neutral, or unhappy face, depending on the result of the counting, and a control that performs the translation between the counting and the face-style attribute.

Rule 6. *Use semantic delegation for semantic or performance enhancement.*

Semantic delegation involves the distribution of domain knowledge across the interactive system. Such distribution relies heavily on the tools at hand and will be discussed further in Section 5.6. In general, semantic delegation is useful for enhancing semantics and performance.

The use of a system may reveal the absence of a concept that would be helpful in accomplishing a task. The problem may be solved in two ways: either the missing functionality may be added to the functional core or the user interface may be modified. The first approach requires access to the source code of the functional core, whereas the second technique requires the functional core to provide the top-level control with enough information to simulate the missing concept. The missing semantic concept is then implemented as an agent in the user interface. As shown in Figure 5.11, the concept of zone in the mobile robot system illustrates such a solution.

High-quality semantic feedback may require frequent round trips between the functional core and the low-level layers of the interface. This long chain of data transfer may introduce performance delays. Because it reduces transmission load between the functional core and the interface, semantic delegation, when possible, provides an easy way to enhance performance. The PAC wall agent will be used to illustrate the technique.

As shown in Figure 5.15, the system provides the operator with the actual length and exact location of the wall being created or resized. This information is updated as soon as the mouse is moved. Clearly, the effective size of a wall is a domain-dependent notion, which should be evaluated by the functional core. On the other hand, the time needed for a round trip between the user interface and the functional core for each mouse movement might exceed the refresh constraint imposed by the human perceptual system [Card, Moran, and Newell 1983]. (In particular, the functional core may run on a different machine in a local area network whose performance may not be easily controlled.) In addition, in the case of the mobile robot, the intelligent supervisor is not interested in transient values; semantic checking, such as of wall intersections, must be performed on stable values only. These observations led to the definition of a wall agent that maintains domain-dependent values and performs the appropriate translations between a line length expressed in pixels and an actual wall length expressed in real-world measurement units.

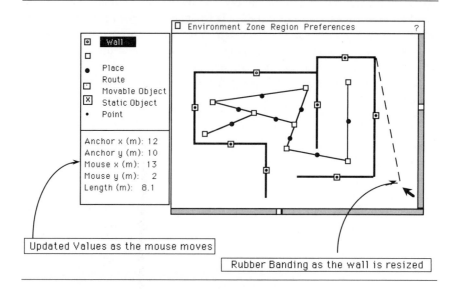

FIGURE 5.15
Rubber banding indicates the current length of the wall, providing the operator
with immediate feedback.

5.5   Human Issues

An interactive system may be considered as a tool or as a collaborator. A tool is
an artifact that does not provide any support for decision making; it is an instrument. A collaborator is a partner that acts toward the accomplishment of a common task; it is an agent.

We observed in Figure 5.5 that an interactive system could be viewed as an
organization of multiple levels of agents: the functional core, the dialogue controller, and a multitude of presentation objects, all acting together with the operator
to accomplish a task. This view of an interactive system, which stresses the active
cooperation of multiple agents, leads to the design of computer systems that are
effective collaborators.

Sequential models of dialogue control have provided useful experience, but
they have failed to support the basics of interaction, such as multithreading.
Although it is not clear yet how to achieve a successful collaboration between an
interactive system and an operator (or a set of operators), experience indicates

that dialogue control conveyed by multiagent models is flexible enough to support opportunistic planning, multithread dialogues, and immediate and informative feedback.

5.6 Engineering Issues

In previous sections we mentioned a number of engineering issues with respect to dialogue controllers:

☐ *Division of functionality.* What functionalities does the dialogue controller include, and what functionalities is the functional core supposed to handle? How does the dialogue controller affect the location of semantic activities?

☐ *Run-time support.* Which application programmer's interface best supports the functionality of an interactive system?

☐ *Models and tools.* What distinguishes a model, an implementation based on a model, and a tool that conveys a particular model?

We next discuss these issues.

5.6.1 DIVISION OF FUNCTIONALITY

The boundary between the functional core and the dialogue controller is not always clear. A number of general rules should be helpful in devising a correct division:

☐ The functional core should be media (or presentation) independent. A functional core is media independent if it is not altered by the replacement of some input/output media with radically different ones and if it remains ignorant of how many times a particular semantic concept is displayed.

☐ The functional core should dynamically provide meaningful semantic feedback. In particular, the dialogue controller should be notified about any creation/deletion/modification of a semantic concept of interest to the operator; any errors, including the level of gravity and the identity of the semantics concepts involved; and the legality of operations (whether or not a semantic operation is currently available).

5.6.2 RUN-TIME SUPPORT

Several criteria may be used to test the power of a system that provides dialogue control support. Some tests are based on the idea that the functional core should be media independent, and others are based on the models, or lack of them, underlying the dialogue controller.

Media independence of the functional core has several implications for the dialogue controller. In particular, the dialogue controller should be able to:

- Implement screen layout policies. In order to perform screen layout, the dialogue controller must have the ability to do arithmetic.

- Handle multiple views of semantic concepts and automatically maintain consistency among them.

In addition to facilitating media independence for the functional core, a dialogue controller should be able to support semantic delegation. In order to support semantic delegation, the dialogue controller must have the ability to define abstractions. For example, in the mobile robot system, the functional core does not contain the notion of zone (the concept concerns not the robot, but the operator). As a consequence, the dialogue controller must be able to define a new abstraction to model the concept of zone.

A model for constructing dialogue controllers provides the designer and implementer with a useful framework. As discussed in the next section, however, there may be a considerable distance between a conceptual framework and a tool that embeds the framework. Clearly, languages for dialogue specification bring additional conceptual help beyond that provided by traditional procedural languages. Such languages, however, should satisfy the criteria we have enumerated so far: arithmetic computation for screen layout, abstraction mechanism for semantic delegation, and automatic maintenance of multiple views of semantic concepts.

5.6.3   FROM ARCHITECTURAL MODELS TO IMPLEMENTATION

An architectural model is a reference framework that guides the process of software organization. As such, it serves different functions than does a tool or an implementation based on the model. We will now discuss some of the distinctions.

Distinctions Between a Model and a Tool.   A model provides guidance in the areas that it specifically models and is neutral in other areas. For example, the PAC model is a framework for defining agents along with their relationships. It can be implemented equally well in C, LISP, or Smalltalk. It can be implemented equally well on top of the Macintosh toolbox or a toolkit based on the X Window System. Because the details of the implementation are not specified, the implementer is free to apply judgment in any area in which the model is neutral.

A tool imposes many more constraints on the user than does a model. A tool embodies a model of a process, either implicitly or explicitly; it embodies a model of the user of the tool (as does any interactive system); it embodies a model of the system on which it is to be used (such as PAC); it works only in a particular set of environments; and it is open to criticisms based on implementation issues such as robustness and performance.

For these reasons, building a tool is much more difficult than defining a model. On the other hand, a good tool is much more useful than a model. Assuming that the implementation decisions are relevant to the user of the tool, much of the work involved in developing a working system has already been accomplished. Instead of having to first understand a model and then decide how to realize that model in the context of a particular system, the user of the tool need only understand the tool and how to use it. Understanding a good tool is easier than understanding a complicated model.

The point of this discussion is that a tool is judged on a different set of criteria than is a model. One set of questions to ask about a tool pertains to the underlying models: the process model (how is it used?) and the system model (what kind of system uses this tool?). Another set of questions pertains to the tool itself, implementation, and ease of use.

Models and Implementation Technology.   In general, there is not a direct mapping between models and implementation technologies. For example, although multiagent models may take advantage of the facilities provided by object-oriented languages, a PAC hierarchy should not be viewed as a hierarchy of classes.

Object-oriented languages provide techniques for conveniently realizing interaction objects, whereas a model such as PAC is a framework for distributing the notions of functional core, control, and presentation at various levels of abstraction. For example, wall agents, which are part of an environment, are subagents in the organization of the user interface. They may be implemented as instances of the class wall, which in turn may be viewed as a subclass of the class line, but certainly not as a specialized version of the class environment. To push further the distinction between an implementation technique and an abstract model, a PAC agent may be implemented as three separate objects or as a unique object that combines the three facets. The appropriate choice in a particular case depends on the programming tools and on the level of abstraction.

At the top level of abstraction, it is clear that the functional core is a distinct entity from the rest of the interactive system. On the other hand, at the bottom level, the decomposition into subagents may be bound by the facilities provided by the tools in the programming environment. For example, the presentation of a wall is implemented by combining the services provided by Xlib to draw the line and by the X Intrinsics to draw the hot spot and to control the appearance of the pop-up menu that lists the set of operations. If we had applied the model rigorously, the pop-up menu would have been designed as a subagent of the wall. The toolkit, however, provides a rather direct way of performing local subdialogues such as that of showing a pop-up menu when selecting a widget. This observation led us to stop the PAC decomposition at the wall level and associate the subdialogue managed by the pop-up menu with the presentation part of the wall.

Similarly, the MVC model stresses the coupling of objects of type model, view, and controller, but the Smalltalk programming environment does not enforce this strong relationship. Instead, the programmer is provided with distinct hierarchies for views, controllers, and models. The implementer can thus exploit the object-oriented facilities to define new classes of views and controllers by specialization. On the other hand, the MVC coupling must be performed by hand in the form of explicit references between a view, a controller, and a model.

5.7 Future

So far we have identified the foundations for dialogue control. The progress of the technology and increasing demands from operators are leading to further requirements and understanding in emerging areas such as cooperative dialogue, collaborative work, and multimodal interaction.

5.7.1 COOPERATIVE DIALOGUE

In general, interactive systems are still designed as tools—not as cooperative partners. For a collaboration to succeed, each partner must maintain a model about the other participants. An interactive system can be considered a collaborator if it maintains a dynamic model of the operator. Unfortunately, most dialogue controllers do not embed any such model.

One difficulty in embedding such a model is to identify which characteristics of the operator are pertinent to the accomplishment of a task: semantic knowledge, syntactic knowledge, physical limitations, problem-solving strategy, information retrieving? Once the operator's characteristics have been determined, the next problem is to dynamically maintain the model.

Dynamic maintenance of such a model involves automatic learning and inference as the operator uses the system. Indeed, data observed by a dialogue controller corresponds to high-level mental operations (such as commands). The dialogue controller should have ben ability to infer the intentions of the operator. An interesting side effect of this property is the automatic evaluation of the distance between the intention and the actual path followed by the operator. The difficulties encountered by the operator can then be automatically detected. The User Interface Design Environment (UIDE) [Foley et al. 1988] is an early step in this direction.

Cooperative dialogue and automatic checking of the psychological validity of a design require the integration of knowledge from multiple disciplines. More interdisciplinary efforts between computer science and cognitive psychology are needed to solve this problem.

5.7.2   GROUPWARE

Groupware refers to "software systems which support two or more, possibly simultaneous, users working on a common task and which provide an interface to a shared environment" [Gibbs 1989, p. 29]. Unlike systems such as database management systems, in which sharing is, for the most part, transparent, groupware makes sharing explicit to operators

The consequence of visible sharing is the design of WYSIWIS user interfaces (what you see is what I see). The concept of multiple views becomes general and distributed over a network. For example, a file may be represented as an icon on two distinct work stations. While one operator drags an icon into the trash, a second operator may simultaneously move the other icon in a different directory.

Concurrent access can be negotiated in a centralized way by the dialogue controller. As in single-user systems, interactive objects notify the dialogue controller of significant events. The dialogue controller, in turn, takes action on the semantic concept and on the other interactive objects representing the concept. Clearly, the implementation of such a mechanism can take advantage of the services provided by distributed object-oriented systems such as Guide [Krakowiak et al. 1990] and Emerald [Black, Hutchinson, and Levy, 1986].

Whereas software issues in groupware can exploit known solutions, models of group behaviour are just beginning to be investigated.

5.7.3   MULTIMODAL INTERACTION

Dialogue models must allow different modalities of interaction through multiple media: graphics, voice, gesture, natural language, and so forth. At present, these modalities cohabit side by side. They are only partially integrated; that is, at a given time, the operator can use only one of the modalities. The next step is to make all the modalities available concurrently. For example, it would be possible for the operator of the mobile robot to say "go here" while pointing with the finger at a location on a map drawn on the screen.

As mentioned in Chapter 4, toolkits are involved in the support for multimedia. The dialogue controller steps in at a higher level of abstraction, closer to domain knowledge. In particular, experience shows that the performance of natural language and speech recognition systems relies heavily on domain knowledge and contextual data. Such information lies naturally in a dialogue controller.

In summary, a dialogue controller should be able to support multiple functional cores, multiple users, and multiple media. No current dialogue controller can support all three, although research is ongoing in each area.

5.8 Summary

This chapter discussed the layer of software that controls the dialogue between the operator and the functional core. The discussion focused on four issues: the types of run-time support provided, the application programmer's interface, the model of dialogue assumed by the dialogue controller, and the architectural model of an interactive system. We looked at several different models for dialogue control and discussed in detail a particular multiagent model. Finally, we gave our views of important future issues.

6

User Interface
Management Systems

As we have seen in the preceding chapters, creating a user interface requires designing and developing both the user interface and the underlying software. A user interface management system (UIMS) is a tool or a set of integrated tools that supports some facet of these tasks. The ultimate goal of a UIMS is to facilitate the design, construction, evaluation, and maintenance of user interfaces. The term user interface development environment (UIDE) has also been used for such a tool set; we have chosen to use the term UIMS because of the large number of currently available systems that call themselves UIMSs. Given the diversity of these tools, however, we will identify and characterize the types of services that a user interface might receive from such a collection of tools in Section 6.1.

One type of service that is receiving increasing attention is the generation of user interfaces from high-level specifications. In Section 6.2 we will present the different approaches to the description of user interfaces and identify their respective strengths and weaknesses. We will then discuss a particular example of a UIMS: Serpent. We will close, as usual, with a discussion of human, engineering, and future issues.

6.1 Types of Services

The services of a UIMS can be classified as supporting the design, construction, evaluation, and/or maintenance of user interfaces. Tools that support design and evaluation are based on the models and concepts discussed in Chapter 2. Tools that support construction and maintenance are based on the models and concepts discussed in Chapters 3, 4, and 5.

We will now briefly consider tools that support each of the phases of the life cycle. Serpent, discussed in Section 6.3, attempts broader life cycle coverage.

6.1.1 DESIGN SERVICES

As we observed in Chapter 2, designing an interactive system involves multiple phases, including:

- Defining a model of the operator,
- Performing a task analysis,
- Defining computer objects that correspond to the task domain, and
- Defining the appearance and behavior of the user interface.

Each stage may be facilitated by suitable tools. In particular, defining a model of the operator and performing task analysis require conceptual and cognitive modeling notations such as Task Action Grammar (TAG) [Payne and Green 1986], Command Language Grammar (CLG) [Moran 1981], and Goal, Operator, Model Selection (GOMS) [Card, Moran, and Newell 1983]. TAG, CLG, and GOMS allow the designer to describe tasks at various levels of abstraction—from the conceptual semantic level to the lexical interaction level. Tools in this area are purely research vehicles for testing various notations and concepts; no task modeling tool is generally available.

The definition of computer objects may be supported by software engineering specification tools described in Davis [1990]. The definition of the user interface is supported with a class of tools called *rapid prototyping tools*. These tools allow the user interface to be specified graphically and may include a simulation or rehearsal facility so that dynamic behavior can be displayed [IEEE 1989].

6.1.2 CONSTRUCTION SERVICES

Since user interface software has a presentation component and a dialogue controller, tools for the construction of user interfaces can be classified according to which of the two aspects they support. Presentation tools include libraries of interaction object classes, resource editors, and presentation specification tools.

- Libraries of interaction objects were discussed in Chapter 4. They range from predefined sets of ready-to-use classes of interaction objects, such as X

Window System-based toolkits and Macintosh toolkits, to programmable constraint systems like Garnet.

☐ Resource editors allow for the definition and modification of the lexical items of a user interface: bit-map, cursor, font, and interaction object editors. Interaction object editors such as ResEdit in the Macintosh environment are useful in two ways. First, they can be used to define new instances from a predefined set of interaction object classes. Second, they can be used to modify the attributes of interaction objects, thus providing control over the initial layout of a display. One fundamental characteristic of resource editors is that they manipulate library items. The library items are passive and have no built-in knowledge of their client. Consequently, such editors are not useful for controlling the dynamic behavior of a user interface. One class of resource editor, called presentation specificiation tool, will be described in more detail in Section 6.2.

Dialogue control necessarily implies the existence of a run-time kernel. Its expression may be programmed by hand or supported by special-purpose specification tools.

☐ As described in Chapter 5, tools for run-time kernels range from reusable and extensible application skeletons to built-in dialogue controllers embedded in user interface generators. User interface generators hide their run-time kernel, whereas application skeletons make the dialogue controller explicit to the programmer.

☐ Dialogue specification tools provide the programmer with special-purpose languages to describe the control of the interaction. They are also a form of user interface generator.

The development of user interfaces is also facilitated by general-purpose software development tools such as debuggers and regression testers. A debugger provides for symbolic examination of an executing dialogue, and a regression tester provides a test set for testing modifications to the dialogue against known expectations.

6.1.3 EVALUATION SERVICES

As mentioned in Chapter 2, evaluation may be performed at various stages, particularly during the design phase or with a running prototype. The design of a user interface can be evaluated with cognitive modeling tools, as well as with more traditional tools developed in the area of computer science.

☐ Cognitive modeling tools such as programmable user models (PUM) [Young, Green, and Simon 1989] and External Task-Internal Task (ETIT) [Moran

1983] support the predictive evaluation of user interface designs. They tell the designer about the usability of a proposed design before it is actually built. A PUM "is a constrained cognitive architecture that can be programmed to simulate an hypothetical user performing some range of tasks with a proposed interface" [Young, Green, and Simon 1989, p. 15]. PUM uses a model of the operator as well as a representation of the tasks to be accomplished with a given user interface. The assumption is that if a PUM is not able to perform the required task, the actual operator will encounter problems with the real system. The prediction provided by ETIT and the "theory of complexity" of Kieras and Polson [1985] are based on an analysis of the mapping between mental tasks and the command space of the user interface.

- Evaluation tools developed in the area of computer science include loggers, simulators, and support for rehearsal. A logger records the physical actions of the operator. An analysis of the observed data may draw the designer's attention to the frequency of use of commands, error and keystroke rates, and effective operator planning (as opposed to the conceptual planning devised by the designers). Such real data may be used as input to predictive tools such as those discussed above. A simulator provides scenario-based output in response to user input. No actual function is performed in a simulator. A special kind of simulator, called a rehearsal tool, is used to test and train operators.

6.1.4 MAINTENANCE SERVICES

Maintenance to a fielded system can be categorized into:

- Correcting errors,
- Enhancing the system on the existing platform, and
- Modifying the system to execute on a different platform.

In general, maintaining a user interface requires the same types of services and methods as are needed to maintain any general-purpose software: version control, documentation, and so forth.

One major motivation for using the levels of abstraction developed in Chapters 3, 4, and 5 is to simplify the effort involved in the maintenance phase:

- Separating the concerns of the user interface from those of the functional core localizes user interface modifications to the presentation layer. Since these modifications are the ones most commonly made to a system, containing them to a few related modules is highly desirable.
- Making explicit the interface between the functional core and user interface software simplifies modifications that affect both components.

◻ Making the functional core media independent allows the fielded system to be transferred to a radically different platform with minimal effect on the functional core.

There are very few general-purpose tools specifically designed for the maintenance phase of user interface development. Since many of the details of user interface software depend on specific operator actions, regression testers that simulate operators are extremely useful. These regression testers are usually developed for specific interactive systems, however, rather than in a general form.

We will now discuss a particular class of specification tools: user interface generators.

6.2 User Interface Generators

A user interface generator automatically produces a user interface from a specification. Figure 5.3 showed the basic components of a user interface generator: a library of interaction objects, a run-time kernel, and a specification tool. Interaction objects were discussed in Chapter 4, and the role of the run-time kernel as a dialogue controller was presented in Chapter 5. In this section we focus on specification issues.

A user interface includes a description of the presentation as well as an expression of dialogue control. A presentation specification tool assists the user interface software designer in constructing static displays from a library of interaction objects and defining links between elements of the displays and the client program. A dialogue control specification tool allows the user interface implementer to describe how interaction objects will be managed. As Figure 6.1 shows, a third type of specification tool uses a high-level semantic description of the functional core to automatically generate the presentation and dialogue control.

We will successively define and evaluate the services provided by these three complementary types of tool.

6.2.1 PRESENTATION SPECIFICATION TOOLS

Definition. Presentation specification tools such as User Interface Manager for X (UIMX) [*Infoworld* 1989] and User Interface Language (UIL) [Open Software Foundation 1989] can be used to define static displays. The user interface software designer instantiates interaction objects from a predefined set of classes,

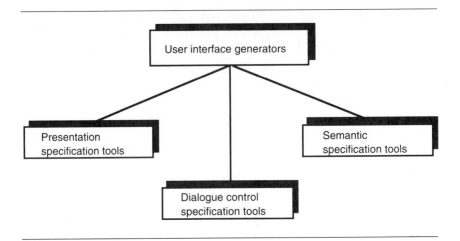

FIGURE 6.1
Different types of user interface generators. A tool can be used to specify the presentation, to specify the dialogue, or to automatically build the presentation and dialogue from a higher level semantic description.

sets their attributes, and defines links with the client programs in the form of callback procedures. Once a desired image has been achieved, a code skeleton is generated that includes the initialization of the interaction objects as well as the skeletons for the callback procedures. The software designer edits the code skeleton to provide for the correct action when the procedure is called and incorporates the completed code into the final interactive system.

Like resource editors, presentation specification tools require the user interface software designer to work at the lexical level of the interaction. Interaction objects produced with presentation specification tools may be linked to a particular client program. For example, in both UIMX and UIL, it is possible to specify the name of the callback procedure to be invoked when a type of event occurs for a particular interaction object.

Some presentation specification tools, such as UIL, are textual. The user interface software designer must learn a special-purpose language and can visualize the effects of the attribute settings only by coding, compiling, and executing the program. This is an awkward method of building static displays. Other presentation specification tools, such as UIMX, are interactive. These tools allow the software designer to describe the presentation through direct manipulation and evaluate the visual rendition of the user interface as it is built.

Strengths and Weaknesses.   To examine the positive and negative aspects of a presentation specification tool, we will return to the mobile robot example. Let us consider specifying the user interface that allows an operator to specify an environment. The user interface for this task has the initial layout shown in Figure 2.14, consisting of a palette and a work space. The palette presents the names of the domain-dependent concepts (such as walls and routes) in the form of physical buttons. The work space contains a menu bar and a graphical representation of the environment being edited.

The palette construction represents the strength of a presentation specification tool. A palette consists of a static collection of buttons. During the specification of an environment, the buttons do not change in number, content, or connection to semantic activities. The button is one of the general-purpose interaction objects contained in the toolkit used by the mobile robot. An interactive design tool allows the developer to see how the palette will appear to the operator (since it does not change during execution). It also allows the developer to connect the buttons to the appropriate action routines, since they do not change during the operator's specification of an environment.

The work space is declared to be a composite widget composed of a drawing area and a menu bar. The menu portion of the work space is defined in a straightforward way, since it can be expressed in terms of general-purpose interaction objects. On the other hand, the description of the content of the drawing area poses two problems:

1. The drawing area, which presents domain-dependent concepts, requires specific interaction objects that may not exist in the predefined set of interaction classes. In this case, the missing interaction object class must be explicitly coded in the client program.

2. The content of the drawing area evolves at run time as the operator edits the environment. For example, the creation of a wall involves selecting the "wall button" in the palette, then drawing the wall in the drawing area. The presentation specification tool provides the mechanism for recognizing which item on the palette has been selected, but it is the responsibility of the software designer to create the instance of the selected object and place it on the drawing area. If the operator subsequently moves the wall, it is the responsibility of the software designer to modify the position attributes of the wall and any other interaction objects attached to the wall.

The example of the mobile robot shows that presentation specification tools are very good for generating static components of a user interface, provided these components can be described with the set of predefined interaction object classes. On the other hand, presentation specification tools deal poorly with the dynamic behavior of components.

Defining special-purpose interaction objects and describing the dynamic behavior of interaction objects require programming in a usual programming language. In turn, programming requires that the developer know the underlying user interface toolkit and make the program conform to a sound architecture.

Presentation specification tools do not provide any architectural framework.

In particular, they do not enforce separation of concerns or media independence for the functional core. Callback procedures attached to interaction objects may mix domain-dependent computation with presentation-dependent features. Dialogue control specification tools, presented in the next section, alleviate this problem.

6.2.2   DIALOGUE CONTROL SPECIFICATION TOOLS

Definition.   Dialogue control specification tools provide the user interface software designer with a special-purpose language for specifying the sequencing rules for interaction objects. Sequencing rules cover a number of dynamic phenomena such as:

☐ The conditions for creating, deleting, and modifying interaction object instances,

☐ The conditions for screen mapping and unmapping of interaction objects, and

☐ Layout computation.

Ideally, a dialogue control specification language should support the requirements identified in Section 5.2. In practice, the options are to specify all the dialogue with a special-purpose language or to specify the dialogue with a combination of programming by demonstration and programming in a general-purpose language. Some UIMSs, such as Serpent, include a special-purpose language. Other tools, such as Interface Builder [Webster 1989] and HyperCard [Harvey 1988], combine programming by demonstration and programming with a general-purpose language.

Programming by demonstration in HyperCard and Interface Builder is limited to the specification of very simple sequencing conditions between interaction objects. Figures 6.2 to 6.5 illustrate the principles of programming by demonstration in HyperCard.

Let us suppose the user interface software designer wishes to link the arrow button shown in Figure 6.2 to the HyperCard HomeCard so that, at run time, when the operator selects the button, the current card is replaced with the HomeCard. To do so, the user interface designer requests that HyperCard provide the properties of the arrow button. In the property list shown in Figure 6.3, the designer selects the "LinkTo..." button. A dialogue box pops up (see Figure 6.4).

The user interface software designer can now look for the desired card by browsing through HyperCard stacks with special commands (not shown here). When the HomeCard is reached, the "This Card" button is selected in the dialogue box (see Figure 6.5). The "LinkTo..." command now having been completed, the dialogue box disappears and the system image returns to the initial state shown in Figure 6.2.

FIGURE 6.2
The arrow button to be linked to the HomeCard.

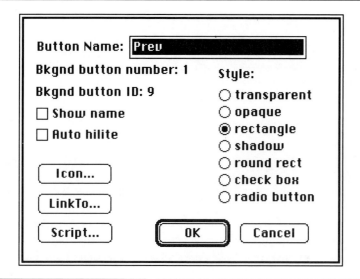

FIGURE 6.3
The property list of the arrow button. It allows the oerator to modify style or other properties.

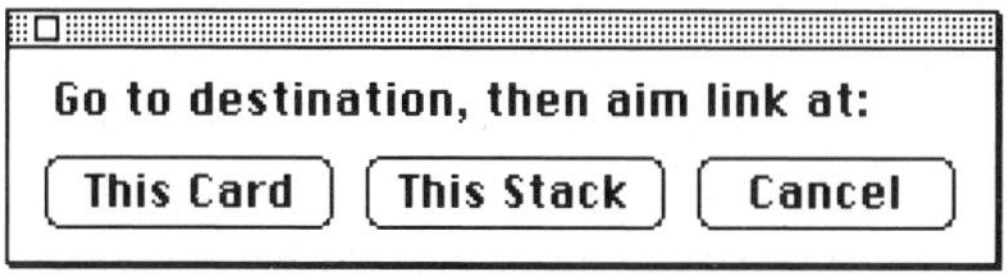

Go to destination, then aim link at:

This Card | This Stack | Cancel

FIGURE 6.4
The "LinkTo" dialogue box allows the operator to specify the target of the arrow button.

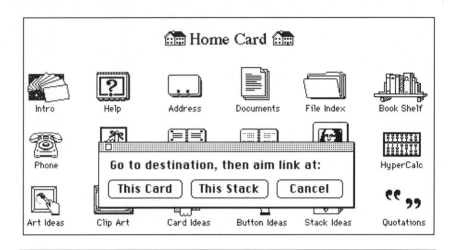

FIGURE 6.5
Selection of the destination card. All the possible targets are represented, and the
operator chooses the one desired.

In this method of programming, code is produced by demonstration. In the
particular case of the "LinkTo" demonstration, HyperTalk code is automatically
produced, gathered in a script, and attached to the interaction object involved in
the demonstration. Figure 6.6 shows the arrow button script resulting from the
"LinkTo" demonstration: when the arrow button receives a "mouseup" event,
control should be passed to the card whose internal identification, 5341, denotes
the HomeCard.

Interface Builder has a similar mechanism for creating simple links. In most
cases, dialogue control must be specified with a general-purpose language:
HyperTalk for HyperCard or Objective C for Interface Builder.

Strengths and Weaknesses.   The strengths of a special-purpose language for
describing dialogue control are as follows:

- It enforces the separation of concerns between the nature of presentation
  techniques and their dynamic relations. This separation greatly enhances
  iterative refinement. It makes possible the programming of different run-
  time behaviors for the same instances of presentation objects.

- It allows the run-time system to automatically determine and enforce the
  relationships between application data and interaction objects and among
  interaction objects themselves.

```
Script of bkgnd button id 9 = "Prev"

on mouseUp
  go to card id 5341
end mouseUp
|
```

FIGURE 6.6
The arrow button script resulting from the "LinkTo..." demonstration. The script is in HyperTalk. Any more sophisticated manipulations must be coded in HyperTalk directly.

The weakness of special-purpose dialogue specification tools is that even simple relationships such as sequencing must be specified textually.

The strength of the mixed programming by example and general-purpose language is that the user interface software designer can specify simple relationships using direct manipulation rather than text. Thus, some relationships can be determined and enforced by the run-time system. One weakness of this approach is that when the relationships are too complicated to be expressed by demonstration, concerns can be intermixed. Also, the user interface software designer must explicitly manage the interaction objects.

Since the strengths and weaknesses of the two approaches are complementary, it follows that a system combining the two approaches should yield the benefits of both. No such system has yet emerged.

So far, we have presented two basic complementary specification types of tools. We now discuss a third approach that implicitly conveys both presentation and dialogue control issues: semantic specification tools.

6.2.3   SEMANTIC SPECIFICATION TOOLS

Definition.   A number of UIMSs, such as Mickey [Olsen 1989], the User Interface Design Environment (UIDE) [Foley et al. 1988], MacIda UIMS [Petoud and Pigneur 1990], and Interactive Transaction System (ITS) [Bennett et al. 1989], are able to derive the presentation and the dialogue control from the specification of the interface between the functional core and the user interface. This specification, expressed with a special-purpose language, describes the semantics of the functional core with regard to the user interface. It includes the definition of high-level data structures and functions, along with the preconditions and postconditions of activation. For example, in the case of the mobile robot system, data structures for walls, routes, and environments would be declared, as well as their corresponding operations. The precondition for the operation "create a mission" would be "the number of environments is greater than 0."

The generation of the presentation relies mainly on a mapping function, which associates data types with classes of interaction objects. For example, an enumerate data type would be presented as a menu of radio buttons. This correspondence may be encoded by the tool, as in MacIda UIMS, or it may be controlled by the user interface designer, as in ITS. Specification provides the designer with more flexibility. In particular, the correspondence between functional core data and presentation objects may be defined by a specialist in human factors and cognitive psychology. This correspondence would, of course, be in accordance with the particular task domain, but it would also integrate general consistency rules. For example, the user interface designer might specify that menus of a certain type always occur on the left and that the "Quit" command always be the last choice on the leftmost menu.

The generation of dialogue control is inferred from the preconditions and postconditions, as well as from the name and type of the operations. For example, an operation is made available to the operator as soon as its precondition is satisfied, and the operation is invoked when its parameters are specified.

Strengths and Weaknesses.   In contrast to the presentation and dialogue tools, which require the user interface software designer to work at the syntactic and lexical levels, semantic specification tools provide a higher level conceptual framework, which guarantees media independence for the functional core.

High-level semantic specification may be exploited in two ways: to make the current state of the system explicit and to generate help. As illustrated in Figure 6.7, MacIda UIMS is able to produce and dynamically maintain a graph that shows what the user has done and what needs to be done to accomplish a task. This graph is automatically derived from the specification of the control flow, which expresses the logical functioning of the functional core. This graph is a good example of how to support the evaluation stage and the elaboration of the plan of actions stage identified in Chapter 2.

For planning automatic help, Senay, Sukaviriya, and Moran [1990] describe how preconditions and postconditions may be used as items in add lists and delete lists of a Stanford Research Institute Problem Solver (STRIPS)-like planner [Fikes and Nilsson 1971]. Once a plan is generated, it can be used to provide procedural help within the operator's current context through various representation techniques such as graphical animated help [Sukaviriya 1988].

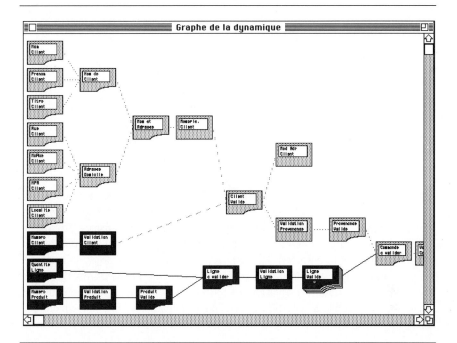

FIGURE 6.7
An example from MacIda UIMS. The graph shows what the operator has done (dark icons) and what needs to be done to accomplish a task (light icons). Icons with broken corners denote data structures, whereas the others represent operations.

The encapsulation provided by high-level specification tools has its drawbacks. In particular, the user interface software designer has no control over either dialogue flow or presentation techniques. In some circumstances it may be desirable to have access to a meta language in order to modify the built-in strategies. ITS is an interesting attempt in this direction.

Another problem related to flexibility (but not confined to semantic specification tools) concerns the set of predefined classes of interaction objects. Interaction objects available in UIMSs are general-purpose entities that may not appropriately convey the semantics of a particular domain concept. One solution is to build a new interaction object, which is a tedious programming task. The alternative is to use the technique pioneered by HyperCard. In HyperCard, drawing and programming activities are combined in a powerful manner. The static output aspect of an interaction object is defined by drawing, whereas the dynamic behavior is expressed in a HyperTalk script [Shafer 1988] associated with the object. An example of the use of HyperCard is provided in Appendix C. Although Hyper-

Card makes possible the animation of images, it does not allow the creation of new classes of interaction objects.

Having presented the types of tools available for specifying user interfaces, we now describe a particular UIMS, Serpent, and show how it deals with the problems identified so far.

6.3   An Example: Serpent

Serpent is a UIMS that has an integrated dialogue specification mechanism and presentation tool. The dialogue specification mechanism is a special language that generates a dialogue controller. The dialogue controller uses a production model to implement the multiagents discussed in Section 5.4.2 and uses a constraint mechanism to enforce relationships among interaction objects. Serpent is designed not only to support the separation of the functional core from the toolkit layer, but also to integrate a variety of toolkits. In order to make the examples concrete, we will use a specific toolkit—the Athena toolkit. In subsequent sections, we will discuss:

- The specification mechanism of Serpent,
- Serpent's interface with the functional core,
- How Serpent supports the inclusion of different types of toolkits,
- The use of Serpent within the life cycle of an interactive system, and
- The relationship between Serpent and abstract models.

6.3.1   SERPENT'S DIALOGUE SPECIFICATION MECHANISM

Slang, Serpent's language for specifying dialogue, is based on the production model. Programs in Slang are collections of "if *condition* then *action*" statements. Slang also uses constraints (see Section 4.3.3) as a method for specifying relationships between domain objects and interaction objects and among various interaction objects. Slang is designed for use by both the user interface designer and the user interface software designer. Simple interactions are easy to specify; when the user interface designer wishes to specify more complex interactions, more complicated Slang concepts must be used.

Our presentation of Slang will begin with the mechanisms for specifying interfaces with a fixed collection of objects. We will then discuss the mechanisms for creating and destroying objects. The latter mechanisms use more complicated production system concepts.

A Simple User Interface.   Figure 6.8 shows two buttons displayed on a screen. The number button, initially set to zero, is incremented whenever the "Push" button is selected. Figure 6.9 gives the Slang program that produces the interface in Figure 6.8. This very simple program demonstrates several features of Slang.

- ☐ Interaction objects in a Slang program are enumerated together with their attributes and methods. The attributes define the presentation, and the methods specify the reaction to operator actions. The example includes three interaction objects: a form that acts as the background, a button that displays the numerical value, and a button that says "Push." The "Push" button has a method, which responds to selection events.

- ☐ Slang allows the specifier to declare local variables. In the example, the local variable counter keeps track of the number of times the "Push" button has been selected.

- ☐ Slang embeds a constraint mechanism. In the example, the attribute label_text of counter_button is constrained to be the same as the variable counter. Whenever counter is modified, label_text is automatically modified by the Serpent run-time system. This use of constraints means that no flow-of-control statement needs to be specified in order to change the value of label_text. In general, Slang programs are declarative in style rather than procedural; that is, they specify *what* is to be done rather than *how* it is to be done.

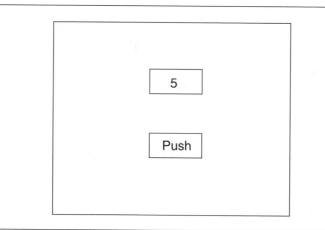

FIGURE 6.8
A two-button user interface built with Serpent, with no dynamic creation of interaction objects. Each time the button labeled "Push" is selected, the number is incremented.

```
VARIABLES:
  counter :  0;
OBJECTS:
  display:  label_widget
    ATTRIBUTES:
    . . .
    label_text:  counter;


  push_button:  command_widget
    ATTRIBUTES:
    . . .
    label_text:  "PUSH";


  METHODS:
    notify:
      counter  := counter + 1;
```

FIGURE 6.9
The Slang program corresponding to the example in Figure 6.8. Three different
objects are used: a background form, a label_widget, and a command_widget.
The local variable counter keeps track of how many times the command_widget
has been selected.

☐   Slang supports dynamic type conversion. None of the local variables or
    expressions within Slang are explicitly typed. All the types are dynamically
    calculated. In the example, the variable counter is maintained as an integer
    and can be incremented in the method. The attribute label_text, however, is
    a string. The conversion from integer representation to string representation
    is handled automatically by the run-time system. The dialogue specifier
    does not need to understand type systems in order to specify and execute
    simple Slang programs.

Creation and Destruction of Object Instances.   In the previous example, the user
interface was built from a fixed collection of objects. In Serpent, the dynamic
creation or destruction of objects is expressed via view controllers. A *view
controller* includes a set of components and a condition under which it is
instantiated. Components may be interaction objects or other view controllers.
When the condition becomes true, the view controller is instantiated. In turn, the
instantiation of the view controller provokes the instantiation of its components.
When the condition becomes false, the view controller instance and the associ-

ated component instances are destroyed. View controllers are the manifestation of the production system model used by Serpent.

Figure 6.10(a) shows a drop-down style menu. Selection of the "Colors" button results in the screen shown in Figure 6.10(b). Figure 6.11 presents the Slang program that specifies this sequence of behavior.

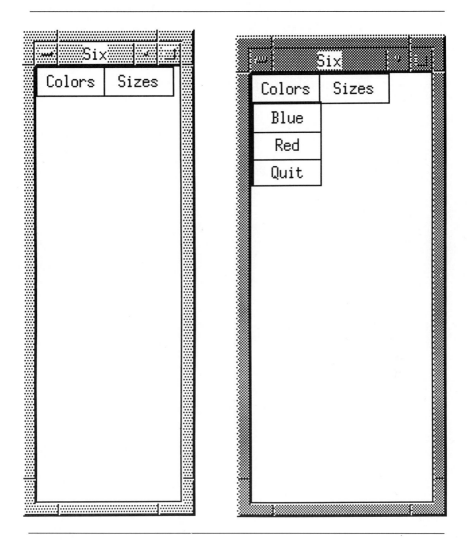

FIGURE 6.10
(a) A drop-down style menu built with Serpent; (b) the color menu generated after the selection of the "Colors" button.

```
#include "sat.ill"

III

/*  This program demonstrates the concept of view controllers with
instantiation conditions.  Initially a menu bar is placed along the top of the
screen with two push buttons labelled Colors and Sizes.  When the Colors
button is selected the view controlled named colors_sub_menu is instantiated
along with its objects and a menu containing RED and BLUE appears.*/


    VARIABLES:
     /* the two variables control the instantiation of the menus */

     display_colors_submenu : FALSE;
     display_sizes_submenu : FALSE;

    OBJECTS:

/* the three objects initially visible to the operator are the background
form and the two buttons forming the menu*/

    menu_bar_form: Xawform
      {ATTRIBUTES:
        height: 500;
        width: 500;
      }

    colors_menu_item: XawCommand
      {ATTRIBUTES:
        parent: menu_bar_form;
        horizdistance: 0;
        vertdistance: 0;
        height: 20;
        width: 50;
        label: "Colors";

      /* the notify method is informed when the operator selects this
      button*/

      METHODS:
        notify: {
          display_colors_submenu := TRUE;
          }
      }
```

FIGURE 6.11
The Slang program for the drop-down style menu infigure 6.10. Separate view
controllers are used to generate the drop-down menus. Instances of these view
controllers are created when the appropriate variables are set to TRUE.

```
sizes_menu_item: XawCommand
  {ATTRIBUTES:
    parent: menu_bar_form;
    horizdistance: 50;
    vertdistance: 0;
    height: 20;
    width: 50;
    label: "Sizes";

  METHODS:
    notify: {
      display_sizes_submenu := TRUE;
        }
    }
```

/* the following view controller controls the instantiation of the colors
menu. It is controlled by the boolean variable display_colors_submenu that is
initially FALSE and is set to TRUE when the operator selects the Colors
button*/

```
VC: colors_sub_menu
  CREATION CONDITION: (display_colors_submenu)

  OBJECTS:

    color_menu_form: Xawform
      {ATTRIBUTES:
        parent: menu_bar_form;
        horizdistance: 0;
        vertdistance : 20;
        height: 60;
        width: 50;
        }

    blue_menu_item: XawCommand
      {ATTRIBUTES:
        parent: color_menu_form;
        horizdistance: 0;
        vertdistance: 0;
        height: 20;
        width: 50;
        label: "Blue";

      METHODS:
        notify: {
          /*  This method is executed when the end user
              selects the blue_menu_item command widget*/
              }
        }
```

FIGURE 6.11
(continued)

```
red_menu_item: XawCommand
    {ATTRIBUTES:
      parent: color_menu_form;
      horizdistance: 0;
      vertdistance: 20;
      height: 20;
      width: 50;
      label: "Red";

    METHODS:
      notify: {
        /*   This method is executed when the end user
        selects the red_menu_item command widget*/
        }
      }

white_menu_item: XawCommand
    {ATTRIBUTES:
      parent: color_menu_form;
      horizdistance: 0;
      vertdistance: 40;
      height: 20;
      width: 50;
      label: "Quit";

    METHODS:
      notify: {
        display_colors_submenu := FALSE;
        }
      }
ENDVC colors_submenu
```

FIGURE 6.11
(continued)

Notice that the local variable display_colors_submenu in Figure 6.11 is initialized to FALSE and is set to TRUE when the "Colors" button is selected. The colors view controller contains the interaction objects that provide the operator with the color options. Thus, when the creation condition of the view controller is realized, the view controller and the embodied interaction objects are all instantiated. When the "Quit" button is selected, the variable display_colors_submenu is set to FALSE, the creation condition becomes untrue (via the constraint mechanism), and the view controller instance and the associated object instances are destroyed. This use of view controllers as instantiation mechanisms becomes powerful when used in conjunction with instances of functional core data. This mechanism is described in the next section.

6.3.2   SERPENT'S INTERFACE WITH THE FUNCTIONAL CORE

Serpent communicates with the functional core through a collection of shared data. This common database has an independent existence. Thus, the interface between Serpent and the functional core is not embedded within parameters of function calls such as callback procedures; it is an explicit declarative interface. The virtues of an explicit declarative interface include the following:

☐ The functional core software designer and the user interface software designer must agree on the information to be available to the operator. They must also agree on the semantic level of commands that can be returned to the functional core. This provides a design-time contract that can be used in error detection and management of subsequent modifications.

☐ Instances of functional core data can be used as the basis for multiple views. Serpent can update multiple interaction objects that depend on a single instance of functional core data (again, using the constraint mechanism).

☐ The functional core can be written in the language the designer prefers. Serpent supports functional cores written in either C or Ada.

The interface between Serpent and the functional core is expressed in a database schema-like language. The specification consists of a list of records, where each record defines a type of shared data. Figure 6.12 shows a portion of the specification for the interface between Serpent and the functional core of a calendar program. As shown in Figure 6.13, the calendar program saves dates and activities.

The interface between Serpent and the functional core for the calendar consists of two classes of data:

1. Data transferred by the functional core to Serpent, such as current appointments for each date, and

2. Data returned from Serpent to the functional core, such as modified and new appointments.

The functional core views Serpent as an active database. The functional core has the ability to create, modify, and destroy instances of shared data. It is also informed of the creation, modification, and deletion of these instances by Serpent. Following are some of the primitives that the functional core can call to communicate and retrieve shared data:

☐ Create transaction

☐ Create instance of record

Calendar: shared data

Appts: record

year:	integer;	! year of entry
month:	integer;	!month of entry
day:	integer;	!day of entry
mid:	string[20];	!midnight appointment
half_twelve	string[20];	!12:30 appointment
.		
.		
.		rest of day

end record;

Command: record

comm:	string[20];	!end user command

end record

end shared data;

FIGURE 6.12
An example of specification of the interface between the functional core and Serpent. The data that constitute the interface consist of a set of dates, times, and associated text. This is the contract that defines the exchanges between the functional core and the user interface software.

- Destroy instance of record
- Add to transaction/modify/delete data for particular instance
- Wait for transaction
- Retrieve type of activity to instance (creation, deletion, or modification)
- Retrieve modifications for a particular instance

Figure 6.14 shows how the constraint mechanism offered by Serpent can be exploited. In this example, the operator is able to construct an arbitrary arithmetic expression, which can be arranged geometrically on the display. The operator chooses arithmetic operators and arguments from a menu and connects them using the connect command. The connection of the output of an arithmetic operator, the input of another operator, or the connection of an argument to the input of an arithmetic operator is displayed by connecting lines. Once an arithmetic operator and an argument are linked, any movement of one of them will result in the automatic adjustment of the connecting lines.

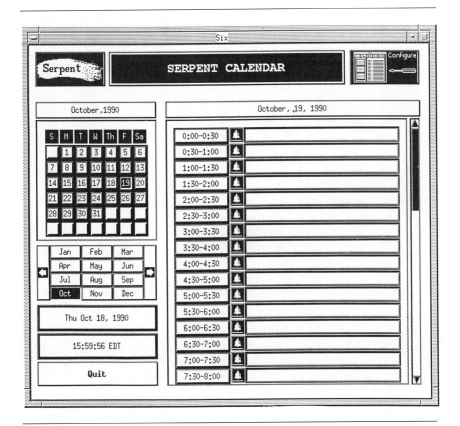

FIGURE 6.13
An interface for a calendar program generated with Serpent. The operator can enter appointments and activities at different times for each date.

The Slang program for Figure 6.14 contains data that define each line, together with its start position and its end position. When an arithmetic operator or an operand is moved, the line's new position is propagated to the data. The constraint mechanism recalculates and redraws the line. Again, the change in position causes the line to be redrawn automatically, without any explicit flow-of-control specification in the Slang program. The line is specified to be dependent on a particular piece of data, the data are specified to be dependent on a position, and any modification to the position causes the line to be updated.

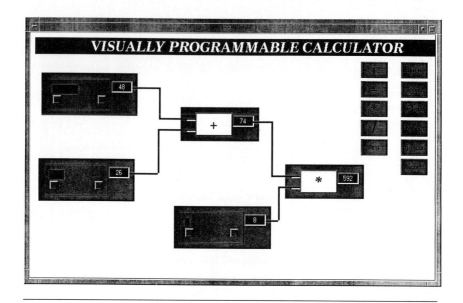

FIGURE 6.14
The constraint mechanism in Serpent maintains the lines in the correct positions whenever the arithmetic operators or arguments are moved. The constraint mechanism is also used to maintain the correct values whenever one of the arguments is modified.

6.3.3   SERPENT AND TOOLKITS

Serpent is intended to remove the functional core, as well as Slang, from any dependence on a particular toolkit or even a particular medium. For this purpose, Serpent uses an explicit interface with the underlying toolkit. The interaction objects within a toolkit are enumerated with the same explicit interface mechanism that is used to communicate with the functional core.

A particular Slang program declares which toolkit(s) it is using and enumerates interaction objects from this (those) toolkit(s) within view controllers. Although the Slang language is itself toolkit independent, a Slang program captures all the dependencies in the use of a particular toolkit. When a new toolkit is to be used, only the Slang program must be modified.

The toolkit integrator must choose the methods that are available for a particular presentation object type. In particular, using compound objects that are not directly supported in the toolkit creates problems with feedback. For example, if two objects are grouped for moving together, each object is responsible for its own feedback when it is moved—there is only individual object feedback, no compound object feedback. The solution is to implement within the toolkit the concept of compound object feedback, but this complicates the integration process.

6.3.4   SERPENT WITHIN THE LIFE CYCLE

Serpent is useful as a prototyping tool as well as a production tool. User interfaces can be built quickly from a specification, and the specification of a user interface is compiled into an executable code, which can be linked to an actual functional core. This use of the same tool for both phases of the life cycle of an application system has the following advantages:

 ☐   Incremental development of the user interface from the prototype into the actual product is possible. If different tools are used for prototyping and production and if there is no interchange mechanism between them, it is impossible for the prototype to evolve into the actual product. The prototype must be used strictly as a specification mechanism, then thrown away.

 ☐   The prototype is necessarily implementable. If different tools are used for prototyping and production, there is no guarantee that the interface designed by the user interface designer can be implemented easily. Since, with Serpent, the same tool is used for both functions, it is not possible to create a prototype interface that cannot be turned into an actual product.

6.3.5   SERPENT AND ABSTRACT MODELS

Section 5.4.2 introduced the multiagent model as a means for developing modular user interface software. Serpent can be seen as an application of the multiagent model. An agent is characterized by an internal state, and it has event receivers and event transmitters. In Serpent, these concepts are all embodied in the notion of a view controller. Each view controller may contain local variables to maintain state. Each view controller responds independently to events directed to its components and each component has attributes that, when modified, transmit events to the underlying toolkit.

   View controllers can be nested so the hierarchy of multiple agents discussed in Section 5.4.2 is also captured in Serpent. At an abstract level, Serpent can be viewed as an implementation of the multiagent model, together with the use of a constraint mechanism to propagate events.

   One way of looking at Serpent is as a method for mapping between disparate collections of objects in an object-oriented system. In order for communicating to take place between an object specialized in the functional domain and a user interface object, either the two objects must communicate directly, which would violate the separation of concerns, or the two objects must communicate through a mediator. This mediator is what we have called a dialogue controller. Serpent then becomes a programmable mediator between disparate collections of objects.

6.4   Human Issues

In general, tools enable certain operator behaviors, are neutral toward other behaviors, and inhibit certain behaviors. In this section we discuss the types of tools available for constructing user interfaces in terms of their effect on behavior. We consider window systems, toolkits, interactive design tools, and user interface management systems.

□ Window systems enable the operator to perform multiple tasks more simply. They do this by managing the screen resource so that the outputs of multiple processes are visible simultaneously. Window systems do not, by themselves, have much impact on the quality or cost of developing a user interface. Since the level of abstraction of a window system is approximately that of the graphic systems that have been available for about a decade, window systems are not going to enable major advances without other layers on top of them.

□ Toolkits enable user interface software designers to construct static interfaces, but only after an extensive learning phase. Because of the reusability of interaction object libraries, interaction objects such as menus and buttons are generally available. Dynamic interfaces involving existing interaction objects are also enabled by toolkits, although the user interface software designer must use appropriate software architectures and must manage the interaction objects without assistance.

□ Presentation specification tools enable designers to construct static interfaces without the extensive learning phase required when a toolkit is used directly. Designers still must learn to use the toolkit in order to create dynamic interfaces, which cannot be constructed with a presentation specification tool. These tools are neutral as to software architectures.

□ User interface management systems enable designers to create dynamic interfaces and use appropriate software architectures. To do so, designers must learn a specialized language or a specialized tool.

User interface specification tools all rely on a set of predefined classes of interaction objects. These libraries have the advantage of defining a consistent style of interaction; however, they support only a limited number of styles. In particular, they do not include facilities for direct manipulation: no support for rubber banding, no mechanism for overlapping or dragging objects across window boundaries. Consequently, the tendency is to replace a difficult-to-express design with a straightforward solution that may not fit the operator's expectation. For example, in the very first version of the mobile robot system, because of the difficulty of generating the desired user interface, the characteristics of walls, such as location and size, were specified in a property sheet rather than through direct manipulation. In subsequent versions, direct manipulation was used; its cost was outweighed by the advantages of the higher quality interface.

Clearly, the final interface represents a compromise between the ideal user interface and the user interface that is most easily constructed. Using a tool for constructing a portion of the user interface makes certain functionalities easy to construct and makes others more difficult to construct.

6.5   Engineering Issues

Very few UIMSs are available for general use. Most of these focus on presentation specification; a few focus on dialogue specification. In any case, UIMSs clearly provide useful support for the development of user interface software. The appropriateness of a particular UIMS depends on the type of user interface to be constructed. The available tools vary in their ability to support different types of construction.

Once a UIMS is identified as providing the desired class of services, the effect of how those services are delivered on the life cycle of the user interface must be analyzed. Since user interfaces are best developed in an iterative fashion, it is desirable to have all of the services integrated in one tool.

Finally, how a particular service is delivered can be examined. We identified a number of evaluation criteria for window systems, interaction objects, and dialogue controllers. Additional criteria are:

▫   How well does the UIMS support the desired architectural model at run time?

▫   How well does the UIMS support the desired types of interfaces?

▫   How well does the UIMS support its operator?

This last point is worth pursuing in slightly more detail. A user interface specification tool has its own user interface, which can be evaluated both for how well it performs its task and for how friendly it is to its operator. Specification tools take different views as to how best to specify a user interface. Some questions to ask are:

▫   How are full-screen user interfaces specified? They typically are difficult to describe, since the user interface of the tool per se consumes screen space.

☐ What facilities does the tool provide for the management of generated user interfaces? Some tools expose the underlying operating system file structure, so the operator must navigate within a directory system; others provide a collection of folders and facilities for managing those folders within the tool.

☐ How extensive are the rehearsal facilities? The software designer should be able to run the interfaces at some level to gain an understanding of the dynamic nature of the interfaces.

We saw in the mobile robot example that one of the first steps in designing the user interface was to change the design to accommodate available technology. User interface design is a trade-off between what is best for the operator and what is best for the designers and implementers of the system. Given the current types of tools, choosing a UIMS involves making compromises between what is desired and what is available.

6.6   Future

Current tools for developing user interfaces put the emphasis on toolkits. They facilitate the production of interactive software, but they do not provide support for the design and evaluation phases or for appropriate software architectures. In the UIMS of the future, we will see both improvement of current techniques and integration of interdisciplinary knowledge. Such combined efforts will have an impact on every phase of the life cycle of user interfaces and will affect every level of abstraction of interactive systems.

6.6.1   INTERDISCIPLINARY EFFORTS

The design and evaluation phases of the user interface life cycle are just beginning to be examined by computer scientists. Closer integration of results in cognitive psychology with those in computer science is necessary both to advance the state of the art in cognitive psychology and to communicate those advances to software developers.

For example, design tools developed in cognitive psychology, such as TAG, CLG, and GOMS, are useful modeling frameworks for task analysis but are representational systems only. They stress the hierarchical decomposition of the task domain, but they do not support task decomposition itself. Similarly, PUM does not provide any solutions—it only makes a predictive evaluation of usability.

Just as task analysis would be significantly enhanced by decision support and predictive evaluation tools, so would the specification of the user interface.

Current specification tools do not offer the user interface software designer any solution, nor do they evaluate the resulting design. High-level semantic description tools such as UIDE [Foley 1988], however, set the foundations for predictive evaluation.

Predictive evaluation performed at the design stage could be associated with run-time deductive evaluation. The latter would be based on automatic measuring of the operator's performance. Currently operator performance is usually captured through modeling and analyzing keystrokes. A high-level specification mechanism, such as that offered by Serpent, allows automatic capturing of operator's actions at a level of abstraction higher than that of keystrokes. In particular, the system could observe the sequence of commands invoked by the operator and from that infer the operator's intentions; the system could then evaluate the discrepancy between the system commands and the mental task planning. This evaluation would identify the difficulties the operator faced; it would also provide the designer with an explanation of the source of the problems. In summary, current log systems need to switch from keystroke level to mental-task level and be completed with a reasoning and modeling process such as that embedded in PUM.

6.6.2 IMPROVEMENT OF COMPUTER SCIENCE TECHNIQUES

Multifunctionality will affect the levels of abstraction of user interfaces, including toolkits for supporting multimedia user interfaces and dialogue controllers for implementing multi-user collaborative systems and for connecting multiple functional cores. This achievement will in turn have an impact on specification tools. Some authoring systems like HyperCard are already able to take multiple media into account, but for output only.

In addition to supporting multifunctionality, computer scientists will continue to work on mastering currently experimental ideas, such as:

- Integrating the presentation and dialogue control specification tools,
- Improving the techniques for defining new interaction objects,
- Defining facilities for general-purpose services such as undo-redo, cut-and-paste, and help, and
- Standardizing the interface with functional cores.

6.7 Summary

In this chapter we discussed the types of tools that are available to support the design, construction, and maintenance of user interfaces. We focused on presentation specification and dialogue specification as the two areas in which tools are currently available.

We hope that we have provided a useful categorization of software tools for user interface development and have shown the relationship between those tools and the requirements for developing useful and functional user interfaces.

The field of user interfaces is in its infancy. Some of the components of an ultimate environment for user interface development are visible, but none is even close to realization. This provides an exciting opportunity to make substantial progress in an area that intimately affects how people interact with, and hence use, computers.

A

A Simple Draw Program Using Xlib

A.1 The User Interface

Chapter 3 described general concepts related to windowing systems. In this appendix, we provide a detailed example of a simple draw program implemented with the primitives provided by Xlib.

Figure A.1 presents the program. Figure A.2 shows the initial picture of the screen. Pressing any key terminates the program. Pressing any mouse button while the mouse is inside the window moves the line to the right.

```
/****************************************************************************
This is a simple example for experimenting
           - window creation
           - basic graphics primitives
           - event mechanism
in X windows.
****************************************************************************/
#include <stdio.h>
#include <X11/Xlib.h>
```

FIGURE A.1
The draw program using XLib.

```
#include <X11/Xutil.h>
main(argc,argv)
    int argc;
    char **argv;
{
    Display *display;                              /* to denote the workstation */
    int screen;                                    /* screen ID of display */
    Window   window;                               /* window ID */
    unsigned int width, height;                    /* window width and height */
     int x = 50, y = 50 ;                          /* window position */
    unsigned long borderwidth = 4;                 /* window border width */
    char *windowname = "My Full Window";
    char *iconname = "My Iconized Window";
    GC gcxor;                                      /* GC to draw in XOR mode */
    XGCValues  gcvalues;                           /* struct for creating GC */
    unsigned long valuemask = 0;                   /* use defaults */
    XEvent event;                                  /* event received */
    XSizeHints sizehints;                          /* size hints for window manager*/

    /* The following initial values should be declared in a resource file
    */
     /* width and height of the rectangle */
     /* position of the rectangle */
    /* initial location of the line */
    unsigned int widthrect=100, heightrect=100;
     int xrect=10, yrect=10;
     int x1=15, y1=0, x2=0, y2=15;

printf("debut\n");

    /*
    * Open the display using the $DISPLAY environment variable to locate
    * the X server.
    */

    if ((display = XOpenDisplay(NULL)) == NULL)
      {
      fprintf(stderr, "%s: can't open %s\n", argv[0],
      XDisplayName(NULL));
      exit(1);
      }

    /*
     * Get screen Id
    */

    screen = DefaultScreen(display);
     /*
```

```
 * Compute window size based on screen size
 */

width = DisplayWidth (display, screen)/3;
 height = DisplayHeight (display, screen)/3;

/*
 * Create the opaque window as a sibling of RootWindow with a
 * black border and a white background.
 */

window = XCreateSimpleWindow(display, DefaultRootWindow(display),
                            x, y, width, height, borderwidth,
                            BlackPixel (display, screen),
                            WhitePixel (display, screen));

/*
 * Initialize size hint property for window manager.
 * flags : marks the relevent items of the structure.
 * PPosition -> window location is set by program.
 * PSize -> window size is set by program.
 * PMinSize -> minimum size for window is set by program.
 */

sizehints.flags = PPosition | PSize | PMinSize ;
sizehints.x = x;
sizehints.y = y;
sizehints.width = width;
sizehints.height = height;
sizehints.min_width = 100;
sizehints.min_height = 100;

/*
 * Always set the minimum properties for window manager
 *  before mapping the window.
 */

XSetStandardProperties( display, window, windowname, iconname,
                       None, /* no pixmap for icon */,
                       argv, argc, &sizehints);

/*
 * Select event types wanted
 */

XSelectInput (display, window,
             ExposureMask | KeyPressMask |ButtonPressMask);
```

FIGURE A.1
(continued)

```
/*
 * Create the graphic context to draw graphics.
 * Specify black foreground since default may be white on white.
 * Draw in XOR mode.
 */

    gcxor = XCreateGC(display, window, valuemask, &gcvalues);
    XSetForeground(display, gcxor, BlackPixel(display, screen));
    XSetFunction(display, gcxor, GXxor);

    /*
     * Map the window to make it visible.
     */

    XMapWindow(display, window);

    /*
     * Loop forever, examining each event.
     * Use first Expose to display graphics.
     * KeyPress to exit, ButtonPress to move a line.
     */

    while (1) {XNextEvent(display, &event);
        switch (event.type) {
        case Expose:
            /* get rid of all other expose events on the queue */
            while (XCheckTypedEvent(display, Expose, &event));
            XDrawRectangle (display, window, gcxor, xrect, yrect, widthrect,
                            heightrect);
            XDrawLine (display, window, gcxor, x1, y1, x2, y2);
            break;
        case ButtonPress:
            /* erase old line */
            XDrawLine (display, window, gcxor, x1, y1, x2, y2);
            /* move the line */
            x1 += 10; y2 += 10;
            /* draw the line at new location */
            XDrawLine (display, window, gcxor, x1, y1, x2, y2); break;
        case KeyPress:
            XCloseDisplay (display);
            exit(0);
            break;
        default:
            break;
        } /* end switch */
    } /* end while */
}
```

FIGURE A.1
(continued)

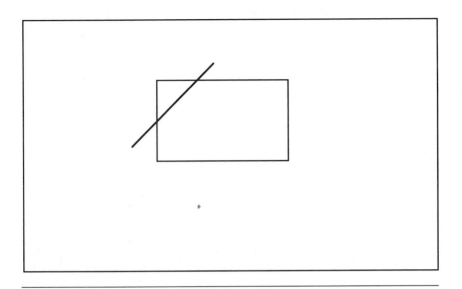

FIGURE A.2
The screen produced by the program presented in Figure A.1

A.2   Comments

XOpenDisplay is a routine from XLib. It opens a connection between the X server and the workstation that executes the program listed in Figure A.1.

DefaultScreen is a macro provided by Xlib to get the internal identification of the screen. This identification is useful for obtaining the physical characteristics of the screen: DisplayWidth, DisplayHeight, BlackPixel, WhitePixel, and so forth.

XCreateSimpleWindow creates the window on which the line and the rectangle will be drawn. The X Window System organizes windows, so hierarchically, "window" is created as a child of some window. In our example, the ancestor is the root window (the window that corresponds to the screen). The root window is obtained with the macro DefaultRootWindow.

XSetStandardProperties allows the programmer to specify a number of requirements to the window manager. Recall that the window manager is yet another client of the X server; its role is to manage the presentation of windows. In our example, we require a desired size, a minimal size, and a location for "window." We do not specify any pix-map for the icon when the window is iconified, but we provide the window manager with a window name (windowname) to be used as a title and a character string (iconname) to be used in place of the window when it is iconified. Such properties are used as hints by the window manager. Not every window manager will take them into account. For example, uwm, a window manager distributed with the X Window System, does not produce a title and thus will ignore our "windowname" parameter.

XSelectInput specifies the types of events "window" will be interested in: exposure, key press, and mouse button events. An exposure event is produced by the server when a window changes its visibility. In our example, "window" will receive an exposure event when it becomes visible. A key event happens when the end user presses a key of the keyboard, and a mouse button event is signaled whenever a mouse button is pressed while the mouse is visiting the window.

Graphics primitives, such as XDrawLine and XDrawRectangle, require the specification of a graphics context. As mentioned in Section 3.5.2, a graphics context is a data structure that captures a number of graphics parameters such as line width, color, and mode. A graphics mode is a boolean function, which combines pixels from a source rendition surface with pixels produced by the graphics primitive. In our example, XCreateGC creates a graphics context, gcxor, initialized with default values (the value of valuemask is 0). XSetForeground sets the foreground attribute of gcxor to the color returned by the macro BlackPixel. This attribute determines the color used for drawing. XSetFunction sets the graphics mode of gcxor as "exclusive or" (GXxor).

Now we are ready to map "window" on the screen with XMapWindow. This request is absorbed by the window manager to produce window decorations such as borders and title. These arrangements are performed asynchronously with regard to our program. As a result, there is no guarantee that "window" is effectively visible upon return from XMapWindow. The programmer needs to be aware of this functioning, since anything drawn in an invisible window is not recorded by the server. In our example, a line and a rectangle must be drawn in "window." To do so, the program must wait for the next exposure event.

The program now enters an infinite loop (while (1)), acquires events (XNextEvent), and processes events according to their type (switch (event.type)). XNextEvent returns the first event queued for the window by the X server. If the queue is empty, the calling process is blocked.

- On the first expose event, all other expose events are eliminated from the window queue with XCheckTypedEvent; the rectangle and the line are drawn with the graphics context gcxor.

- On any mouse button press, the line is erased and moved to the right. Erasing the line consists of redrawing the line at the current location in Xor mode. The Xor mode restores the source pixels to the values they had before the line was drawn.

- On reception of a key press, the connection is closed and the program terminated.

B

A Simple Draw Program Using the HP Toolkit

B.1 The User Interface

Chapter 4 presented the services and the general functioning of toolkits. This appendix contains an enriched version of the simple draw example, implemented with the HP toolkit. The HP toolkit is a public domain toolkit available with the X Window System, Version 11, Release 3. The goal is to help the reader to appreciate the difference between the levels of abstraction provided by a window manager and a toolkit.

Figure B.1 presents the program. Figure B.2 shows the screen after the end user has elected the "Draw Line" and the "Draw Rectangle" buttons.

```
/* **************************************************************************
           A very simple DRAW program using HP widgets.

           - Press "Quit" button to exit
           - Press "Draw Line" button to draw a line
           - Press "Draw Rectangle" button to draw a rectangle
           - Press "Move Line Left" to move the line to the left
           - Press "Move Line Right" to move the line to the right.
   ************************************************************************** */
#include <stdio.h>
#include <X11/Xlib.h>
```

FIGURE B.1
The draw program using the HP toolkit.

```c
#include <X11/StringDefs.h>
#include <X11/Intrinsic.h>
#include <X11/Xutil.h>
#include <Xw/Xw.h>
#include <Xw/WorkSpace.h>
#include <Xw/Form.h>
#include <Xw/RCManager.h>
#include <Xw/PButton.h>

#define RIGHT 1
#define LEFT 0

void quit_callback ();
void drawline_callback ();
void drawrectangle_callback ();
void movelineright_callback ();
void movelineleft_callback ();

unsigned int widthrect = 100, heightrect = 100;
int xrect = 10, yrect = 10;
int x1=15, y1 = 0, x2 = 0, y2 = 15;
GC gcxor;                                    /* GC to draw in XOR mode */
XGCValues gcvalues;                          /* struct for creating GC */
int n;
Arg wargs[6];
Display *canvasdisplay;                      /* the display of canvas widget */
Widget toplevel, canvas, form, commands;
Widget quitb, drawlineb, drawrectb, movelineleftb, movelinerightb;

void main (argc, argv)
        int argc;
        char *argv[];

{
  /*
   * Establish a connection with the X server.
   * Initialize X toolkit.
   * Create the toplevel window.
   */

     toplevel = XtInitialize (argv[0],      /* name: to determine the resources */
                        "Draw",             /* class: to determine the resources*/
                        NULL,               /* options */
                        0,                  /* noptions */
                        &argc, argv); /* command line arguments */

  /*
   * The toplevel window contains a form.
   */
```

FIGURE B.1
(continued)

```
form = XtCreateManagedWidget ( "form",          /* for ressource */
                               XwformWidgetClass,
                               toplevel,       /* parent */
                               NULL,           /* no args */
                               0);             /* no args */

/*
 * Create the column to hold the command buttons in the form.
 */

commands = XtCreateManagedWidget (   "commands", /* for resource */
                                     XwrowColWidgetClass,
                                     form,     /* parent */
                                     NULL,     /* no args */
                                     0);       /* nargs */

/*
 * Insert the  buttons in the commands column.
 * For doing so:
 *      - label specified in a resource file
 *      - assign a call back procedure to be called when button released.
 *
 */

quitb = XtCreateManagedWidget ( "quit", /* for ressource */
                                XwpushButtonWidgetClass,
                                commands, NULL,  0);
XtAddCallback (quitb, XtNrelease, quit_callback,
               NULL); /* no client data for the callback procedure */

drawlineb = XtCreateManagedWidget ( "drawline", /* for ressource */
                                    XwpushButtonWidgetClass,
                                    commands, NULL, 0);
XtAddCallback (drawlineb, XtNrelease, drawline_callback, NULL);

drawrectb = XtCreateManagedWidget ( "drawrect", /* for resource */
                                    XwpushButtonWidgetClass,
                                    commands, NULL, 0);
XtAddCallback (drawrectb, XtNrelease, drawrectangle_callback, NULL);

movelinerightb = XtCreateManagedWidget ( "movelineright", /* for resource */
                                         XwpushButtonWidgetClass,
                                         commands, NULL, 0);
XtAddCallback (movelinerightb, XtNrelease, movelineright_callback, NULL);

movelineleftb = XtCreateManagedWidget ( "movelineleft", /* for resource */
                                        XwpushButtonWidgetClass,
                                        commands, NULL, 0);
```

FIGURE B.1
(continued)

```
    XtAddCallback (movelineleftb, XtNrelease, movelineleft_callback, NULL);

    /*
     * Create the drawing surface.
     * Memorize the display it  belongs to.
     */

    canvas = XtCreateManagedWidget ( "canvas", /* for ressource */
                                    XwworkSpaceWidgetClass, form, NULL,
                                    0);
    canvasdisplay = XtDisplay (canvas);

    /*
     * Create the graphic context to draw in canvas.
     * Use background and foreground color of canvas
     * Draw in XOR mode.
     */

    n = 0;
    XtSetArg (wargs[n], XtNforeground, &gcvalues.foreground); n++;
    XtSetArg (wargs[n], XtNbackground, &gcvalues.background); n++;
    XtGetValues (canvas, wargs, n);
    gcvalues.function = GXxor;
    gcxor = XtGetGC (canvas, GCFunction | GCForeground | GCBackground,
                    &gcvalues);

    /*
     * Show the toplevel widget and siblings.
     */

    XtRealizeWidget (toplevel);

    /*
     * Obtain events from the queue and
     * let the toolkit dispatch them to the appropriate widgets.
     */

    XtMainLoop ();
} /* end main */

void quit_callback (w, client_data, call_data)
    Widget w;                /* widget for which the callback is registered */
    void *client_data;       /* parm specified by the client in the XtAddCall.. */
    void *call_data;         /* contains data provided by the widget */
{
    printf ("Begin exiting ... please standby ... \n");
    fflush (stdout);
    exit (0);
}
```

FIGURE B.1
(continued)

```
void drawline_callback (w, client_data, call_data )
   Widget w;
   void *client_data;
   void *call_data;
{
   XDrawLine (canvasdisplay, XtWindow(canvas), gcxor, x1, y1, x2, y2);
}

void drawrectangle_callback ( w, client_data, call_data )
   Widget w;
   void *client_data;
   void *call_data;
{
   XDrawRectangle ( canvasdisplay, XtWindow(canvas),
                       gcxor, xrect, yrect, widthrect, heightrect);
}

void movelineright_callback ( w, client_data, call_data )
         Widget w;
          void *client_data;
          void *call_data;

{
   /* erase old line */
   XDrawLine (canvasdisplay, XtWindow(canvas), gcxor, x1, y1, x2, y2);

   /* move line to new location and draw */
   x1 += 10;
   y2 += 10;
   XDrawLine (canvasdisplay, XtWindow(canvas), gcxor, x1, y1, x2, y2);
}

void movelineleft_callback ( w, client_data, call_data )
   Widget w;
   void *client_data;
   void *call_data;

{
   /* erase old line */
  XDrawLine (canvasdisplay, XtWindow(canvas), gcxor, x1, y1, x2, y2);

   /* move line at new location and draw */
   x1 -= 10;
   y2 -= 10;
   XDrawLine (canvasdisplay, XtWindow(canvas), gcxor, x1, y1, x2, y2
}
```

FIGURE B.1
(continued)

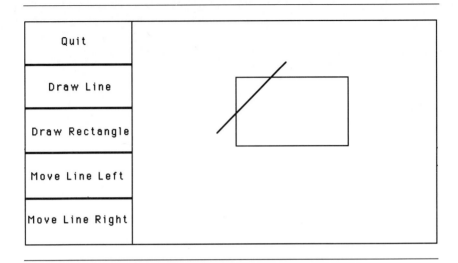

FIGURE B.2
The screen after a rectangle and line have been created.

B.2 Comments

Figure B.3 shows the hierarchy of widgets used in the example. "toplevel" is the interface with the window manager. It contains a form widget, which is the parent of a work space (canvas) and of a comands widget. The commands widget is a container for the set of push buttons.

The first statement of the program, XtInitialize, opens a connection with the X server (it embeds an XOpenDisplay), initializes the toolkit, and creates the toplevel widget. The second parameter, "Draw," is used by the resource manager to look for the resources defined in a resource file. Figure B.4 shows such a file. Notice that the prefix "Draw" appears in all of the resource definitions.

XtCreateManagedWidget is a primitive provided by the Intrinsics. It creates an instance of a widget class as a child of an existing widget. In our example, form is an instance of XwformWidgetClass and is a child of toplevel. XwformWidgetClass is a constant defined in the HP toolkit that identifies the class formWidgetClass implemented in the HP toolkit.

The form is populated with two children: the commands widget and the canvas widget. The commands widget is a row-column widget. It is a composed widget that includes a geometry manager to control the spatial layout of the

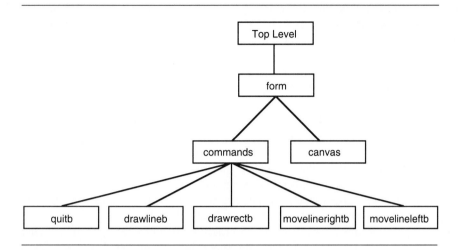

FIGURE B.3
The hierarchy of widgets used in the example.

```
####################################################
# Draw: Class resource file the simple draw program #
####################################################

Draw*commands.columns:            1
Draw*quit.label:                  Quit
Draw*drawline.label:              Draw Line
Draw*drawrect.label:              Draw Rectangle
Draw*movelineright.label:         Move Line Right
Draw*movelineleft.label:          Move Line Left
Draw*canvas.xRefName:             commands
Draw*canvas.xAddWidth:            True
Draw*canvas.xAttachRight:         True
Draw*canvas.xAttachLeft:          True
Draw*canvas.xAttachBottom:        True
Draw*canvas.xAttachTop:           True
```

FIGURE B.4
A resource file.

children. The children are the buttons quitb, drawlineb, drawrectb, and so forth. Notice that the first parameter in XtCreateManagedWidget("commands", ...) is a string ("commands") that identifies the resources associated with the widget in the resource file. In particular, the first line of the resource file, Draw*commands.columns: 1, indicates that the commands widget includes only one column. The labels for the buttons are specified similarly in the resource file.

Resources for the canvas widget need some explanation. Resources xAddWidth, xAttachRight, xAttachLeft, xAttachBottom, and xAttachTop specify the position of a widget within its parent relative to another child. Here the reference widget for the canvas widget is the commands widget (Draw*canvas.xRefName: commands in the resource file). The values specified for xAddWidth, xAttachRight, xAttachLeft, xAttachBottom, and xAttachTop imply that the canvas widget is placed to the right of the commands widget and that its height is limited to that of the commands widget.

XtAddCallback specifies which procedure to call when an action occurs. For example, when the action XtNrelease occurs for quitb, function quit_callback will be called. Action XtNrelease occurs when, for example, a mouse button is released while the mouse cursor is within the button. Callback procedures must conform to a standard signature. This signature includes three parameters: the widget for which the callback is invoked, parameters specified by the client when the procedure was registered, and some data, which depend on the widget class.

XtRealizeWidget(toplevel) maps the toplevel widget and its children on the screen. The program is ready to listen to events.

XtMainLoop() encapsulates an infinite loop, just like the one described in Appendix A. It acquires events and dispatches them to the appropriate widgets. For example, when the end user selects the "Quit" button, XtNRelease becomes true and the procedure quit_callback is automatically invoked.

C

A Simple Draw Program
Using HyperCard

C.1 The User Interface

Chapter 6 identified one promising way of specifying user interfaces: combining specification by demonstration with specification by programming. Although imperfect as a user interface prototyping tool, HyperCard is a pioneer of this technique. This appendix presents the simple drawing example elaborated with HyperCard.

Figure C.1 shows the initial picture of the screen. A palette of buttons presents the functions of the application system: quit the system, draw a shape (either a rectangle or a line), move the line, and erase the work space.

Figure C.2 shows the screen after the operator has created a rectangle and a line. The system is very crude. The operator can draw only one rectangle and only one line with a fixed size and location.

C.2 Constructing the User Interface Interactively

The palette of buttons and the work space have been constructed interactively from HyperCard objects. Object classes in HyperCard include stack, card, background, button, and text fields.

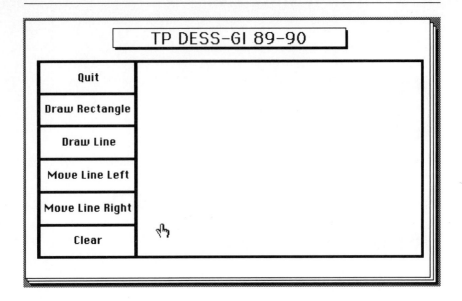

FIGURE C.1
The initial screen.

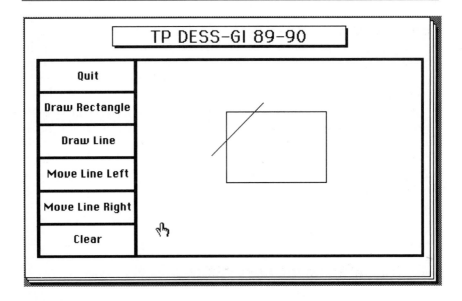

FIGURE C.2
The screen after a rectangle and a line have been created.

A stack is a collection of cards that are logically related. A card is a rendition surface that can be populated with a background, pictures, buttons, and text fields. Our drawing application system has one card which belongs to a particular stack. New stacks and new cards are created by selecting the "New Stack" and "New Card" items, respectively, from the File and Edit pop-up menus (see the menu bar at the top of Figure C.3).

A background is a rendition surface that is visible through a card. A background may be associated with several cards, in which case the items in the background are visible through all the cards. In our example, the outlines of the work space and of the palette have been constructed in the background and therefore are protected from the drawing primitives that are performed at run time on the card. (These primitives will be invoked to draw and erase the rectangle and the line in the work space.) Drawing is performed as in MacPaint: The operator selects a tool in the tools palette and then creates a picture. (Figure C.3 shows the tools palette.) In the example, the outlines in the background have been drawn with the rectangle and line tools.

We need now to create a button that will invoke the function of the application system. Figure C.3 shows how to create an instance of the button class. The

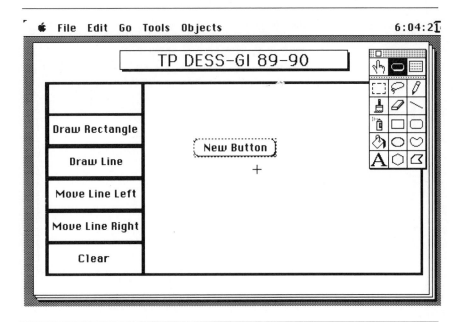

FIGURE C.3
The creation of an instance of the class button.

selection of "Button" in the tools palette switches HyperCard into button mode. "Button" in the tools palette turns black; then a pop-up menu associated with "Objects" in the menu bar appears and lists the applicable operators, including "New Button." Figure C.3 shows the screen after "New Button" has been selected. A button instance has been created with the default label "New Button." The designer can then move and resize the button with the mouse or edit its properties.

Figure C.4 shows "New Button" placed at the desired location. We need now to edit its properties to change the default values. Figure C.5 shows the property list for the newly created button. By editing the "Button Name" field, we can specify a new label: "Quit." By selecting the "LinkTo" item, we can instruct HyperCard by demonstration, so that pressing the button at run time will lead to another card.

"LinkTo" brings up a dialogue box for linking, as shown in Figure C.6.

In the link mode, we can browse through stacks of cards and indicate which card should be linked to the button. For example, after selecting the "LinkTo" item, we can browse through HyperCard stacks until we reach the "Home Card." As shown in Figure C.7, the Home Card displays a list of HyperCard stacks. To

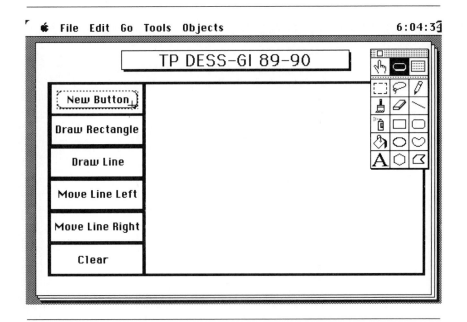

FIGURE C.4
"New Button" has been moved with the mouse to the desired location.

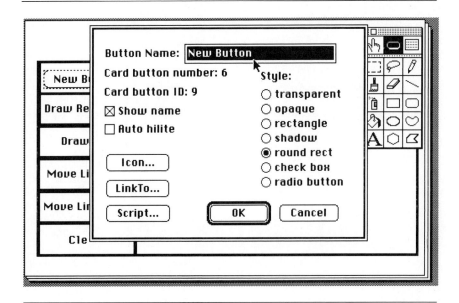

FIGURE C.5
Editing the attributes of "New Button."

link the "Quit" button to the Home Card, we simply press the "This Card" button of the dialogue box while the Home Card is visible. Selection of the "Quit" button at run time will then automatically lead to the Home Card.

Our demonstration through mouse actions and menus selections has resulted in the creation of a particular program called a script. The role of scripts is explained in the next section.

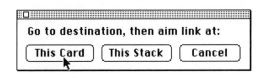

FIGURE C.6
A dialogue box makes the link mode explicit.

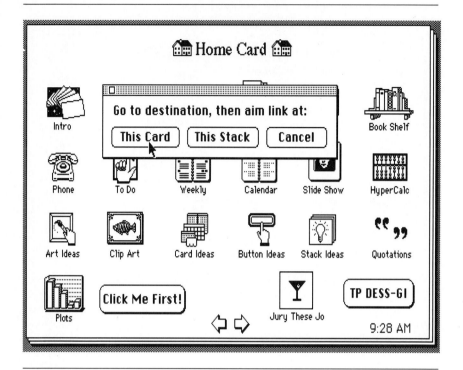

FIGURE C.7
Linking the "Quit" button to the Home Card. Notice in the bottom right corner of the card the "TP DESS-GI" button, which is linked to the card shown in Figure C.1.

C.3   Scripts

A script is a HyperTalk program associated with an object, such as a stack, a card, a background, or a button. It is composed of a sequence of event handlers. An event handler describes a sequence of actions to be executed when a condition becomes true. HyperTalk conditions are very simple expressions. For example, an event type such as "mouseUp" can be used as a condition. Figure C.8 shows the script built automatically by HyperCard when we linked the "Quit" button to the Home Card: if the "Quit" button is selected with the mouse, the condition "mouseUp" will become true and the HyperTalk statement "go to card ...." will be executed. Notice that the Home Card is identified as item 5341 of stack "Home."

```
on mouseUp
    go to card id 5341 of stack "Home"
end mouseUp
```

FIGURE C.8
The script for the "Quit" button.

Statements in HyperTalk reflect the physical gestures you normally use when building and editing a picture with an application system such as MacPaint. Figure C.9 gives a flavor of the editing primitives provided by HyperTalk. The script associated with the "Clear" button is a textual representation of the physical actions an end user would perform with MacPaint to erase the contents of the work space: choose the select tool from the palette, "Select" the contents of the drawing surface, and then use the command "Cut" from the Edit pop-up menu of the menu bar.

In addition to statements for editing and constructing pictures, HyperTalk includes algorithmic features such as local and global variables, procedures, and conditional and loop statements. Figure C.10 shows the script associated with the "Draw Line" button. The variables $x1$, $y1$, $x2$, and $y2$, which denote the end points of the line, are declared as global variables. These variables are shared with the scripts executed to move the line (see Figure C.12). As with a MacPaint-like application system, drawing a line consists of selecting the line tool in the palette, then dragging the mouse in the work space.

Figure C.11 shows the script associated with the "Draw Rectangle" button. It is similar to that of the "Draw Line" button.

```
on mouseUp
    choose select tool        — select the objects to be deleted
    doMenu "Select All"       —deselect any object that may already have been
                                 selected
    doMenu "Select"           — select all the painted objects
    doMenu "Cut Picture"      — cut the selected painted objects
    choose browse tool        — return to normal browse mode
end mouseUp
```

FIGURE C.9
The script for the "Clear" button.

```
on mouseUp
  global x1                        — global variable used in move line left
  global y1                        — and move line right event handlers
  global x2
  global y2
  put 245 into x1                  — initialize variables
  put 150 into y1
  put 305 into x2
  put 90 into y2
  choose line tool                 — start to draw a line
  set lineSize to 1                —optional: line width sets to 1
  drag from x1,y1 to x2,y2         — draw the line
  choose browse tool               — return to normal browse mode
end mouseUp
```

FIGURE C.10
The script for the "Draw Line" button.

Figure C.12 contains the script of the "Move Line Left" button. Again, the programming paradigm is inspired by the physical actions performed with a graphics editor. The underlying graphic model for HyperTalk, however, is pixel based. As a result, HyperTalk has no notion of graphical objects such as lines or rectangles. In our example, we need to move a line. One crude way of performing


```
on mouseUp
  global rectx1
  global recty1
  global rectx2
  global recty2
  put 250 into rectx1
  put 100 into recty1
  put 400 into rectx2
  put 200 into recty2
  choose rectangle tool
  drag from rectx1,recty1 to rectx2,recty2
  choose browse tool
end mouseUp
```

FIGURE C.11
The script for the "Draw Rectangle" button.

```
on mouseUp
                                   — we don't check whether the line
                                     moves outside the workspace
    global x1
    global y1
    global x2
    global y2
    global rectx1
    global recty1
    global rectx2
    global recty2
    choose eraser tool             — erase current line
    drag from x1,y1 to x2, y2
    put x1 - 10 into x1            — compute new line coordinates
    put y1 - 10 into y1
    put x2 - 10 into x2
    put y2 - 10 into y2
    choose line tool               — draw new line
    drag from x1,y1 to x2,y2
    choose rectangle tool          — redraw the rectangle
    drag from rectx1,recty1 to rectx2,recty2
    choose browse tool             — return to normal mode
end mouseUp
```

FIGURE C.12
The script for the "Move Line Left" button.

this action consists of erasing the current line with the eraser, then drawing the line at the new position. Unfortunately, the eraser tool has a fixed thickness and therefore may erase more pixels than desired. In our example, the rectangle must be redrawn.

Bibliography

Adobe. *PostScript Language Reference Manual.* Addison-Wesley, Reading, Mass., 1985.

Ahlers, K. L., and A. Dwelly. *OUTILS: Towards a User Interface Management System for Graphical Interaction.* ECRC (European Computer-Industry Research Centre) Technical Report, Munich, Germany, 1986.

Anderson, J. R. *The Architecture of Cognition.* Harvard University Press, Cambridge, Mass., 1983.

ANSI/IEEE. ANSI/IEEE Standard 729–1983." *Software Engineering Standards.* IEEE, New York, 1989.

Baddeley, A. Short Term Memory for Word Sequences as a Function of Acoustic, Semantic and Formal Similarity. *Quarterly Journal of Experimental Psychology,* 18, 1966, pp. 362–365.

Balkovich, E., S. Lerman, and R. P. Parmelee. Computing in Higher Education: The Athena Experience. CACM, 28(11), 1985, pp. 1214–1224.

Barnard, P. J Cognitive Resources and the Learning of Human-Computer Dialogs. In *Interfacing Thoughts, Cognitive Aspects of Human-Computer Interaction,* J. Carroll, ed. MIT Press, Cambridge, Mass., 1987, pp. 112–159.

Barnard, P. J., N. V. Hammond, J. Morton, J. B. Long, and I. A. Clark. Consistency and Compatibility in Human-Computer Dialogue. *International Journal of Man-Machine Studies,* 15, 1981, pp. 87–134.

Bass, L. J. A Generalized User Interface for Applications Programs (II). *CACM,* 28(6), 1985, pp. 617–627.

Bass, L. J., E. Hardy, R. Little, and R. Seacord. The Incremental Development of User Interfaces. In *Engineering the Human-Computer Interface,* North-Holland, Amsterday, 1990.

Bennett, W. E., S. J. Boies, J. D. Gould, S. L. Green, and C. F. Wiecha. "Transformations on a Dialog Tree: Rule Based Mapping of Content to Style. *Proceedings of the ACM*

SIGGRAPH Symposium on User Interface Software and Technology, Williamsburg, Va., November 1989. ACM, New York, 1989, pp. 67–75.

Binding, E., L. Schmandt, K. Lantz, and B. Arons. Workstation Audio and Window-Based Graphics: Similarities and Differences. In *Engineering the Human-Computer Interface*, North-Holland, Amsterday, 1990.

Black, A., N. Hutchinson, and H. Levy. Object Structure in the Emerald System. *Proceedings of the OOPSLA '86 Conference*, Portland, September, 1986. ACM, New York, 1986, pp. 78–86.

Bly, S., and J. K. Jarret. A Comparison of Tiled and Overlapping Windows. *Computer Human Interaction Conference Proceedings,* Boston, April 13–17, 1986. ACM, New York, 1986, pp. 101–106.

Bobrow, D. G., and M. Stefik. *The Loops Manual.* Knowledge Systems Area Technical Report KB-VLSI-81-13, Xerox, Palo Alto, Calif., 1981.

Boehm, B. A Spiral Model of Software Development and Enhancement. *IEEE Computer*, 21(5), 1988, pp. 61–72.

Boies, S. J., J. D. Gould, S. E. Levy, J. T. Richards, and J. W. Schoonard. *The 1984 Olympic Message System—A Case Study in System Design.* IBM Research Report RC-11138, Yorktown Heights, N.Y., 1985.

Borenstein, N. *The Design and Evaluation of On-line Help Systems.* Carnegie-Mellon University Technical Report CMU-CS-85-151, Pittsburgh, 1985.

Borning, A. H. Graphically Defining New Building Blocks in ThingLab. *Human Computer Interaction*, 2(4), 1986, pp. 269–295.(a)

Borning, A. H. Defining Constraints Graphically. *Computer Human Interaction Conference Proceedings*, Boston, April 13–17, 1986. ACM, New York, 1986, pp. 137–143.(b)

Butler, J. Device Independent Graphics Output for Microsoft Windows. *Byte*, 8(12), 1983, p. 49.

Callahan, J., D. Hopkins, and B. Shneiderman. An Empirical Comparison of Pie vs. Linear Menus. *Proceedings of the CHI '88 Conference*, May, 1988. ACM, New York, 1988, pp. 95–100.

Card, S., and A. Henderson. A Multiple, Virtual-Workspace Interface to Support User Task Switching. *Proceedings of the CHI+GI '87 Conference.* ACM, New York, 1987, pp. 53–59.

Card, S., T. Moran, and A. Newell. *The Psychology of Human-Computer Interaction.* Lawrence Erlbaum Associates, Hillsdale, N.J., 1983.

Cardelli, L. *Building User Interfaces by Direct Manipulation.* Digital Systems Research Center Technical Report 22, Palo Alto, Calif., 1987.

Carroll, J. M., ed. *Interfacing Thoughts.* MIT Press, Cambridge, Mass., 1987.

Carroll, J. M., and C. Carrithers. Training Wheels in a User Interface. *CACM*, 27(8), 1984, pp. 800–807.

Carroll, J. M., and R. L. Mack. Metaphor, Computing Systems, and Active Learning. *International Journal of Man-Machine Studies*, 22(1), 1985, pp. 39–57.

Cohen, E. S., A. M. Berman, M. R. Biggers, and J. C. Camaratta. Automatic Strategies in the Siements RTL Tiled Window Manager. *Proceedings of the 2nd IEEE Conference on Computer Workstations.* IEEE, New York, 1988.

Conklin, J. Hypertext: An Introduction and Survey. *IEEE Computer*, 20(9), 1987, pp. 17–41.

Coutaz, J. A Layout Abstraction for User System Design. *ACM SIGCHI*, January, 1985, pp. 18–24. (Also in Carnegie-Mellon University Technical Report CMU-CS-84-167, Pitttsburgh, 1984.)

Coutaz, J. Abstractions for User Interface Design. *IEEE Computer,* 18(9), 1985, pp. 21–34.

Coutaz, J. The Construction of User Interface and the Object Oriented Paradigm. *ECOOP'87*, The European Conference on Object Oriented Programming, Paris, June, 1987, pp. 135–144.

Coutaz, J. PAC, an Implemention Model for Dialog Design. *Interact'87*, Stuttgart, September, 1987, pp. 431–436.

Coutaz, J. Interface Homme-Ordinateur: Conception et Réalisation. Ph.D. dissertation, Université Joseph Fourier, Grenoble, France, December, 1988.

Crowley, J. Coordination of Action and Perception in a Surveillance Robot. *IEEE Expert*, 2(4), 1987, pp. 33–43.

Date, C. J. *An Introduction to Database Systems*, vol. 1, 3rd ed., 1981. Addison-Wesley, Reading, Mass., 1981.

Davis, A. M. *Software Requirements Analysis and Specification*. Prentice Hall, Englewood Cliffs, N.J., 1990.

Ditton, E. A. and R. A. Ditton. Amiga Animation. *Byte*, 11(9), 1986, pp. 241–248.

Fikes, R. E., and N. J. Nilsson. STRIPS: A New Approach to the Application of Theorem Proving to Problem Solving. *Artificial Intelligence*, 2, 1971, pp. 189–208.

Foley, J. D., W. C. Kim, S. Kovacevic, and K. Murray. *The User Interface Design Environment*. Department of Electrical Engineering and Computer Science Technical Report GWU-IIST-88-04, George Washington University, Washington, D.C., January, 1988.

Forgy, C. L. *The OPS83 Report*. Carnegie-Mellon University Technical Report CMU-CS-84-113, Pittsburgh, 1984.

Gibbs, S. J. LIZA: An Extensible Groupware Toolkit. *Proceedings of the CHI'89 Conference*, April, 1989. ACM, New York, 1989, pp. 29–35.

Goldberg, A. *Smalltalk-80: The Interactive Programming Environment*. Addison-Wesley, Reading, Mass., 1984.

Gosling, J. Partitioning of Functions in Window Systems. In *Methodology of Window Management*, F. R. A. Hopgood, ed. Springer-Verlag, New York, N.Y.,1986, pp. 101–106.

Gosling, J., and D. Rosenthal. A Window Manager for BitMapped Displays and Unix. In *Methodology of Window Management*, F. R. A. Hopgood, ed. Springer-Verlag, New York, N.Y., 1986, pp. 115–128.

Gosling, J., D. Rosenthal, and M. Arden. *The NeWS Book, An Introduction to the Network/ Extensible Window System*. Springer-Verlag, New York, N.Y., 1989.

Gould, J. D. How to Design Usable Systems. In *Handbook of Human-Computer Interaction*, M. Helander, ed. North-Holland, Amsterdam, 1988, pp. 757–789.

Green, M. W. *The Design of Graphical Interfaces*. Computer Systems Research Institute Technical Report CSRI-170, University of Toronto, Canada, April, 1985.

Grudin, J. The Case Against User Interface Consistency. *CACM*, 32(10), 1989, pp. 1164–1173.

Hansen, W. J. User Engineering Principles for Interactive Systems. *Proceedings of the Fall Joint Computer Conference*, 39, 1971, pp. 523–532.

Harel, D. Statecharts: A Visual Formalism for Complex Systems. *Science of Computer Programming*, 8(3), June, 1987, pp. 231–274.

Harvey, G. Understanding HyperCard for Version 1.1. Sybex Books, San Francisco, Calif., 1988.

Hayes, F., and N. Baran. A Guide to GUIs. *Byte*, 14(7), 1989, pp. 250–257.

Hayes, P. J., P. Szekely, and R. Lerner. Design Alternatives for User Interface Management Systems Based on Experience with Cousin. *Proceedings of the CHI'85 Conference*, April, 1985. ACM, New York, 1985, pp. 169–175.

Hayes-Roth, B., and F. Hayes-Roth. A Cognitive Model for Planning. *Cognitive Science*, 3, 1979, pp. 275–310.

Hermann, M., and R. Hill. Abstraction and Declarativeness in User Interface Development—the Methodological Basis of Composite Object Architecture. In *Engineering the Human-Computer Interface*, North-Holland, Amsterdam, 1990.

Hill, R. D. Supporting Concurrency, Communication and Synchronization in Human-Computer Interaction. Ph.D. dissertation, Department of Computer Science, University of Toronto, January, 1987.(a) [See also Supporting Concurrency, Communication and Synchronization in Human-Computer Interaction—The Sassafras UIMS. *ACM Transactions on Graphics*, 5(2), April, 1986, pp. 179–210.]

Hill, R. D. Event Response Systems—A Technique for Specifying Multi-thread Dialogues. *Proceedings of the CHI+GI'87 Conference*. ACM, New York, 1987, pp. 241–248.

Hodges, M. E., R. M. Sasnett, and M. S. Ackerman. A Construction Set for Multimedia Applications. *IEEE Software*, January, 1989, pp. 37–43.

Hopper, K. Architectural Design: An Analogy. In *User Centered System Design*, D. A. Norman and S. W. Draper, eds. Lawrence Erlbaum Associates, Hillsdale, N.J., 1986, pp. 9–24.

Hullot, J. M. SOS Interface, un Générateur d'Interfaces Homme-Machine. *Actes des Journées Afcet-Informatique sur les Langages Orientés Objet*, Bigre+Globule, 48, Publ. IRISA, Campus de Beaulieu, 35042 Rennes, January, 1986, pp. 69–78.

Hutchins, E. L., J. D. Hollan, and D. A. Norman. Direct Manipulation Interfaces. In *User Centered System Design*, D. A. Norman and S. W. Draper, eds. Lawrence Erlbaum Associates, Hillsdale, N.J., 1986, pp. 87–124.

IEEE. Special Issue Devoted to Rapid Prototyping. *IEEE Computer*, May 1989.

Ilog. Aïda, Environnement de Développement d'Applications. *Manuel de Référence Aïda, Version 1.32*. Ilog, Paris, France, March, 1989.

Infoworld. UIMS Quickens Progamming for Open Look, Motif. *Infoworld*, December 11, 1989, p. 42.

ISO (International Organization for Standardization). *Information Processing Systems—Computer Graphics—Graphical Kernel System (GKS) Functional Description*. ISO IS 7942, July, 1985.

ISO (International Organization for Standardization). *Information Processing Systems—Computer Graphics—Programmer's Hierarchical Interface to Graphics (PHIGS) Functional Description*. ISO DP 9592, October, 1986.(a)

ISO (International Organization for Standardization). *Information Processing Systems—Computer Graphics—Techniques for Interfacing Graphical Devices (CGI) Functional Description*. ISO DP 9636, December, 1986.(b)

Jacob, R. J. K. An Executable Specification Technique for Describing Human-Computer Interaction. In *Advances in Human Computer Interaction*, H. R. Hartson, ed. Alex Publishing, Norwood, N. J., 1984.

Karsenty, S. Graffiti: Un Outil Interactif et Graphique pour la Construction d'Interfaces Homme-Machine Adaptables. Ph.D. dissertation, Université de Paris-Sud, Centre d'Orsay, December, 1987.

Kieras, D., and P. G. Polson An Approach to the Formal Analysis of User Complexity. *International Journal of Man-Machine Studies*, 22, 1985, pp. 365–394.

Knuth, D. E. TEX and Metafont: New Directions in Typesetting. Digital Press, Bedford, Mass., 1979.

Krakowiak, S., M. Meysembourg, M. Riveill, H. Nguyen Van, and C. Roisin. Design and Implementation of an Object-Oriented Strongly Typed Language for Distributed Applications. *Journal of Object Oriented Programming*, in press.

Krasner, G. E., and S. T. Pope. A Cookbook for Using Model-View-Controller User Interface Paradigm in Smalltalk-80. *Journal of Object Oriented Programming*, August/September, 1988, pp. 26–49.

Lewis, C., and D. A. Norman. Designing for Errors. In *User Centered System Design*, D. A. Norman and S. W. Draper, eds. Lawrence Erlbaum Associates, Hillsdale, N.J., 1986, pp. 411–432.

Linton, M. A., J. M. Vilssides, and P. R. Calder. Composing User Interfaces with Interviews. *IEEE Computer*, February, 1989, pp. 8–22.

Mikelsons, M. Prettyprinting in an Interactive Programming Environment. *Proceedings of the ACM Sigplan SIGOA Symposium on Text Manipulation*, June, 1981. ACM, New York, 1981.

Miller, G. A. *The Psychology of Communication*, 2nd ed. Basic Books, New York, 1975.

MIT. X *Toolkit Library—C Language Interface, X protocol, Version 11*. MIT, Cambridge, Mass., 1987.

Moran, T. The Command Language Grammar, a Representation for the User Interface of Interactive Computer Systems. *International Journal of Man-Machine Studies*, 15, 1981, pp. 3–50.

Moran, T. P. Getting into a System: External-Internal Task Mapping Analysis. *Computer Human Interaction '83*, Special Issue of the SIGCHI Bulletin. ACM, New York, 1983, pp. 45–49.

Morris, J. H., M. Satyanarayanan, M. H. Conner, J. H. Howard, D. S. H. Rosenthal, and F. D. Smith. Andrew: A Distributed Personal Computing Environment. *CACM* 29(3), 1986, pp. 184–201.

Myers, B. A. Tools for Creating User Interfaces: An Introduction and Survey. *IEEE Software* 6(1), 1989, pp. 15–23.(a)

Myers, B. A. Encapsulating Interactive Behaviors. *CHI'89 Conference Proceedings*, Special Issue of the SIGCHI Bulletin. ACM, New York, 1989, pp. 319–324.(b)

Newell, A., and S. Card. Straightening Out Softening UP: Response to Carroll and Campell. *Human Computer Interaction*, 2(3), 1986, pp. 251–267.

Norman, D. A. Design Rules Based on Analyses of Human Error. *CACM*, 4, 1983, pp. 254–258.

Nye, A. *Xlib Programming Manual for Version 11. The Definitive Guides to the X Window System*, vol. 1. O'Reilly & Associates, Sebastopol, Calif.,1988.

Norman, D. A. The Trouble with Unix. *Datamation* 27, 1981, pp. 556–563.

Norman, D. A., and S. W. Draper, eds. *User Centered System Design*. Lawrence Erlbaum Associates, Hillsdale, N.J., 1986.

Olsen, D. R. A Programming Language Basis for User Interface Management. *CHI'89 Conference Proceedings*, Special Issue of the SIGCHI Bulletin. ACM, New York, pp. 171–176.

Olsen, D. R., and E. P. Dempsey. Syngraph: A Graphical User Interface Generator. *Computer Graphics*, July, 1983, pp. 43–50.

Open Software Foundation. OSF/*Motif, Programmer's Reference Manual, Revision 1.0*. Open Software Foundation, Cambridge, Mass., 1989.

Payne, S. J., and T. R. G. Green. Task-Action-Grammar: A Model for the Mental Representation of Task Languages. *Human Computer Interaction*, 2, 1986, pp. 93–133.

Petoud, I., and Y. Pigneur. An Automatic Visual Approach for User Interface Design. In *Engineering the Human-Computer Interface*, North-Holland, Amsterdam, March, 1990.

Pfaff, G. E., ed. *User Interface Management Systems*. Eurographics Seminars, Springer-Verlag, New York, N.Y.,1985.

Quint, V. Une Approche de l'Edition Structurée des Documents. Ph.D. dissertation, Université Scientifique Technologique et Médicale de Grenoble, 1987.

Reason, J. and K. Mycielska. *Absent Minded? The Psychology of Mental Lapses in Everyday Errors*. Prentice Hall, Englewood Cliffs, N.J., 1982.

Relles, N. *The Design and Implementation of User-Oriented Systems*. University of Wisconsin Technical Report 357, Madison, July, 1979

Rose, C., and B. Hacleer. *Inside Macintosh*. Addison-Wesley, Reading, Mass., 1986.

Ross, D. T. and K. L. Schoman. Structured Analysis: A Language for Requirement Definition. *IEEE Transactions on Software Engineering*, New York, N.Y., 1977.

Samuelson, P. Why the Look and Feel of Software User Interfaces Should Not Be Protected by Copyright Law. *CACM*, 32(5), 1987, pp. 563–572.

Scapin, D. L. *Guide Ergonomique de Conception des Interfaces Homme-Machine*. Rapport INRIA 77, October, 1986.

Scheifler, R. W., and J. Gettys. The X Window System. *ACM Transactions on Graphics*, 5(2), April, 1986, pp. 79–109.

Schmucker, K. MacApp: An Application Framework. *Byte*, 11(8), 1986, pp. 189–193.

Schulert, A. J., G. T. Rogers, and J. A. Hamilton. ADM—A Dialog Manager. *Proceedings of the CHI'85 Conference*, April, 1985. ACM, New York, 1985, pp. 177–183.

Senay, H., P. Sukaviriya, and L. Moran. Planning for Automatic Help Generation. In *Engineering for Human-Computer Interaction*, G. Cockton, ed. North-Holland, Amsterdam, 1990, pp. 293–308.

Shafer, D. *HyperTalk Programming*. Hayden Books, Indianapolis, 1988.

Schneiderman, B. *Designing the User Interface: Strategies for Effective Human-Computer Interaction*. Addison-Wesley, Reading, Mass., 1987.

Sibert, J. L., W. D. Hurley, and T. W. Bleser. An Object Oriented User Interface Management System. *SIGGRAPH'86*, 20(4), 1986, pp. 259–268.

Simon, H. A. *The Sciences of the Artificial*, 3rd ed. MIT Press, Cambridge, Mass., 1984.

Sukaviriya, P. Dynamic Construction of Animated Help from Application Context. *Proceedings of the ACM SIGGRAPH Symposium on User Interface Software*, Banff, Alberta, Canada, October, 1988. ACM, New York, 1988.

SUN Microsystems Inc. *NeWS Manual*. SUN Microsystems Inc., Mountain View, Calif., 1987.

Sutton, J., and R. Sprague. *A Study of Display Generation and Management in Interactive Business Applications*. IBM San Jose Research Laboratory Technical Report RJ2392(#31804), San Jose, November, 1978.

Tanner, P., and W. Buxton. *Some Issues in Future User Interface Management Systems (UIMS) Development*. IFIP Working Group 5.2 Workshop on User Interface Management, Seeheim, West Germany, November, 1983.

Tulving, E. Precis of Elements of Episodic Memory. *The Behavioral and Brain Sciences*, 7, 1984, pp. 223–268.

Vander Zanden, B.T. Constraint Grammars—A New Model for Specifying Graphical Applications. *Proceedings of the CHI'88 Conference,* May, 1989. ACM, New York, 1989, pp. 325–330.

Wasserman, A. Extending State Transition Diagrams for the Specification of Human-Computer Interaction. *IEEE Transactions on Software Engineering,* 11(8), 1985.

Webster, B. F. *The NeXT Book.* Addison-Wesley, Reading, Mass., 1989.

Young, R.M., T. R. G. Green, and T. Simon. Programmable User Models for Predictive Evaluation of Interface Designs. *Proceedings of the CHI'89 Conference,* May, 1989. ACM New York, 1989, pp. 15–19.

Index